T0283456

IN THEIR NAMES

IN THEIR NAMES

The Untold Story of Victims' Rights,
Mass Incarceration, and the
Future of Public Safety

LENORE ANDERSON

THE
NEW
PRESS

NEW YORK
LONDON

Requests for permission to reproduce selections from this book should be made through our website: https://thenewpress.com/contact.

Published in the United States by The New Press, New York, 2022
Distributed by Two Rivers Distribution

ISBN 978-1-62097-712-5 (hc)
ISBN 978-1-62097-776-7 (ebook)
CIP data is available

The New Press publishes books that promote and enrich public discussion and understanding of the issues vital to our democracy and to a more equitable world. These books are made possible by the enthusiasm of our readers; the support of a committed group of donors, large and small; the collaboration of our many partners in the independent media and the not-for-profit sector; booksellers, who often hand-sell New Press books; librarians; and above all by our authors.

www.thenewpress.com

Book design and composition by Bookbright Media
This book was set in Adobe Garamond and Janson Text

Printed in the United States of America

To the remarkable leaders with whom I have partnered for the last decade and to the thousands of people who have joined together through tireless activism in pursuit of safety for all, I offer this book in your honor. You are organizers, experts, and advocates, but most of all, you are healers—healing generations of harm caused by systems of neglect and dehumanization. My partnership with Robert Rooks is the foundation, and many other leaders, whose stories I share here, including Aswad Thomas, Tinisch Hollins, Shakyra Diaz, Aqeela Sherrills, David Guizar, Ingrid Archie, Adela Barajas, Jay Jordan, and many more, have worked alongside us for years, advocating for change in legislative hearing rooms, in front of television cameras, on the steps of state capitols, and on stages big and small. I hope this book does justice to your wisdom, power, and impact.

To Kioni, Nyame, Tehya, and Jael. May my generation do everything possible to make the world more safe and just for yours.

Contents

PART I

A Marriage of Convenience

1

A Traumatized Nation

Aswad was twenty-six years old and two weeks away from moving across the Atlantic Ocean to start his basketball career in Europe when he woke up in a hospital bed and learned that he might never walk again. Eight hours earlier, on his way home, the recent college graduate had stopped at a convenience store in his neighborhood in Hartford, Connecticut. It was a warm summer night in 2009, and Aswad ran in to buy a bottle of orange juice. As he left the store, two young men holding guns appeared in front of him. They asked for his wallet. Aswad panicked and turned away. Instantly, he heard bangs—nine shots, it would turn out. He felt himself falling.

Two of the nine bullets hit Aswad. One went through his left shoulder and tore across his back, and the other hit him in the lower back, lodging right next to his spine. Using the dwindling strength left in his arms, Aswad dragged himself along the concrete sidewalk and back into the store. He looked up at the terrified clerk, who was holding a phone. Then he passed out.

When he woke, Aswad found himself in a hospital bed with tubes running everywhere, into his body and all around him. His family stood by his bed with vacant, tear-filled gazes. He soon learned his lungs had collapsed, he couldn't talk or move his lower body, and his shoulder was shattered. The young basketball star lay in that hospital bed for ten days, swinging from feelings of shock and anxiety to extreme physical agony. Every eight hours, the nurses had to change the bandages on his shoulder and back. He had never felt such excruciating pain. Dr. Marshall, the physician who had performed emergency surgery on Aswad the night he was shot, visited him regularly to see how he was doing. Aswad was lucky, he said. When Aswad had arrived in the ambulance, the doctor was not sure he was going to make it. And, had the bullet to his lower back entered a razor's edge closer to his spine, he could have been paralyzed. Aswad felt relieved to have survived and that he would walk again, but Dr. Marshall told him that the likelihood of ever playing basketball competitively was very slim.

Ten days later, Aswad was discharged from the hospital in a wheelchair, with a machine to help him breathe and a large plastic bag stuffed with four different types of medication and a stack of discharge papers. He had been shot just days before he was scheduled to start his post-college professional career overseas, and that meant he was unemployed and uninsured at the time. It also meant he did not have his own place to live. So, after he left the hospital, he stayed on the couch in the small apartment his mother shared with one of Aswad's older brothers, not far from where the shooting took place. For many months, he rarely left that couch. He was in near-constant physical pain and was devastated by the drastic changes he faced. Every part of his life felt broken. How could he go outside again without being a target? How would he make a living? How could he avoid putting hardships on his family? The medical bills from the ambulance, emergency surgery, and hospital stay started piling up. And his Elms College student loans—tens of thousands of dollars—would soon need to be paid as well.

"Everything I worked toward was gone," Aswad recalled years after the shooting. "Falling into debt, straining my mother, trying to figure out my new life. Whenever I moved, pain shot through my body. With every loud noise, I was flooded with adrenaline. Every time I closed my eyes, I was being shot again. Every time I opened my eyes, I was facing financial and emotional problems I couldn't easily solve."

Aswad suffered from chronic panic attacks, night sweats, and post-traumatic stress disorder. He could barely talk about the profound grief he was experiencing because he was worried how it might affect his already distraught family. A soft-spoken, earnest person and the youngest of five children who hates to burden others, he did not want to put too much emotional weight on his loved ones.

Interactions with the investigators on the criminal case added to Aswad's distress: a battery of questions about what happened and about things he could not remember of the split seconds that changed everything. He felt as if every question implied it was his fault—his fault that it happened or his fault that he didn't recall much. The tone of condemnation and suspicion softened only when investigators found out about his promising basketball career that was cut short. Trips to the hospital were overwhelming too, made up of a long list of things he needed to do to heal his damaged body: medications, instructions, things to monitor, more appointments. He was traumatized and overwhelmed. That quick and seemingly inconsequential stop for orange juice had, in an instant, rerouted the path of his entire life.

The trauma and shock of an altered life that Aswad experienced is hard to fathom—and a frighteningly common experience in the United States. At least one in four Americans become a victim of crime during the course of their lives, and more than half of these are victims of violent crime. This is likely an undercount.[1] Add in Americans who have lost a family member to violence—in criminal justice speak they are often called "co-victims" because the traumatic aftermath of a loved one's violent death causes life-altering psychological anguish that is similar to those who are directly victimized by violent injury—and the magnitude of impact is even higher. Victimization adds up to roughly 3 million people *annually* who have had their lives altered by violence, with many more people, from family members to friends and community residents, also bearing the brunt.[2]

Like Aswad, those who survive becoming a victim or losing a family member to a violent death are often plagued by a wide range of catastrophic repercussions in nearly every aspect of their lives, including traumatic stress. Health experts have uncovered the ways trauma can drastically interrupt well-being, often leading to a lifetime of negative consequences, including chronically poor health, economic instability, and early death. The documented experiences of crime survivors across the United States are proof of this. They report that trauma impedes a person's capacity to recover and regain stability in far-reaching dimensions, including losing the ability to maintain jobs or housing, struggling with family responsibilities or being unable to stay in school, coping with trauma by self-medicating with drugs or alcohol, and experiencing chronic levels of stress, hyperawareness, insomnia, exhaustion, dissociation, and hopelessness. Depression and anxiety arising from trauma also damage physical health, such as the development of ailments, including heart disease, diabetes, and other life-threatening maladies, creating additional lifelong burdens beyond the emotional and economic impacts. Multiply this by the millions who have been harmed by violence without getting recovery help and the picture of debilitating trauma begins to look like a national public health emergency. It is not an overstatement to say that the United States is a traumatized nation.

In addition to the weight of managing traumatic stress, many survivors also experience *victimization debt*—this is the financial burdens and liabilities arising from victimization that can cause ripple effects, quickly driving victims and co-victims into poverty or economic stagnation. People without health insurance who become victims of crime often face mountains of medical debt, and those who suffer life-altering physical injuries, like Aswad, become unable to maintain prior employment pathways, struggle to pay bills that were incurred prior to victimization, and lose access to credit or become ineligible for loans. Many victims are also forced to rely on family members or friends to find safe places to live; to help care for children when the strain of negotiating life postinjury is too great; or to provide transportation if they can no longer drive, afford car costs, or experience too much hyperarousal to rely on public transportation. The financial and emotional burdens of recovery are steep.

Americans from all walks of life enter the ranks of victims. The difference between safety and physical harm, between stability and trauma, and between one life and an altogether different one can be as random and unexpected as stopping at a convenience store to buy orange juice. However, victimization data reveal that in fact it usually isn't all that random. A large-scale pattern underlies the madness. The effects of violence and crime are not evenly distributed across all demographics at the same rate; instead, different degrees of privilege produce different degrees of insulation. In particular, race and socioeconomic status, which all too often define where you live and work, dramatically influence the likelihood of becoming a victim of crime.

While the attempted robbery and shooting that Aswad survived was random, the fact that he became the target of a crime was not. Demographically speaking, it would have been near impossible for Aswad to escape victimhood in his lifetime. An African American male, Aswad grew up in Highland Park, just outside of Detroit, Michigan. When he was a child, Highland Park was largely a low-income, African American community that knew the devastating effects of neighborhood violence all too well. Data show that those who are most vulnerable to becoming victims are our nation's youth; Americans of color; people from low-income backgrounds; lesbian, gay, or transgender people; and those with disabilities.[3] And the disproportionate vulnerability these demographic groups face is even greater when looking at the likelihood of becoming a victim repeatedly. Yes, crime is ubiquitous in the United States, but crime is also concentrated: low-income communities of color are disproportionately affected, and young people from these communities are disproportionately impacted in the extreme.[4]

That fateful day in the convenience store was not Aswad's first life-altering brush with gun violence. When he was just ten years old, his best friend, Reubin, also ten, was killed in a drive-by shooting. The two boys had been inseparable, a pair who did homework together, played games and sports together, and motivated each other to dream big. Their childhood lives were intertwined, just as they imagined their teenage and adult futures would be. That is, until Reubin's horrific death sent shock waves throughout the community and flooded Aswad's young life with indescribable grief. Being so young, Aswad "didn't know how to process death," especially the death of his best friend, and it terrified him.[5] And that was just the beginning. By the time he was eighteen, he had lost more than thirty friends and neighbors to gun violence. The chronic aftereffects of so much trauma shaped his life, and the absence of real support to deal with these surroundings was as constant a theme as was the war zone–like violence he witnessed.

Millions of people in the United States have experienced the same kinds of post-trauma impacts that Aswad experienced. The terrible irony of this crisis is that even as every year more victims must reckon, mostly on their own, with life-changing traumas and financial debt arising from crime and violence, the United States is coming out of four decades of unprecedented political attention to the plight of victims of crime and exponential growth in the criminal justice system—the very system purportedly tasked with protecting victims, through both stopping crime and ostensibly attending to the needs of those who have been victimized.

Through the so-called tough-on-crime era of the last forty years, proclaimed concern for crime and victims has been elevated over almost every other political issue in American politics. Driven by attention to what politicians in the 1980s called the overlooked victims, drastic changes have emerged in the operation of criminal justice. And the most powerful political movement at the center of these sweeping changes—which fueled tough-on-crime and criminal justice expansion—was the victims' rights movement. During the same time period in which Aswad, his family, and his community struggled to find safety, the political cause for the rights of victims was driving a sea change in American crime policy. That victims' rights movement has now influenced nearly every aspect of American political life and nearly every aspect of the justice system: from courtroom protocols, to police and prosecutorial practices, to sentencing decisions, to the size and power of corrections agencies. The United States went from having virtually no laws related to victims on the books in the 1970s to enacting literally thousands of law changes in every single state in the nation and federally in the decades since. From the 1980s to 2010s, *over 32,000* laws seeking to advance victims' rights were enacted.[6] In terms of legislative accomplishments, the victims' rights movement has been one of the most successful political movements in U.S. history.

Through this unprecedented political action and media attention, the victims' rights movement won big, at least conceptually. Three main types of policy reform emerged to advance protection for victims. Victim assistance programs sought to provide financial and emotional support to survivors. Criminal court procedural rights sought to elevate the standing of victims in criminal cases. And the expansion of criminal justice bureaucratic power sought to protect victims from repeat crime and to catch more people committing crime—an expansion that included everything from procuring more resources for investigation and surveillance to expanding pretrial detention, making prison sentences longer and longer, emphasizing punishment over rehabilitation, severely curtailing release opportunities for people in prison, and considerably increasing budgets for law enforcement, prosecution, and corrections. In other words, the victims' rights movement essentially functioned politically as a steady regimen of steroids for the criminal justice system, resulting in the system's extraordinary growth and power.

But these massive changes did not help Aswad, or millions like him. In 2009, the year he was shot, the national incarceration rate reached its highest point in U.S. history, higher than it has ever been since, and the federal crime victims fund had swelled to an unprecedented $4.8 billion, more than double what it had been just two years prior.[7] But that extreme incarceration rate and groundswell of money for victims did not prevent the harm Aswad experienced or help him in the aftermath. Where were all those victims' rights when he was traumatized by violence?

Disturbingly, victim assistance was nonexistent in his experience. No one in a justice system obsessed with punishment mentioned anything to him about places to go for help or even interacted with him as a person struggling to adjust. When he found out about victims' rights, nearly ten years later, Aswad was stunned to learn that this type of help existed. He called his relatives who had also been victims of gun violence. "Did you ever hear about victim assistance or victim compensation?" he asked.[8] His father, who was shot in the chest in the 1980s, had not. His brother, who was shot in the 1990s, had not. His cousin, who uses a wheelchair after being shot in the back, had not. His friends from his old neighborhoods of Highland Park and Hartford had not either. And Dr. Marshall—his emergency room doctor—also didn't know about these funds. In fact, in many of their post-op visits, the doctor had lamented to Aswad about how little help existed for the hundreds of victims he operated on annually.[9]

Aswad's survey of loved ones victimized by violence is consistent with national statistics. Despite the proliferation of victim assistance programs, few victims access these services or attain available compensation. Research has shown that less than 10 percent of violent crime victims receive help from victim services agencies and two-thirds of all crime victims report never receiving mental health or financial assistance to recover from harm—despite being entitled to this assistance.[10] This includes victims, like Aswad, who lack awareness of services that may be available. But it also includes victims who are aware that such assistance exists but who find it impossible to access it because of its limited availability or its prohibitive costs or because they, as victims, are wrongly deemed ineligible by those in charge of implementing the programs. For the small percentage of survivors who *do* benefit from certain services, very few receive such help by way of the justice system. Instead, more than nine in ten of survivors who do get help report relying on informal networks of family or friends or receiving assistance from people they meet in the health care system, not from the criminal justice system.[11]

This is especially true for victims of color from low-income communities. Disparities in access to assistance reveal an alarming reality: those who are demographically more vulnerable to becoming victims of crime are also less likely to attain recovery assistance. In other words, the most harmed are the least helped. Victims who do find out about assistance options, including victim compensation, from the justice system typically learn about it as part of the support offered to victims where there is a criminal prosecution (although, like Aswad, not all learn about it even through this channel). But most crimes do not result in criminal prosecutions. In fact, the majority of crimes are not reported to the justice system, and of the crimes that *are* reported, less than half result in a prosecution.[12]

So, for far too many survivors of crime, particularly young people of color from low-income communities, when there's no prosecution, there are no criminal court rights and there is also no assistance. Reflecting and compounding the disparities in who most often becomes a victim, as well as the disparities in who obtains victim assistance, are the disparities in which crimes result in criminal justice prosecution, disparities that also fall along race, socioeconomic, and age lines.[13] It is as if an invisible hand is excluding the very people most vulnerable to being victims from ever benefiting from the victim assistance or procedural rights enacted across the country in their names.

How is it possible that the most harmed remain the least helped by our systems of public safety? This neglect happens because, even though the law-and-order-oriented victims' rights movement birthed new rights and assistance in the name of victims, it also cemented a *hierarchy of harm*—the justice system's long-standing hierarchical lens through which victims are seen or unseen. This is a hierarchy that falls primarily along race and socioeconomic lines, of whose harm receives official recognition and response, and whose does not—of which victims matter the most to our systems of public safety and which do not.

Despite all the rhetoric, law changes, new investments, and political attention, the justice system that was bolstered to advance victims' rights continually fails to *see* most crime victims. Instead, for too many victims the larger effect of the victims' rights movement was not courtroom rights or recovery help. Rather, the movement simply added fuel to grow the budgets and power of criminal justice bureaucracies across the nation. Victims' rights became the moral justification for expanding criminal justice power, but the resulting criminal justice bureaucracies have been largely incapable of providing protection and help to most victims of crime.

Those bureaucracies often ended up further victimizing the very people in whose name they grew. Instead of becoming responsive to more victims, criminal justice bureaucracies became a political powerhouse: the voice of public safety in policy making and the lobby that orchestrated the expansion of what is now widely understood as America's broken system of mass incarceration.

This book reveals the long-standing chasm that exists between victims of the most common forms of crime—the people helped least by the victims' rights political agenda—and the massive criminal justice system that emerged in their names. It illustrates how the pro-victim rhetoric of the law-and-order political agenda has been deceptive. Instead of providing support to more victims or effectively addressing the cycle of crime, it has propagated mass incarceration, cemented discrimination against victims, and worsened many victims' relationship with the criminal justice system. The book also describes how the political mythology of the justice system as the voice of public safety disserves most victims by contributing to cycles of unaddressed trauma, which is a leading cause of subsequent violent crime.

In the name of protecting victims, mass incarceration's bureaucracies have misdirected the very resources needed to alleviate cycles of trauma and have blindfolded the public to the real safety needs of most victims. Confronting these difficult truths is necessary if we are to replace mass incarceration with a new approach to safety that more effectively prevents crime and helps those who are victimized by it.

How is it possible that calling for an expansion of the criminal justice system to care for crime victims has hurt so many victims? In theory, the growth and power of a movement spotlighting how victims have been ignored should have been all to the good. To be sure, there have been shifts that have benefited some. Today, at least on paper, victims have more legal rights than ever before, and massive public investments have been made in victim compensation and assistance programs, creating an entirely new set of service agencies that did not previously exist. That's very important, even if those rights and services do not reach most survivors.

All this has come into being because the victims' rights movement, while rightfully identifying the invisibility of most victims in the American criminal justice system, unfortunately, and perhaps unwittingly, placed that very system at the center of the policy solutions offered to fix the problem. This was not the exclusive solution offered, but it was certainly the predominant one.[14] The law-and-order brand of politics that emerged as a political force around the same time as—and in concert with—the nascent victims' rights movement, was focused on increasing the power of the

justice system to arrest and incarcerate. Ultimately, those solutions
to crime problems, which strengthened criminal justice bureaucracies, came to represent the goals of both law-and-order advocates
and many victims' rights advocates. At the height of the victims'
rights movement in the 1990s, victims' political action groups
stood arm in arm with law enforcement groups and prison lobbyists calling for expanded criminal justice powers. And this became
a political strategy that was virtually unassailable. After all, who
would disagree with victims' groups calling for more investments
into our systems of public safety?

On its face, the link between victims' rights and law-and-order
politics seems clear. In the early days, victims' advocates expressed
frustration with a nonresponsive justice system, and prosecutors
and police complained that people facing conviction had more
rights in court than victims did. There were plenty of real-world
examples of victims being ignored that could back these arguments
up. The American justice system as originally conceived was not
centered on victims' needs, voices, or interests; it was designed as
a system in which the state—representing the people—pursued
criminal legal cases against the perpetrators of crimes. This adversarial system was a contest between the state and suspects in which
the only outcomes were either punishment or acquittal. Victims
never had much legal standing, influence, or even relevance in that
setup.

So, in the name of protecting victims, the argument went, it was
urgent to roll back defendants' rights, give victims more influence
in court processes, aggressively pursue more punishment to prevent dangerous people from remaining out on the streets, and give
more balance to the justice system in favor of the victim. Prison
expansion was applauded, extreme sentencing grew popular, and
political careers were cemented through standing up for victims
by enacting changes that made the justice system more powerful.

Investment in criminal justice bureaucracies took off. Every state
in the nation built more prisons, ratcheted up sentence lengths, and

expanded police, probation, courts, prosecutors, and sheriffs—you name it, if it was part of the criminal justice system, politicians stood in line to throw dollars at it. The set of bureaucratic agencies that make up the U.S. criminal justice system went from relative political insignificance to a behemoth set of institutions that had (and has) the political capacity to influence elections, push through legislation, and secure exponential budgetary growth.

The effects of that expansion have been immense. As of 2020, more than 2 million people in the United States work in the justice system. Indeed, the number of people working in criminal justice rivals the workforce of the nation's entire agriculture sector. One in every eight state employees works in the corrections system.[15] It's an enormous network of institutions that has grown to eclipse most state and local government investments in everything from higher education to mental health to parks and recreation. As part of this unprecedented growth, the cost of running the U.S. criminal justice system has ballooned. The United States spends more than $80 billion annually on prisons alone; this doesn't include police, sheriffs, courts, probation and parole departments, prosecutors, or defense attorneys. In 2017, the Bureau of Justice Statistics estimated that, taken together, the total annual investment in the U.S. criminal justice system is more than $300 billion—larger than the entire budget of any state, even California, a state that has the fifth largest economy in the world.[16]

Through these immense bureaucracies, the United States now incarcerates more people per capita than any nation on the planet. Nearly 2 million people are incarcerated in the United States, representing a 500 percent increase over the last fifty years.[17] Russia incarcerates roughly half as many people per capita as the United States does, and China—which many Americans assume to be a gulag nation because of its authoritarian political system—incarcerates about one-fifth as many people.[18]

In the wake of the victims' rights legal revolution, the discretion and power of criminal justice bureaucracies have grown along with their budgets. Years of new policing authority laws and court decisions have whittled away Americans' rights to be protected from unwarranted search and seizure.[19] Police have gained immense authority to stop, search, arrest, and detain people for just about any reason at just about any time. In parallel, prosecutorial authority has grown. As mandatory sentencing regulations expanded, these laws handed greatly increased discretion and power over to prosecutors.[20] Prosecutors now have the ability to charge people with crimes that come with mandatory minimum sentence terms and to secure plea deals that quickly result in convictions. It is much easier to secure a plea deal or conviction when the penal code mandates what will happen if people are found guilty at trial. *If you take a plea deal to a lesser charge, you'll get ten years, but if you fight the case and we go to court, you'll face a mandatory twenty-year sentence.* This is the oft-heard "offer" that many people facing charges encounter.

What have been the effects of this growth in criminal justice discretion and power on communities, particularly communities most harmed by concentrated crime? The very real human costs of these internationally unique incarceration practices are now a defining feature of many American neighborhoods, neighborhoods that pleaded for more safety and help for victims and received instead unprecedented levels of arrest, prosecution, and imprisonment, an extreme response that spread poor health, led to family disintegration, and destroyed community stability.

The racial disparities embedded in mass incarceration are nothing less than extreme. One in three Black men will be imprisoned at some point in his life, as will one in six Latino men. By contrast, just one in seventeen white men will be imprisoned over the course of his lifetime.[21] At every level of the justice system, disparities in treatment across race demographics are prevalent. People of color, especially Black Americans, are more likely to be stopped by police, to be charged by prosecutors more heavily, to be held in detention pretrial, and to receive a stiffer sentence in court and face longer prison terms with fewer chances for release.[22]

This growth in imprisonment also exacerbates rather than mitigates trauma. Once people are convicted and sentenced, they very often experience trauma at the hands of the system that claims to have incarcerated them to protect others. Sheriffs and wardens who run prisons and jails often have wide leeway to engage in torture-like tactics as disciplinary measures and even to prevent timely release. The use of solitary confinement or isolation in response to violence or rule breaking is often permissible, as are limiting visitation or contact and meting out bodily violence.

Moreover, after serving their time, people with prior criminal records are ineligible for many areas of employment, many professional trade licenses, and many supervisorial roles within specific job markets. In a very real sense, a prison sentence doesn't end when the formal sentence ends. The near-permanent punishment facing people with convictions increases instability, community degradation, economic losses, and chronic ill health and precipitates early death.[23] And people of color with records are even less likely to attain housing, stable jobs, and a host of other vital supports compared with their white counterparts with records. It is a stigma that, as Michelle Alexander described in *The New Jim Crow*, has created what amounts to a caste system in America.

Empowered by the political perversion of calls for victims' rights, the U.S. criminal justice system has grown over just a few decades into an unparalleled juggernaut—an extraordinarily expansive array of institutions that wield immense power to intervene in the lives of everyday Americans with excessive punishment and a lifetime of social exclusion. Remarkably, all of this has been accomplished without effectively addressing the actual needs of most victims—neither their needs for help recovering from harm nor their preferences for how people who have caused harm are held accountable: in survey after survey, victims reveal a strong policy preference for a justice system that emphasizes accountability through rehabilitation over excessive punishment.[24]

* * *

This carceral growth combined with chronic victim disregard has devastating consequences for public safety as well. The excessively punitive system now often *adds to* trauma more than it addresses trauma, a response that contributes to the cycle of crime. Fresh out of law school in 2001, I began working with parents of incarcerated youth to help them get their children out from behind bars. I set out to expand parents' voices in juvenile court, to help parents push courts to see the children facing criminal charges in front of them as children—as somebody's *child*—and to consider the devastating effects of incarceration on their development and future. Yes, these youth committed crimes, but they could be held accountable without being shipped off to warehouse-style prisons where isolation, violence, and degradation were commonplace. When given different options, like mental health treatment or restorative justice, surely everyone would agree that imprisonment only makes matters worse for these kids.

I learned many things those early years as an advocate for alternatives to incarceration for youth. Painfully, the availability of alternative options to harsh incarceration—and the parents advocating for them—rarely changed court outcomes. The mostly low-income parents of color were rarely viewed as legitimate voices in a court process that sought to churn through dockets and close case files, without ever evaluating its own biased assumptions about the teens in front of them. I also witnessed the consequences of imprisonment: kids in solitary confinement for months or even years, daily fighting and suppression from guards, harsh cement cellblocks hardening young minds, places literally designed to cut youth off from humanity.

But for many of the young people I encountered who were facing incarceration, their day of sentencing was not the most difficult thing that had happened in their young lives to date. David, for example, had witnessed more than a dozen murders before his fifteenth birthday, while Angela had been placed in foster care after suffering from sexual abuse at home, only to be sexually abused again in the foster care system.

The youths came from different backgrounds, but virtually all of them had been victims long before they were ever arrested for *committing* a crime. Unseen and unsupported, they were survivors of life-altering harm many years before the day of their first arrest. Most had been victims of numerous acts of violence before ever getting into trouble themselves, bearing with them the emotional scars of repeated traumas experienced over the course of years. And most of the time they hadn't received any help—no interventions to assist them in coping with extreme stress, depression, sleeplessness, and near-constant fear. These personal burdens went unaddressed, regardless of how drastic an effect the traumas had on their young lives. Time and again, these children became victims, and nothing happened, or nothing helpful happened, in response to the influence of violence on *their* lives. Where were *their* victims' rights when they needed them, before they broke the law?

The experience of these youth, starting with disregard when they were unprotected and hurt and including placement in a trauma-inducing environment after they commit a crime themselves, is a very common cycle for many people entering our justice system as defendants. Most people who commit violence were previously victims who did not regain safety. Ignoring people who are unprotected and traumatized has been a dysfunctional part of our public safety system for generations. Yet helping these young survivors recover from trauma long before they resorted to committing crime would almost certainly have done more for public safety than locking them up after they traumatized someone else.

That was twenty years ago, in the midst of the nation's tough-on-crime era of unparalleled criminal justice system expansion. A lot has changed since then. The perils of extreme incarceration growth have been well documented and hotly debated. It is now almost universally accepted and popularly understood that the United States has a criminal justice problem. In many parts of the country, in both blue and red states, criminal justice reforms have emerged, and incarceration has started to decline.

The groundswell of support for such change is long overdue. But criminal justice is a system that is extremely difficult to change, especially when violence rates shift up, as gun violence did during the COVID-19 pandemic years of 2020 and 2021, and political attention again swings toward politicians who want to appear anti-crime and pro-victim. One of the key recurring obstacles to change is the persistent notion in policy-making arenas that the purpose of our criminal justice system is to protect victims. For a long time—and it is still the case in many parts of the country today—those advocating for criminal justice reform have been seen as standing *against* the interests of crime victims. When policy reform proposals emerge, public officials in statehouses across the country ask familiar questions: But what about victims? Is this reform going to be safe? These questions have had the power to stop many reforms from being enacted, or to severely limit them, no matter how popular, thoughtful, or effective the proposed reforms may be. The policy arguments about being careful with justice reform because *we don't want to create more victims* is a common theme that regularly stifles the breath of policy change.

But what is so vexing about this "Is-it-safe?" debate about reform is just how little of the debate is informed by the realities of crime, violence, and victimhood in the United States. Already, millions of people do not experience the justice system as a place in which to seek protection and help. And millions of crime incidents happening annually could be prevented through appropriate interventions and support when vulnerable people, especially young people, experience trauma. Without prevention or healing built into the DNA of our public safety systems, it is hard to imagine how a beefed-up justice system will ever truly deliver safety.

From the founding of the United States to the present day, protecting victims from harm has been a far cry from the actual purpose or capabilities of American criminal justice. For more than half of the nation's history, for example, the American justice system did not even provide Black Americans or many other demographic groups with a legally cognizable claim to safety. And even when the laws changed to obligate the justice system to serve all communities, that difference in human recognition was deeply baked into daily operations.

Two hundred years after the justice system was founded on a severely limited definition of who had a right to safety, a modern-day law-and-order political strategy co-opted a true victims' rights movement for the purpose of strengthening criminal justice agencies. That co-opting was part of a long-standing tradition of failing to see most crime victims as people deserving safety or support. For generations, America's racialized criminal justice system has left millions on their own to protect themselves, without a legal system that acts equally on behalf of all harmed people.

For most people hurt by crime and violence, mass incarceration operates a bit like a parallel universe. On the one hand, there is pervasive disregard for so many victims: no shock at the suffering, no concerned response from public systems, no access to support to manage the trauma and financial burden. On the other hand, there is this behemoth system of justice bureaucracies, with immense power to arrest and incarcerate, capable of worsening life outcomes for the people who encounter it, while doing little to address the trauma of either those who are harmed or those who commit harm. These bureaucracies turn lives and communities upside down, all in the name of protecting victims.

The fact that decades of investments in criminal justice have been justified in service of protecting victims of crime, when most victims haven't seen the justice system offer any real protection or help, is perhaps the most sinister and ironic aspect of mass incarceration. Mass incarceration in the name of safety, and disregard for most victims, are two sides of the same coin. If the systems of public safety do not offer true equal protection to all Americans, then those systems have no moral legitimacy.

Now that the need for criminal justice reform has moved from the margins of public debate to increasingly mainstream acceptance, our nation has an opportunity to undo the corrosive legacy of law-and-order politics that, hiding behind the language of victims' rights, fueled mass incarceration. But to achieve the potential of transformation, we must understand, and change, our public safety systems' foundational purpose as it relates to victims. The notion that our current criminal justice system protects and helps victims stands out as a major—perhaps the biggest—political roadblock to ending mass incarceration and giving victims real protection and support.

This book argues that unearthing—and resetting—the relationship between victims of crime and the criminal justice system is required to replace mass incarceration with an approach to public safety that provides *everyone* with a better chance at safety.

Part 1, "A Marriage of Convenience," makes the case that, while mass incarceration was justified as necessary to protect victims, it has done more harm than good in their names. Chapter 2 describes how this happened—how the call for victims' rights in the 1980s and 1990s morphed into a political movement that offered moral cover for mass incarceration but turned a blind eye to millions of victims.

Part II, "The Hierarchy of Harm," brings to light why this happened. Massive growth in criminal justice did not offer more protection because there has been a hierarchy of harm built into the bones of American criminal justice. While victims' rights may have sought to protect more victims, the effort never upended the foundational reality that not everyone who is victimized in the United States is seen as a victim. Chapters 3 and 4 provide a historical snapshot of the legal exclusions to the right to victimhood, and Chapter 5 provides a glimpse into the modern-day manifestations of this discrimination.

Part III, "Poisonous Priorities," describes the impact of this hierarchy of harm on public safety. Beyond failing to help most victims in the aftermath of crime, disregard for most victims has also led to the wrong public safety policy priorities. Chapter 6 describes how the mass surveillance strategies that emerged to protect victims, ignored most victims and even pushed many into the justice system, and Chapter 7 describes how the tough penal code sentencing changes, often enacted in the name of high-profile victims and touted as good for safety, failed to impact crime in a meaningful way.

Part IV, "Hurt People and Healed People," unmasks what the nation's true safety priorities should be. If our nation's public safety systems were truly focused on helping victims and improving safety, we would understand the cycle of trauma and address it, instead of making matters worse. Chapter 8 presents the often overlooked but obvious reality that a lot of crime and violence is traceable back to unaddressed exposure to trauma. Chapter 9 exposes the devastating truth that, instead of building an approach to safety that considers this fact, many American criminal justice practices contribute to the cycle of trauma.

Part V, "A New Safety Movement," offers some key solutions to answer the question: what should our systems of public safety be doing instead? These chapters offer four core solutions to more appropriately honor victims and stop the cycle of harm. Chapter 10 calls for a new victims' right: a right to trauma recovery. Chapter 11 calls for a new lens to examine safety issues, starting with listening to those most harmed and least helped. Chapter 12 lays out a new set of public safety investments, putting public money in the right places to better prevent crime. Chapter 13 offers a new way of thinking about achieving justice. The last forty years of mass incarceration have not brought about justice for most harmed people. It's time to change how we define it and reset our expectations about how to achieve justice for those harmed.

In the legislative and political arenas where decisions about public safety policies and budgets are made, tunnel vision tends to limit who has a say. Most of the time criminal justice agencies dominate debates and wield immense moral authority. Viewing these agencies as the sole—or even main—vehicle for protecting victims and advancing safety must be abandoned. The solutions, and leaders, capable of achieving shared safety are right in front of us, building new models, including community-based trauma recovery services, violence prevention strategies, mental health assistance, and reentry support. These models grow stronger by the day and the leaders growing these approaches are emerging as the new public safety stakeholders. Now it is time for political decision-makers to catch up.

2

How the Call for Victims' Rights Led to Mass Incarceration

The heartache of remembering October 1, 1993, for Jess and Annie Nichol has not gotten much easier over the years. Losing their twelve-year-old sister, Polly Klaas, to kidnapping and murder when they were in grade school changed everything. There was life before that day, then a very different existence after. As it turned out, this tragic event would have a similar impact on criminal justice in the United States. It was one way before Polly's death and another way after.

Polly's murder was as unimaginable as it was horrific. On an otherwise normal evening in Petaluma, California, six-year-old Annie went to sleep in her mother's bed so that her older sister, Polly, could have a sleepover in their shared bedroom with Polly's two best friends. Wearing one of Polly's T-shirts as a nightgown, Annie reluctantly went to bed, upset that she was not allowed to join in the older girls' fun. Jess, Polly's stepsister, also twelve years old at the time, had stayed at her mom's house that night. Hours later, flashing lights on the ceiling of Annie's mother's bedroom woke Annie up from sleep. When she walked into the kitchen, she saw police officers everywhere. Looking for confirmation that what she was witnessing wasn't anything to worry about, Annie glanced at her mother's face. Any trace of possible calming explanations vanished, and she knew something terrible had happened.

Through tears, Annie's mother explained that Polly had been kidnapped. A strange man with a knife had entered the bedroom where Polly and her friends were getting ready for bed, and after tying the girls up, he had abducted Polly at knife point. Annie sat in the living room rocking chair all night, staring at the front door and waiting for Polly to return. "That is the moment my childhood ended," Annie recalled.[1]

Over the course of the next few weeks, one of the largest missing person searches in U.S. history ensued. The Federal Bureau of Investigation (FBI) joined with local and state police and descended on Petaluma to investigate, while hundreds of people volunteered to search for Polly. The phrase "Bring Polly Home" became a rallying cry, making national and international news.[2]

The outpouring of support offers was unprecedented. Actress Winona Ryder, also from Petaluma, offered $200,000 in reward money. It was the first time the internet was used to aid in the search for a missing person, with over 2 billion images of Polly distributed worldwide. In the end, more than four thousand people volunteered to help look for the missing girl.[3] The outrage and horror the crime evoked generated thousands of news stories, with shocked parents all over the world holding out hope that Polly would be found alive.

In the wake of Polly's abduction, young Jess and Annie's world turned upside down. Trying to focus on school or to live any kind of normal life was impossible while they struggled to process their emotions and manage the stares and whispers from classmates, not to mention the near-constant swarming of police and reporters. In December of that year, the search came to a devastating conclusion. Law enforcement arrested Richard Allen Davis, who had been recently paroled from state prison after decades of cycling in and out of incarceration. He confessed and brought police to the site where he had buried Polly's remains. The FBI agents who had become a fixture in Jess and Annie's home for those two surreal months broke the traumatizing news to the family. An overwhelming new wave of grief came in tandem with the need to rush to a hotel in a different town to avoid the media swarm.[4] Press from all over the world reported on the private tragedy that had become a painful public saga.

But it was far from over. For Jess and Annie, the search had ended but the spotlight remained. Celebrities endeavored to blunt the pain and to bring some joy to the girls' lives. Winona Ryder invited the girls to the premiere of the Hollywood movie *Reality Bites*, where they met Leonardo DiCaprio and other big stars on the red carpet. Actor and comedian Robin Williams took the girls for lunch. "Everything was so confusing," Jess recalled. "We got to hang out with celebrities, but all of this was happening because Polly was gone. It was impossible to reconcile. It felt so hollow."[5] The subsequent attention confused them even more when it morphed into a political cause. Justice for Polly became a flashpoint that fueled California, and the nation's, already growing tough-on-crime movement.

Polly's grieving father, Marc Klaas, devastated by his horrific loss as anyone would be, joined with California lawmakers and law enforcement to call for sweeping changes to state criminal law. The movement to enact "Three Strikes and You're Out" emerged, with Marc Klaas lending his voice and the memory of Polly to support this new cause. The slogan matched the simplicity of the proposed law: anyone with a prior serious felony conviction would receive a sentence twice as long for a new felony, and anyone with two prior felony convictions would receive a sentence of twenty-five years to life for a third felony offense. Only one other state in the nation at the time had ever enacted anywhere near such a strict measure. Washington had passed a three-strikes law the year prior to its introduction in California, although the Washington law, which applied the harsh sentencing scheme to a smaller list of offenses, was not as expansive as the sentencing elements of California's proposal.[6] Governor Pete Wilson called a special legislative session specifically devoted to passing tough-on-crime legislation, and Three Strikes was soon passed both legislatively and by way of citizen initiative.[7]

As California sped toward passage of the Three Strikes policy, the movement for stricter sentencing in the name of Polly Klaas grew to national proportions. In December 1993, Mr. Klaas met with and became close to newly elected president Bill Clinton, who promised to champion tougher sentencing laws in honor of Marc's daughter. The next month, Clinton called for Three Strikes in his nationally televised State of the Union address. "When you commit a third violent crime, you will be put away for good. Three strikes, and you are out!" he exclaimed to loud applause. Despite the public clamor of support, this position was surprising to some members of Clinton's own party and administration. Philip Heymann, the president's deputy attorney general, left his post over his opposition to what he referred to as a "just plain dumb" policy. "This is a proposal that will require our grandchildren to support over-aged, retired street robbers for 30 years, [in prison] long after they are no longer dangerous," Heymann said.[8]

President Clinton incorporated the Three Strikes and You're Out policy into the comprehensive crime legislation he was championing and began regularly invoking Polly Klaas's name in speeches and media interviews about the legislation. The Violent Crime Control and Law Enforcement Act of 1994 included dozens of tough-on-crime provisions, including protocols to expedite the death penalty and financial incentives for states to pass strict sentencing laws. States could receive money to build prisons, for example, if they passed "truth-in-sentencing" laws that required people in prison to serve at least 85 percent of their sentence prior to release. The *Los Angeles Times* called the bill the "most expensive and far-reaching crime bill ever considered by Congress."[9]

Invoking Polly Klaas's name became common among elected officials at all levels of the political system. She was referenced thousands of times by politicians across the country campaigning for lengthy mandatory sentencing laws. For Annie and Jess, this led to increased spotlight and more surreal experiences. Within just a few months of the confirmed death of her sister, seven-year-old Annie traveled to the White House to be on an ABC News television special hosted by Peter Jennings in which President

Clinton answered questions from children. There was something morbidly voyeuristic about the whole saga. When the special aired, ABC showed video footage of Annie in her home, standing in front of ropes and bells she had fashioned around her bedroom door "to keep the bad guys out," before showing her at the White House with other children, ready to ask a question of the president. Annie told Clinton that she feared she would be killed before she had a chance to grow up to be an adult, and she wanted to know what he was going to do about that. He choked up and responded by talking about the importance of increasing public safety and the help his crime bill would offer.[10]

In March 1994, five months after Polly's abduction, the California state legislature passed the Three Strikes bill, which Governor Wilson quickly signed into law. Soon after, Clinton's 1994 crime bill made it through the U.S. Congress, with overwhelming majorities in both houses voting in favor—in the Senate, ninety-five senators lined up in support of the legislation—and the president signed it into law with Marc Klaas by his side at the signing ceremony. The laws popping up around the country to mandate lengthy sentences for hundreds of crimes, combined with new federal incentives to enact truth-in-sentencing requirements, drastically lengthened the amount of time people entering prison would stay locked up, increasing average sentence lengths from a few years to a few decades virtually overnight. Across the political spectrum, these tough-on-crime measures garnered widespread support. When some voiced opposition, they were rounded on as being anti-victim.

Shortly after Three Strikes passed California's legislature, California politicians went even further and proposed a broader version for the California ballot, enshrining the law constitutionally. It was so sweeping that Marc Klaas expressed reservations about the measure. But his change of position was not well publicized. Legal reporter Bill Ainsworth wrote in the *Legal Times*, "[a] few months ago, [Klaas's] speeches at victims' rallies and his meetings with [California governor] Wilson and Clinton topped the news. By contrast, his new stance against the measure has received scant coverage."[11]

Voters enacted the Three Strikes ballot measure in November 1994 with overwhelming support: 72 percent voted yes.[12] The wildly popular California ballot measure caught the attention of politicians across the country. Within three years, more than half of the states in the country had passed similar three-strikes laws.[13] Arguably, no single law in the nation has led to more incarceration than California's Three Strikes, considering its direct impact in the nation's most populous state as well as how its passage spurred the replication of other tough sentencing measures nationwide.

Thirteen-year-old Jess was very aware of California's Three Strikes ballot measure campaign. At first, she was excited that something was being done in response to her sister's horrific death. But once she heard people talking about who would be affected by the measure, she felt heartsick. "I remember thinking, 'Wait, what qualifies? So, if somebody does a petty theft or has drugs, they're going to get a strike for that?' I was appalled."[14] Young Jess's concerns were warranted. During the first eight months of implementation, 70 percent of all the thousands of three-strikes sentences issued in courtrooms across California were for nonviolent and nonserious offenses, including theft and drugs—a trend that continued for nearly two decades.[15]

After the enactment of the California law, the state's already exploding prison population grew even more.[16] Over the next ten years, California's prisons became so overcrowded that officials started triple bunking people in cells and turning gymnasiums into dormitories filled with bunk beds. With the number of incarcerated people increasing year after year, prison conditions quickly became dangerous, unsanitary, and extremely violent. The staff were overwhelmed. One person died every week in a California prison as a result of medical neglect.[17] These were largely preventable deaths, but there was simply not enough medical staff to stem the rising tide of maladies that resulted from overcrowding.

Unlike her older sister Jess, Annie was too young to grasp the political developments that emerged in the aftermath of the loss of their beloved sister, or the way their loss had become inseparable from a political crusade that was driving up incarceration at an exponential rate. Both girls vividly recall, however, growing to hate the attention. As young adults they moved away from California, settled into new lives removed from childhood memories, and stopped talking about their loss to avoid triggering the gasps, guilt, and discomfort that swirled with every mention.[18]

While young people today are unlikely to know who Polly Klaas was, her name is still well known to many Americans who watched the nightly news in the 1990s. Yet the fact that her murder is one of the most well-known homicides in U.S. history doesn't bring much peace of mind to Jess and Annie. What they experienced felt like trauma on top of trauma.

"Many people's intentions were good, but the pain was never acknowledged," Jess recalled. Annie elaborated: "It was like we were acknowledged as victims, but we also never really felt seen or heard in that." She added, "Polly was being presented as this symbol of a justice system that wanted to incarcerate more people. There's the Polly that we knew, and then there's this Polly Klaas figure who is unrecognizable. It doesn't make sense that this would be her legacy."[19] Yet, over time, this painful legacy only grew.

The story of how the horrific murder of a white child in a small town came to affect the lives of millions of Americans and to catalyze mass incarceration began long before Jess and Annie's world was upended. It can be traced back to the birth of the U.S. victims' rights movement, whose origins historians date to the 1960s, when victims' rights became a new cause championed by a disparate range of political players from such divergent perspectives as the law-and-order and the feminist movements.[20]

During the tumultuous 1960s era of social justice activism and unrest, the U.S. Supreme Court, led by Earl Warren, issued several groundbreaking opinions that transformed the U.S. criminal justice system. These ranged from recognizing every accused person's right to a defense attorney to prohibiting the admission of evidence in a trial that was obtained illegally, all the way through to requiring Miranda rights be read to suspects in an effort to prevent coerced confessions. These decisions gave legal meaning to the presumption of innocence until proven guilty, a constitutional concept that, until the Warren court weighed in, did not have much influence in the real-world practice of criminal justice. Poor people in particular chronically lacked effective mechanisms to defend themselves against criminal charges or to protect their liberty when police sought to detain them.

Reactions to the Warren court decisions fell primarily along political lines. Conservative political leaders—also reacting to the civil rights and human rights movements that were transforming American society at the time—lambasted the Warren court as issuing decisions that would hamstring police and lead to a crime wave. As Frank Carrington, a conservative thought leader and celebrated champion of the early victims' rights movement, claimed, "We've gone overboard in favor of the criminal and someday the chickens are going to come home to roost."[21] Carrington was one of the first executive directors of Americans for Effective Law Enforcement, a conservative political action group founded to represent the interests of law enforcement and victims when "everyone else" was taking the side of defendants. He joined with law enforcement leaders to distribute talking points memos for politicians, amicus briefs in court cases, and legislative policy proposals—all geared toward strengthening law enforcement and "balancing out" the interests of crime victims with those of defendants.[22]

These law-and-order origins of victims' rights advocacy were fueled by political attention to shifting crime rates in the late 1960s and early 1970s, when racialized concerns about urban riots and increased crime rallied middle-class white voter support for stringent laws and politicians who championed crime control. Republican president Richard Nixon, in 1968, turned up the volume on urban crime hysteria, intentionally seeking to drum up white fear of Americans of color to drive white votes. Michigan and New York became the first two states to pass mandatory minimum sentencing laws focused on lengthy penalties for drug crimes, and other states soon followed suit.[23]

Beyond the law-and-order rhetoric escalating in the political arena, new data also raised questions about the justice system's capacity to help victims. In 1974, the federal government conducted what became the first-ever victimization study, a survey of American households about their experiences with crime and violence. Previously, crime reported to law enforcement was the only official data source on the incidence of crime. The victimization study brought forth a major revelation: crime and violence occurred at much greater rates than previously understood, because most people did not actually report crime to law enforcement.[24] Shockingly, unreported crime represented a larger portion of crime than reported crime did. From the reasons given, a theme of low trust in the justice system emerged, sparking a range of responses from the federal government and criminal justice officials.

Chief among these reactions was the development of programs to incentivize victim and witness cooperation with law enforcement. Victim compensation—programs to provide victims and witnesses who cooperate with law enforcement with financial reimbursement for losses incurred from crime—spread, as well as new efforts to train police and prosecutors in more sensitive approaches to engaging with victims. The impact of trauma on crime victims also became more acknowledged as an issue, and victim assistance organizations emerged to provide survivors with a range of support, from civil legal services to counseling.

On a parallel track, leaders in the feminist movement began drawing attention to the disregard that victims of domestic violence and sexual assault experienced in justice system interactions. Diverse grassroots organizations held speak-outs and protests to raise awareness, to legitimize the experiences of rape and domestic abuse survivors, and to call for more help to stop these largely ignored epidemics. An early victory came in 1972 with the establishment of the first rape crisis centers in the country, places victims could turn to get help, including hotlines, referrals, and aid in navigating the frequently hostile criminal justice system.[25] The centers also became places for the seeding of political action to advocate for new criminal justice practices to take these crimes more seriously. Domestic violence organizations similarly won new public investments in hotlines and services. Proposals to marshal public resources to stop rape and domestic abuse ranged from the establishment of shelters, crisis assistance, and civil legal services to calls for increased law enforcement responsivity. Some advocates also called for mandatory arrest in domestic violence cases and tougher mandatory incarceration.[26]

The victims' rights movement that emerged from these early divergent political influences grew to become one of the most potent political forces in U.S. history. Calls for victims' rights were premised initially on the perception that while people accused of committing crime were securing more legal rights in criminal proceedings, victims of crime were not. Providing courtroom rights for victims to be notified of case information, to speak at criminal proceedings, or to obtain compensation were among the reforms championed, along with more victim services. While reforms resulted in new dollars for both criminal justice agencies and victims, the resources for victims were mostly funneled through law enforcement. This funding created important victim assistance programs, but it also meant that the organizations working most closely with law enforcement grew in size and in visibility, while grassroots victims' rights organizations that promoted other safety solutions were overshadowed.[27]

What is more, as the law-and-order brand of the victims' rights movement matured in the 1980s and 1990s, it developed a platform that went far beyond courtroom remedies or services—calling for more punitive responses to people convicted of committing crimes, including fewer "amenities" for people in prison and ever-lengthening sentences, with fewer opportunities for release. Victims' rights advocates and law enforcement together championed thousands of law changes along these lines, at both the state and federal levels.

Nationally renowned victims' rights advocate Anne Seymour remembers the early days of victims' rights well. The former public affairs director of Mothers Against Drunk Driving (MADD) and co-founder of the National Center for Victims of Crime, she describes the era as one with few distinctions between the calls to support victims and the calls to toughen the justice system. When corrections leaders for Texas governor Bill Clements invited her to speak on behalf of victims at a prison construction groundbreaking ceremony in 1989, she put on the hard hat, grabbed the shovel, and stood proudly for the cameras. "That's what we thought at the time," she said.

Over time, the most politically shrewd elements of the nascent victims' rights movement morphed into a political cause that was virtually indistinguishable from the growing tough-on-crime political agenda. Demands for unrelenting punishment became a political call to action in the name of victims and public safety that for decades was a political third rail, a set of untouchable and unassailable policy priorities.

Nowhere was the call for a more punitive response to crime more evident than in Jess and Annie's home state of California. California has a long list of "firsts" in the history of the victims' rights movement: the first state to establish a victim compensation program, the first state to pass a victims' bill of rights, and the first state to enact more punitive sentencing explicitly in the name of victims' rights.

In 1965, California created the nation's first victim compensation program, to provide financial support to victims or witnesses cooperating with law enforcement. "Most of us have been shocked and outraged," said Governor Pat Brown at the time, "by well-publicized incidents in which witnesses have failed to assist law enforcement."[28] A few years later, in 1970, Ronald Reagan's election as California governor gave a big boost to the national law-and-order movement developing in response both to rising crime and to the liberal judges perceived to be hamstringing police with their rulings. Reagan popularized law-and-order rhetoric in California politics, with his team launching complaints about the "pro-criminal" California Supreme Court that were similar to those complaints being launched against the Warren court nationally.[29] Toward the end of Reagan's second term, after the California Supreme Court struck down a "use a gun, go to jail" law passed in the legislature in 1975, Reagan's political team, including his chief of staff, Edwin Meese, orchestrated a campaign to unseat California Supreme Court justice Rose Bird for being soft on crime, using the notion that Bird was "anti-victim" to bolster the case. While Bird narrowly defeated this first attempt (she was unseated later), the anti-Bird effort elevated victims' rights into mainstream political discourse.[30]

In 1978, California's newly elected governor Jerry Brown signed the first "determinate sentencing" law, urged by liberals as necessary to eliminate disparities in sentencing. The oft-heard concern was that some people received two-year sentences while others received ten years for the same crime. The bill would also serve to empower the legislature to set mandatory sentence lengths for any crime. The effort to enact determinate sentencing was also motivated by intense pressure from increasingly organized law enforcement groups that sought to expand their power, both political and substantive, in part in response to the California Supreme Court's overturning of the "use a gun" law and other rulings.[31]

Then, in 1980, when Ronald Reagan became the first California governor in history to become president of the United States, the California political brand of victims' rights became a national movement. From 1980 to 1982, two major developments—one in California and one through Reagan's leadership nationally—drastically changed the course of criminal justice politics and policy making.

In 1981, a group of law-and-order California legislators and law enforcement political action groups announced their intention to place a first-of-its-kind ballot initiative before voters. Dubbed a Victims' Bill of Rights initiative, the measure proposed sweeping changes to California judicial procedure and sentencing and created specific criminal court rights for victims: it enacted victims' rights to restitution, to provide an "impact statement" during the sentencing phase of a criminal court proceeding, and to attend parole hearings. It also called for a stricter bail system, the enactment of mandatory sentencing rules, limits on plea bargaining, and an abolition or limitation of many defenses related to insanity or mental illness.[32]

Thus, in the name of victims, Proposition 8 sought significantly to increase the power and authority of criminal justice bureaucracies. The preamble proclaimed, "The rights of victims pervade the criminal justice system, encompassing not only the right to restitution . . . but also the more basic expectation that persons who commit felonious acts causing injury to innocent victims will be appropriately detained in custody, tried by the courts, and sufficiently punished."[33] The Proposition 8 campaign was driven by what one historian called a "feverish rhetoric" that California was a "crime jungle" and needed to get tough to better protect victims.[34] The measure was so sweeping that even some in law enforcement spoke out against it as going too far and being likely to create chaos in the courtrooms.[35] A legal scholar at the time wrote, "Although the title 'victims' bill of rights' appealed to a broad range of voters, the actual text of the proposed law contained very few provisions directly addressing victims' concerns."[36] Nonetheless, the proposition passed in June 1982 and sent a message to politicians across the nation that standing up for victims—or at least posturing about their rights—was a popular political choice.[37]

Over the same time period, President Reagan created the nation's first task force on crime victims. Shortly before California voters were slated to vote on Proposition 8—and egged on by some of the same California leaders advancing the proposition—in March 1982, President Reagan spoke to the press about crime. Standing on the White House lawn in front of a small group of people, including law-and-order victims' rights architects Frank Carrington and Edwin Meese, the telegenic Reagan intoned in his Hollywood cowboy voice: "The innocent victims of crime have frequently been overlooked by our criminal justice system, and their pleas for justice have gone unheeded. So, I'm signing today an executive order establishing the President's Task Force on Victims of Crime. This Task Force will conduct a thorough review of national, state, and local policies and programs that affect victims of crime and report back to me and the Attorney General with their findings and recommendations."[38]

The establishment of Reagan's Task Force proved to be a watershed moment, cementing the strength of the victims' rights movement. Made up of leaders in law enforcement and victim advocates, together with law-and-order strategists including Frank Carrington, the Task Force traveled the country, holding hearings. Then its members crafted an extensive report laying out a series of priority recommendations, ostensibly to help victims of crime. The suggestions included legislative action, training for criminal justice agencies, and involvement of private sector leaders. The twelve core recommendations for government action, similar to provisions contained in California's Proposition 8, combined prohibitions on pretrial release and parole release with courtroom rules protecting victims as witnesses in trials, as well as the establishment of support programs for those victims who cooperated with law enforcement investigations.[39] The resulting criminal court–focused recommendations—a combination of victims' procedural rights and a limit on releasing people facing charges or convicted—became an advocacy blueprint for victims' rights and public safety for years to come. The fix for overlooking victims of crime was to strengthen the justice system, to bestow significantly enhanced power on criminal justice officials, and to harshen the sentences meted out to those who committed crimes. While an expanded victims' voice in criminal court has provided more visibility to some victims, many other needs of those victims went unaddressed, as the solution to protecting victims of crime became primarily focused on juicing up the justice system's strength.

In the decade after the passage of California's Proposition 8, as prison populations began to swell, the power of law enforcement lobby groups increased as well. One of the supporters of Proposition 8, and a growing political voice in California's state capital, was California's prison guards' union, the California Correctional Peace Officers Association (CCPOA). A couple of years prior, a savvy political operative named Don Novey—characteristically in a fedora with a fiery personality—became the head of the union.

Within a remarkably short period of time he would elevate the union to become what was considered the most powerful lobby group in California for more than twenty years, from the 1980s through to the first decade of the 2000s. Novey's guards' union was politically aggressive: lobbying the legislature, donating to candidates, and building big coffers to show heft in policy debates about criminal justice. From 1987 to 1992, the union contributed more than $3 million to political campaigns.[40] These investments paid off handsomely, as they won multiple salary increases and successfully fended off several prison-reform measures.[41] Prison guards in California were paid more than their peers in any other state and more than twice the national median wage.[42] And the prison guards' lobby would remain powerful for years to come: they spent more than $32 million on lobbying and political contributions from 2000 to 2010 alone.[43]

Arguably, Mr. Novey's most politically impactful achievement came in 1980, when he met Harriet Salarno. Salarno had lost her daughter, Catina, to horrific violence when Catina's former high school boyfriend shot and killed her on the steps of the University of the Pacific campus, just as she was entering the school on her first day as a new student.[44] Ms. Salarno turned her grief and devastation into action, and ten years after her daughter's death organized a large protest at the California Parole Board to prevent the release of her daughter's killer. The protest grabbed the attention of Mr. Novey, who reached out. Within a year, with funding from Novey's prison guards' union, Ms. Salarno had launched a new victims' political action group: Crime Victims United.[45]

In addition to funds, the prison guards' union gave Crime Victims United (CVU) office space to lobby the state for more punitive criminal justice policies.[46] And lobby they did. With sponsorship from the guards' union, they met with legislators, proposed legislation, and organized victims' rights rallies at the state capitol. In April 1998, "Build more prisons, now!" was the chant that rang out as a crowd gathered in front of the beautiful California State Capitol Building during National Crime Victims' Rights Week, an annual gathering in Sacramento organized by Salarno's group, which over time had become a rally for tough-on-crime policies. Another year, the group filled the capitol lawn with seven hundred cardboard coffins, representing California homicide victims, and Don Novey rallied the crowd for tougher policies. Sitting governors from both parties religiously attended the annual event over the years, to maintain their reputations as "pro-victim."

In the political arena, few disagreed with the victims' rights call for longer and longer sentences. At least half the laws the group advanced were not related to victims' procedural rights—they were about strengthening the criminal justice system's ability to surveil, arrest, incarcerate, make incarceration conditions harsher, and prevent the release of people serving time inside prisons and jails.

"Before their alliance with Novey, victims' rights groups lacked political sophistication," wrote *Sacramento Bee* reporter Bill Ainsworth in 1996. Novey's relationship with Salarno "helped take the victims' rights movement from the political fringes to one of the strongest lobbies in Sacramento . . . and set the foundation for the unprecedented success in 1994 of law-and-order politics."[47]

By the 1990s, the California guards' union had roughly thirty thousand members and an annual budget of more than $20 million. With numerous lobbyists representing them in the state capital, their slogan was "the toughest beat in the state."[48] Working in tandem with Crime Victims United, they essentially steamrolled California's legislative leaders, who spent years passing longer and longer mandatory sentences in the name of crime victims.[49]

Over the course of eight years, the prison guards' union contributed more than $1 million to Crime Victims United and their political activity. Together, these groups drove literally thousands of pieces of legislation. In the state assembly and senate, the scope of their influence was unparalleled. In 1995 alone, for example, Crime Victims United championed and passed more than one hundred bills to mandate tougher sentences and fewer parole opportunities for people in California's sprawling prison system. This group, side by side with the guards, took on a bully-like quality in the halls of Sacramento. Representatives of Crime Victims United, together with the prison guards, threatened elected officials with punishment on Election Day if they refused to support the group's agenda of maximum penalties and fewer privileges for people in prison.[50] Beyond the legislature, they also wielded power at the ballot box. The prison guards' union was instrumental in the success of the Three Strikes ballot initiative in 1994.[51]

Their methods proved contagious. In addition to other states replicating Three Strikes and You're Out, elected officials across the country began ramping up all kinds of tough-on-crime promises to win elections. In 1998, Jeb Bush, then the Republican candidate for governor of Florida, ran a campaign focused on getting tough on crime, including a promise to enact a 10-20-Life law, "modeled after California," to establish mandatory minimum sentencing laws.[52] A real estate developer and the son of former president George H.W. Bush, Jeb Bush ran twice: once in 1994, when he narrowly lost to the incumbent, and again in 1998, when he won in a landslide. In both campaigns, Jeb Bush positioned law and order as a key plank in his platform.

By 1998, that rhetoric was like a speeding locomotive, capable of demolishing all in its tracks. Jeb Bush referred to himself as a "hang 'em by the neck" conservative, a candidate who believed it was time to "emphasize punishment over treatment." Touting his 10-20-Life plan, he declared, "It's kind of an old fashion idea. But the more you [punish people who use guns illicitly], the more people don't commit crimes with guns." Within ninety days of getting elected, Jeb Bush signed three major pieces of criminal justice legislation to mandate lengthy sentences for various crimes. These included his 10-20-Life law. After the fact, he would tell interviewers that he considered these reforms to be among his most important achievements as governor.[53]

From California to Florida, the political commentary and catchphrases were very familiar: standing up for innocent victims and incarcerating violent criminals became the twin slogans of the time. Politically astute politicians and criminal justice lobbies saw the power of messages related to victims and safety. The concept of victims' rights offered substantial political clout to criminal justice agencies advocating for more discretion and more money. The politics of American criminal justice were transformed.

One sunny afternoon in April 2012, the California State Senate Public Safety Committee held one of its regular every-other-Thursday hearings to discuss proposed bills. These meetings were generally predictable: bill authors presented their proposed legislation, members of the committee offered comments and asked questions, and witnesses testified in favor of or against the proposed laws. Then a long line of lobbyists and special interest groups added their comments—the everyday machinery of politics and lawmaking.

On that April day, Senator Mark Leno, a Democrat representing San Francisco's Eleventh District, took the podium and presented a bill that seemed eminently reasonable—so reasonable, in fact, that there wasn't much debate among the committee members. Leno's bill proposed authorizing county sheriffs to move people who were terminally ill from the jails to health care facilities for medical care and hospice. The cost of keeping sick people in the final stages of life incarcerated was enormous, and the state was facing a simultaneous incarceration-crowding crisis and budget crisis, so taking humane and cost-effective steps like this seemed like a no-brainer. "We are talking about permanently medically incapacitated people with six months or less left to live, that pose no risk to public safety. These are individuals that need 24-hour care, many cannot even get up to go to the bathroom by themselves," Leno explained. "So, this bill moves these individuals into a medical setting, reducing burdens and costs on the jails."[54]

When it was time for stakeholder input, a representative of Crime Victims United stood up to testify against the bill. Characterizing the legislation as an affront to victims of crime, she opposed it on principle because it released people from incarceration, even if they were terminally ill and with only a few months left to live.[55]

Lobbyists for victims' groups insisted that even comatose, terminally ill people must stay physically incarcerated—despite the enormous cost to taxpayers, the inhumanity of the practice, and the distress caused to people who work inside jails—out of fairness to victims.

The comments stood in stark contrast to what many victims from cities with high homicide rates and low conviction rates report as their top concerns. Few victims living in communities with little reprieve from violence ever see justice in a courtroom or receive assistance to recover from a crime. The primary safety

concerns they report are certainly not the management of terminally ill detainees. Victims in these situations report problems such
as struggling to get phone calls returned when investigations hit
walls or cases go cold, an inability to pay medical bills when compensation applications are rejected, difficulty finding new places
to live in safer neighborhoods, and fear that the justice system will
not protect them from retaliatory violence if they testify in court.
Despite these realities on the ground, victims' rights political activists in the state capitol were focused on expanded criminal justice
authority, extreme sentences, and reduced release options for incarcerated people—a focus that greatly influenced state politics and
policies but brought little relief to millions of victims.

One observer of the hearing that day in Sacramento knew only
too well how unrepresentative those comments ostensibly on
behalf of victims were. Robert Rooks, the head of the California
branch of the National Association for the Advancement of Col-
ored People (NAACP), sat in disbelief.[56] Though he was new to
California at the time, he was personally familiar with the national
problem of the gap between criminal justice political rhetoric and
the experiences of most crime survivors. Shortly after getting a
master's degree in social work at the University of Connecticut,
Robert started his post-college career as a community organizer in
Hartford, knocking on doors in the city's low-income neighborhoods and talking to residents about their concerns. Too much violence and too little crime prevention always topped the list: moms
keeping their children inside out of fear of bullets flying outside,
teenagers missing school to avoid being jumped, elderly couples
staying inside around the clock to avoid robberies or shootings.

One door he knocked on belonged to Geraldine, another
mother who worried for the safety of her children, the youngest
of whom was a young high school basketball star, Aswad Thomas.
She and other residents started attending community meetings
with Robert where they talked about the criminal justice over-
enforcement/under-enforcement contradiction: plenty of arrests

for crimes like drugs but no relief from violence. "The lack of safety in Black communities has been seen by too many policy makers as a problem inherent to the people from those communities, rather than as a problem happening *to* them," Robert later wrote in an opinion editorial about victims' rights.[57]

Soon, Robert became the executive director of a Hartford-based justice reform advocacy organization called A Better Way Foundation. He joined with other advocates to change Connecticut's criminal laws related to drug crimes—some of the most draconian in the nation—to reduce incarceration and to expand treatment for residents in need. Alongside the call for Three Strikes and You're Out that was burgeoning across the country in the 1990s, another tough-on-crime policy pillar that spread like wildfire in that era was mandatory incarceration penalties for drug crimes, which drove many racially disparate incarceration practices. In Connecticut at the time, one out of every seven Black men, coming from just three neighborhoods, was admitted to prison, costing the state roughly $50 million a year.[58] The drug arrests never seemed to make much of a dent in the number of drug users or in the lack of safety in the neighborhood. "Reducing drug penalties is a good idea, but where are the treatment programs? We have been pushing for treatment, but no one listens," residents told Robert.

That stuck with him. Having grown up in Dallas, Texas, in the 1980s, he understood what the Hartford residents were talking about. In a matter of a few years, after crack cocaine had arrived in the neighborhood, his Dallas community went from church picnics and barbecues to boarded-up houses, empty streets, and incessant sirens. Community leaders called on local officials for help. But instead of treatment, the criminal laws stiffened, the police department acquired paramilitary equipment, and Robert went from losing neighbors and loved ones to addiction to losing them to incarceration and neighborhood violence as new policing tactics ramped up the war-like street environment. "My community cried out for help when drugs and guns hit. We got mass incarceration in response—a response that only hurt the community more," he said.

When Robert was in middle school, his mother moved him out of the increasingly dangerous neighborhood to a safer suburb. By the time he graduated with his master's degree years later, four of his five best grade school friends from the old neighborhood had been killed. And later, a Dallas police officer shot and killed the fifth friend while he was experiencing a psychiatric crisis. Attending the funerals of his grade school friends changed everything. In 1996, after seeing his best friend, PJ, the friend who had taught Robert "how to crease [his] jeans and gave [him] the courage to ask a girl for her phone number," in a casket, Robert pledged to become a community organizer.

Talking to Hartford residents, Robert and local leaders set out to organize an effort that would honor the community's urgings. The money being poured into prisons could be better spent in communities for treatment. He built one of the first community-led "treatment-not-incarceration" campaigns in the country. The campaign urged legislators to equalize the sentencing disparity between crack cocaine and powder cocaine and to put the money saved from incarcerating fewer people into treatment.

Criminal justice bureaucracies came out in force against it. Corrections officials, prosecutors, police, and even judges opposed the legislation. It would make Connecticut unsafe, they all claimed. That wall of bureaucratic opposition in the name of safety was a daunting barrier. Community meetings, legislative visits, media interviews—it was round-the-clock work to build support for the cause. Despite the drumbeat of criticism, Robert and his allies succeeded at getting a bill passed in the legislature, a remarkable feat in that era. Then the day came for Republican governor Jodi Rell to decide whether to sign it. Facing immense pressure from criminal justice bureaucracies, Rell vetoed the bill.

Robert and the hundreds of campaign volunteers were devastated. They marched to the capitol in protest. Seeing the response, the governor called on the legislature to propose an alternate bill, and within two weeks a new bill passed and she signed it into law, making Connecticut the first state in the nation to equalize sentencing disparities between crack and powder cocaine and the first to require community-based investments in treatment to support reduced incarceration.

"Those bureaucracies were so stuck on this idea that the way they did things was just how things were done, and the people impacted didn't have any right to suggest another way. 'Safety' was their job, and their job only," Robert remembered. "The bureaucracies blocked everything. They had a safety monopoly in politics. It took community organizers years of organizing before elected officials were forced to look at the issue another way. It shouldn't take all that for the community, for everyday survivors, to be seen."

Watching the narrative related to victims that played out in the Sacramento hearing that day in 2012 was another turning point for Robert. Whether it was criminal justice bureaucracies in Connecticut claiming that treatment instead of incarceration would hurt safety, or it was victims' political action groups in California opposing prison release, no matter how infirm the people in prison were, the views expressed by those who were considered public safety stakeholders were, he felt, dangerous. He left that hearing motivated to try a new approach: "I knew it was time to do something different and had heard about this new organization aiming to reach out to victims from the communities hardest hit. I joined Californians for Safety and Justice to help build that new safety movement."

Twenty-seven years after their sister's tragic death, Annie and Jess, in the summer of 2020, made the decision to wade into the public sphere again. As adults, they had never spoken out or even identified themselves publicly. But Jess revealed she had never been comfortable with California's Three Strikes law and the growth of mass incarceration that seemed to emanate directly from the victims' rights campaign waged in her sister's name, and that gnawing feeling had never gone away. In 2020, witnessing some of the largest protests in U.S. history taking place all over the country, with unprecedented calls for an end to racial discrimination and mass incarceration, Annie and Jess knew they had to take action.[59] They began researching the criminal justice system and meeting with reform organizations. They penned an essay in the *Los Angeles Times* against mass incarceration, one of the *Times's* most shared opinion pieces in 2020.[60] They then launched "A New Legacy" podcast to educate the public about the issues. Writing about this project for *Elle* magazine in 2022, they commented:

> It's difficult to describe how strange it is to be connected to this legacy of mass incarceration and the pervasive injustice of three strikes, which happened as a result of the worst trauma we've experienced, and then to carry the shame and the pain of that legacy. . . .
>
> Our childhoods were spent in a painful spotlight, and part of the trauma we went through was not only enduring the loss of our sister in this violent way, but also everything that happened after. We've been part of a story that's been used in the true crime genre. . . . There's something to be said for the way that we sensationalize very specific stories, but in doing so, we allow people to bypass larger realities and systems we're all a part of.[61]

From a narrow political perspective, the victims' rights movement partnership with law enforcement agencies was incredibly successful, in part because of its foolproof message as the voice of public safety. But decades later, with the benefit of hindsight, the success of the victims' rights movement looks a bit like a Pyrrhic victory. Despite various aims, the result was primarily mass incarceration.

Ultimately, the law-and-order brand of the victims' rights movement effectively gave justice agencies immense political and financial power—a power that hurt victims more than it helped.

PART II

The Hierarchy of Harm

3

Victims Seen and Unseen

In 2015, Renata Singleton, a New Orleans accountant for a local elementary school and a single mother of three, was arrested and booked into Orleans Parish Prison. Just two years prior, a federal judge had mandated local officials to clean up the notorious jail's deplorable conditions, including lack of sanitation, inadequate medical care, and rampant violence. "Rapes, sexual assaults and beatings are commonplace throughout the facility," the complaint that led to the federal court mandate read. "Violence regularly occurs at the hands of sheriff's deputies as well as other prisoners."[1]

Change was slow going for years following the decree. When Renata walked inside the jail, she was terrified and in tears. Having never been in trouble with the law, she had no idea what to expect. She could not sleep or eat. And even more concerning than the toxic jail environment was how her children were going to handle her incarceration. After one phone call, during which her fifteen-year-old daughter cried nonstop, Renata decided "it was too much" emotionally for the children to hear her in jail, so she stopped calling home.[2] After five days of incarceration, she finally met with a judge. She sat in court wearing an orange jumpsuit, handcuffed and chained. "I felt like a failure," she recalled.[3] The judge decided to release her, requiring her to wear an ankle monitor and to appear in court the next day.

When she returned home, harder than trying to explain to her children about the crime that landed her in jail was trying to explain that she had actually committed *no* crime. In fact, she was jailed for being a crime *victim*.[4]

Six months before she ended up in jail, her boyfriend had scared her when he grabbed and smashed her cell phone, and so she called the police. They arrived soon after and arrested him without incident for misdemeanor battery and property damage. Renata left the relationship and later told investigators that she did not want to pursue charges. They were no longer a couple and she wanted to move on. The New Orleans District Attorney's Office decided to pursue the misdemeanor case against the ex-boyfriend anyway, and to force Renata to provide courtroom testimony, they arrested and jailed her—and set the bail bond at $100,000.

Renata sat in jail, panicked and petrified, for five days, all because the prosecutor wanted to convict someone else. When she appeared in court as promised the day after her release, the case had already been closed; the ex-boyfriend, who had been immediately released on a $500 bond upon his arrest, had pled guilty and received probation. He never spent a single day in jail.

From that day forward, Renata's relationship with the justice system completely changed. "I probably won't call the police again, as long as it isn't life-threatening," she told the *New Yorker* in 2017.[5] As shocking as the prosecutor's decision to have Renata arrested and jailed sounds—surely this must have been just one rogue prosecutor with no moral compass—Renata's experience was not isolated. In fact, over a five-year period, from 2012 to 2017, more than 150 *victims* and witnesses to crime were incarcerated by the New Orleans District Attorney's Office.[6] Nearly all of them were low-income people of color. Many were victims of domestic violence or sexual assault, although victims of human trafficking, gun violence, and other crimes were jailed as well. Some victims, like Renata, were jailed for a few days, while others were incarcerated for months at a time.[7]

When this New Orleans practice came to light, it grabbed national headlines and caused an uproar, including a lawsuit on behalf of Renata and other jailed victims. Yet New Orleans is far from the only place where prosecutors have opted to incarcerate victims. Legally, if a prosecutor believes the victim is a material witness to the prosecutor's case and the victim does not want to testify or may not make it to court, the prosecutor can ask the court to issue a warrant and have the victim jailed until the trial date, no matter how damaging the impact of jail is on the victim or the victim's family.

While the frequency of the practice varies widely and many justice officials use less drastic methods to secure victim testimony (including ankle monitors, home detention, and video depositions), the starkest consistency in terms of when victims are jailed is their demographic profile. The victims who get arrested are virtually always low-income people of color who do not have enough money to post bail or to hire their own lawyer to represent their interests or challenge their incarceration. They are arrested *without the right to a court-appointed lawyer* and incarcerated until the trial date, all to ensure the prosecutor can get a conviction.

Legal challenges to jailing victims have revealed dreadful incidents across the country. In 2016, prosecutors in Washington County, Oregon, jailed a victim of sexual misconduct by a prison guard. The victimization happened while she had been previously incarcerated in state prison. The victim's bond was set twenty-five times higher than the bond set for her assailant. He posted bail immediately, while she sat in jail for fifty days, unable to buy her freedom. At trial, he was convicted and sentenced to sixty days in jail, only ten days longer than she had served.[8]

Human trafficking victims as young as thirteen years old have been incarcerated by federal prosecutors in trafficking prosecutions. Victims report suffering immense life consequences as a result of being jailed. Some have lost jobs or homes while they languished in jail; others have suffered mental breakdowns or have experienced extreme anxiety and depression. Their children have been traumatized by their sudden absence, and some victims have even been victimized *again* while they were incarcerated. In 2018, in Houston, Texas, for example, a prosecutor jailed a rape victim, who also had mental illness, for nearly a month. During that time, she was beaten by other residents and staff and denied her mental health medication.[9]

How could it be that these victims of violence—the very people the justice system is supposed to protect—are being jailed as part of the response to the crime they suffered?

Part of the answer lies in the legal definition of a victim, something that is very different from the commonsense understanding of the word. Under criminal law, crime victims are little more than a means to an end; their status essentially equates to that of any other witness or piece of evidence. They don't have standing to bring criminal cases—only the government can do that. A victim's only official role in criminal court is to help the prosecutor secure a conviction. And some attorneys are willing to put *some* victims through humiliation, degradation, and extreme stress, all in the name of securing that verdict.

This kind of treatment is part of what the victims' rights movement sought to remedy. The political movement to create basic rights for victims secured constitutional amendments in state after state that command the justice system to treat all victims with dignity. Yet decades after victims' rights bills swept the country, victims are still being disregarded and even incarcerated. And the legal reality that victims are essentially nothing more than witnesses in court is not the only reason they are treated this way. There is a deeper, more influential reason: the victims who get jailed are not really viewed as victims at all, either inside or outside the courtroom.

To be treated with dignity, as so many victims' rights constitutional amendments demand, requires that you be seen as a victim in the first place. Not every victim is afforded the privilege of being recognized as, or treated like, someone who has suffered from a criminal act—not in the eyes of justice system officials, politicians, or the media. Not all people who have been the object of a criminal act get to be "victims."

Being viewed as someone who deserves dignity and as someone whom the law seeks to protect from crime has, historically, been a status reserved for a privileged few. While the stories of those recognized as innocent victims can dominate news headlines, and calls for justice for those victims can transform entire legal and political systems, many of the people hurt by crime and violence every day—in fact, many of the people most vulnerable to being hurt—are not afforded dignity, concern, or visibility in courtrooms, newspapers, or statehouses. They are not viewed as innocent, the harm they have suffered is discounted, the repair they deserve is ignored. And at times they are treated the same way as—or, like Renata, even worse than—the people who harmed them are treated.

There is a pervasive, unspoken hierarchy of harm at work that determines which victims get the privilege of being treated as deserving victims in American criminal justice and which do not get that privilege. How the justice system treats victims is frequently determined by this hierarchy of whose harm matters and whose harm does not. This is a hierarchy that operates underneath the surface at every level of the justice system. And that hierarchy, which falls primarily along racial, socioeconomic, and gendered lines, is the lens through which most victims' worth is evaluated. The hierarchy ranges from being seen as wholly innocent and deserving of justice to being criminalized, literally blamed for the harm suffered, and deemed unworthy of protection.

Through this hierarchy, millions of people hurt by crime do not experience a justice system that offers concern or protection or that treats them with dignity. Victims of domestic violence are blamed for their victimization or are jailed for their fear of testifying. Victims of rape or trafficking become reluctant to report the crime, when doing so will result in even more humiliation or traumatic exposure. Gun violence victims in urban neighborhoods are reflexively assumed to be engaging in high-risk behaviors or to be committing crime at the time of the shooting. Neighborhood violence victims are blamed for causing the harm they suffer, left to endure painful, violent injuries that the justice system does not properly investigate, and end up more vulnerable to becoming victims again. Victims at the bottom of the harm hierarchy suffer more than just disregard. They are more vulnerable and less safe precisely because of their invisibility.

As the failings of mass incarceration began gaining mainstream attention in the 2010s, many of the miscarriages of justice that have operated in American criminal justice for generations are coming to light and driving change. Millions of Americans now recognize some of the deepest harms that happen too often within criminal justice—from executing innocent people and incarcerating people for petty drug crimes to shielding police who break the law from facing prosecution. Many years of grassroots activism, political power building, and policy reform advocacy mean that these miscarriages of justice live more visibly in the collective consciousness than ever before—important signs of long overdue progress. But the exclusion of millions of everyday crime victims from being treated as people who have a right to safety remains a stark and often overlooked failure of justice. This chapter and the following two seek to make this failure visible by mapping out the hierarchy of harm that determines who is recognized as a victim deserving of protection and who is discriminated against as a victim, and how that distinction has fundamentally undermined the very bedrock of American criminal justice from the beginning. This is arguably the *first* miscarriage of justice, the cardinal sin on which all other justice system failings rest—one that has persisted over generations despite substantial systemic reforms.

Being recognized in American criminal justice as a crime victim requires several components. First, the harm you suffer, whether it's theft, violence, or abuse, must be recognized as a crime. Then, the justice system must seek to protect you from the harm. Additionally, when you are harmed, you must be provided a voice in the justice process—you must be given the opportunity to report or to testify as to what happened. And finally, the harm suffered must be deemed worthy of an official response, meaning there is a legal mechanism for accountability and restitution. In some ways, and for some victims, the justice system achieves those base-level functions. But for other crime survivors, arguably most of them, the justice system fails. These victims are excluded from official victimhood and remain unprotected by law.

The hierarchy that excludes most victims from recognition and redress is not new. Even a cursory look at the origins of U.S. criminal justice reveals a system that was not built to protect most victims. To the contrary, it was constructed from a very limited definition of who has a right to be safe, beginning with the definition of what constituted a crime and going on to include who could report crimes and testify in court and who could expect accountability or compensation. While the justice system's role and capacities have, in recent generations, been transformed, along with the rest of American society, these origins have influenced the development of American criminal justice to the present day and continue to determine the effectiveness of our public safety systems. Looking back at its roots shows us how our justice system operates to exclude most victims from protection, rights, and safety, and this awareness can help illuminate the path to repair.

The Roots of Disregard: Controlled but Unprotected

In 1853, American abolitionist William Goodall wrote in his treatise *American Slave Code*, "The slave who is but a *chattel* on all other occasions . . . becomes a *person* when he is to be punished! . . . He [or she] is under the *control* of law though *unprotected* by law."[10]

The American criminal justice system began and evolved with very different purposes and rules, depending on who was being violated and who was doing the violating. In colonial America, courts were venues for punishing people who broke moral codes, arbitrating commercial disputes, and a place for the very few—primarily land-owning white males—to seek justice in response to specific harms they suffered. In the words of the legal historian Lawrence Friedman, these systems tended to be "cheap, informal, and accessible."[11] Each colony had its own unique system. In most places, victims themselves were the party who prosecuted the case, investigated the crime, and brought the evidence to a judge or jury, who decided the outcome. Victims could hire sheriffs to arrest or could hire local prosecutors, but victims themselves were largely in charge of presenting the evidence to the judge and asking for punishment or remedy.[12]

Of course, this victim-led pursuit of justice against lawbreakers in the early days of American history did not extend far. Landless and poor white people didn't have the means to do much about any violations they may have suffered; the money and resources needed to investigate cases likely eluded them. Native Americans were not recognized as citizens of the colonies, so they had limited standing to bring claims of wrongdoing to local judges. And married white women, legally and financially dependent on their husbands, were limited in their ability to pursue cases against people who may have violated them.

No group of people was more thoroughly and explicitly excluded from the protection of the law at the outset of American criminal justice than Black Americans. Two completely different and contradictory legal systems formed the basis of the development of American criminal law: the laws of slavery made up a separate legal system from the early common law, citizen-initiated justice. Slave Codes were among the first written laws in the colonies.[13] Long before penal codes or just about any other criminal laws were written down, Slave Codes were drafted that, beyond defining people of African descent as property without inherent rights, explicitly excluded enslaved Black Americans from being protected by law while also mandating that every facet of their lives was controlled by it.[14] These laws made it a crime for enslaved persons to protect themselves from harm and legalized violence against them.[15] Some Slave Codes even delineated the types of violence white people could mete out, up to and including "accidental death" arising from punishment, a gruesome reminder that abhorrent and morally wrong acts are not by default illegal.[16] What was recognized in common law as a crime was not considered a crime under the laws of slavery when the victim was a Black American. The hierarchy of harm was official and was explicitly defined through the development of two entirely different legal systems. Being categorized as a victim is not a right until it is legislated as one—and for two and a half centuries, elite white Americans had a monopoly on victimhood.

Once the United States became a nation, the common law approach to justice, essentially available to elite white men only, changed significantly. However, for Black Americans, the controlled but unprotected framework that legally codified a hierarchy of harm did not.

On the heels of the American Revolution, early American criminal legal practices began to change from being citizen-initiated and informal to being state-initiated and more formalized. In other words, the state, rather than the victim, began to emerge as the legal entity that took action against those who committed crimes.[17]

This developed in part out of concern for protecting the rights of those accused of crime, not out of concern for helping victims. Putting the state in charge of responding to crime through formal procedures created a more standardized system to ensure that people accused of crime were subjected to a fair process. Protecting citizens from being unfairly stripped of liberty, at least for those Americans with recognized humanity, was a core concern leading to the overthrow of British rule. The U.S. Constitution and new state laws created rights for the accused to due process and to confront accusers in court. To manifest these new rights, the state became responsible for prosecuting crime, and criminal court procedures were codified. Putting the state in charge of prosecutions legally diminished the role of victims—specifically those who had recognized rights to safety—in court. A victim went from being a party to the case under colonial common law (the plaintiff who prosecuted the crime) to being a witness—the person who could testify in court, presented as part of the state's prosecution against the accused.[18]

Meanwhile, the opposite legal construct for enslaved Black Americans, birthed in the Slave Codes, was maintained, and even strengthened. As criminal laws and procedures were formalized, enslaved people remained subjected to the separate laws of slavery, which excluded Black Americans from being legally recognized as victims or protected by law. White enslavers were granted immense authority to control enslaved people in just about any manner they desired, including using violence.[19] Few matters related to how enslavers treated enslaved people ever entered criminal courts because enslavers had near-total legal control. In many of the slave states, the primary instance in which harming an enslaved Black person was considered a crime was if the white person causing the harm did not own the enslaved person—in which case, the victim of the crime was the white enslaver, not the enslaved person. The enslaved person was recognized only as a vessel for the property interest of the enslaver.[20] So, even in these rare instances in which a criminal court acknowledged that a harm happened, it was somehow not the enslaved person who suffered, only the enslaver.

Enslaved Black Americans also lacked a meaningful right to self-defense. They could not strike a white person, have a weapon, protect their own children from violence, run away, or take just about any action to stop violence or abuse.[21] While some state Slave Codes offered a self-defense exception to the rule that enslaved persons were not permitted to lift a hand against white people, the exception was not honored in the actual operation of criminal justice. For example, in 1855, in *Missouri v. Celia*, a twenty-year-old enslaved woman was convicted and executed for killing Robert Newsom, an enslaver who purchased her when she was fourteen years old for the explicit purpose of sexually molesting her. He abused her for years before she physically fought back and killed him. Her defense attorney argued that Missouri laws prohibiting rape applied, and therefore Celia was allowed to protect herself from the crime of rape. The judge disagreed. After determining that rape laws in Missouri did not protect enslaved people, because as property their bodies were under the control of enslavers, the judge prohibited the jury from considering a claim of self-defense in deciding the case.[22] The defense's attempt to argue that Celia was a rape victim and that criminal laws outlawing rape could protect her was a rare challenge to the laws of slavery at the time. When the media reported on the verdict, which was widely covered in American newspapers, the underlying victimization of Celia was never mentioned, only the homicide and conviction.[23] An enslaved woman had no right to be protected from violence and had no right to protect herself from it either.

Beyond lacking a legal right to safety or self-defense, enslaved Black Americans were also prohibited from testifying against white people in court, being deemed to lack competency to testify against white people in any legal matter, whether civil or criminal. Black Americans living free of enslavement in the North were also prohibited from testifying against white people, with few exceptions.[24]

Even when the law recognized that crimes against free Black Americans were actually crimes, the inability to testify reinforced the hierarchy of harm and made it nearly impossible to be a victim in actuality. In a criminal court process where the state, not the victim, is the party taking action, the right to testify in court is essential to being protected by law. Victim testimony is one of the key mechanisms used to file criminal charges against someone and to secure convictions, and it is the primary way that victims are visible as part of criminal court processes. Outlawing Black Americans from being heard in court essentially legalized crimes against them

by white people, even in states where Black Americans were considered free citizens. Without the right to testify, the right to report
a crime or to be protected by law from that crime becomes largely
meaningless. Historian and law professor Alfred Avins wrote in
1966 that the inability to testify against a white person "withdrew
the substance of the protection of the laws in many cases and only
left a shadow."[25]

In a horrifying legal contradiction, however, enslaved Black
Americans were legally acknowledged to be full human beings
when they were accused of *committing* crimes.[26] When they were
charged with criminal acts, they suddenly were held fully responsible for their behavior and even in some states afforded basic
criminal procedural rights, such as a right to an attorney and to
refrain from self-incrimination. Startlingly, legislators and judges
promoted these procedural rights not to protect the life and liberty
of the accused but rather to protect the property interests of the
enslaver.[27]

While Black Americans had no legal claim to safety when they
were victims of violence, they were held to account in criminal
courts for crimes they committed. Enslaved Black Americans were
legally capable of being guilty but almost never legally afforded
innocence. The singular exception to this never-innocent rule was
when they were called on to testify as victims of crime committed
by other Black Americans.[28] The only time their victimization was
legally valuable was when helping prosecutors in pursuit of con-
victing another Black person.[29]

Historians have documented the unconscionable ways Black
Americans, with no right to protection and no ability to testify
against whites or to attain justice for harms suffered, were manipu-
lated, stolen from, abused, and killed by white Americans acting
with impunity.[30] And the justice system did nothing to help. This
was not a small number of people living under violent rule with
no protection from harm. At the time of emancipation, one in five
Americans was an enslaved Black person.[31]

While there is no comparable experience of the total dehuman-

ization embedded in the explicit control by law without the protection of law, other groups of people also lacked legal claims to safety
despite widespread experiences of victimization. White women,
for example, faced limited protections from crimes committed
against them by their spouses. White men were permitted "to beat
their wives, children, and free domestic servants," and their victims found no safe harbor in criminal courts.[32] While unmarried
white women were legally recognized as adult human beings, for
much of the colonial era and early American history, once they
were married, white women were legally defined as dependents of
their husbands under the legal concept of coverture.[33] They were
essentially children in the eyes of the law and were unable to seek
protection from the justice system in cases of domestic violence
or marital rape, which were considered the purview of the private
family affairs of white men.[34]

Even when domestic violence was officially outlawed and classi-
fied as a crime—which didn't occur in all states until 1920—for
generations, the criminal justice system was reluctant to intervene
in the privacy of a white man's household.[35] The North Carolina
Supreme Court, for example, famously held in 1868, in affirming
an acquittal of a white man charged with assaulting his wife, that
"[t]he laws of this State do not recognize the right of the husband
to whip his wife, but our courts will not interfere to punish him for
moderate correction of her, even if there had been no provocation
for it. . . . Family government being in its nature as complete in
itself as the State government is in itself."[36] The rights of white children to be safe from violence in the home were similarly limited
under this notion of the privacy of family affairs. Child abuse was
rarely prosecuted. Both white women and children, however, could
have reasonable expectations of legal protection against crimes
committed outside the household, and they were able to testify in
court.[37] Both could act as witnesses in criminal prosecutions and
could testify against the accused.[38]

While different groups of Native American people and nations
developed different legal relationships to the colonies and early

U.S. government, they collectively faced a lack of protection in American criminal courts and also were not viewed as people who have a right to seek justice for harms committed against them. Many of the atrocities suffered by Indigenous people were carried out by the federal government and U.S. military. Claims against the U.S. government for abuses and violence were typically not the purview of state justice systems, no matter how atrocious the abuses were. For example, after winning the Battle of the Washita in 1868, George Armstrong Custer invited his officers to rape Native American women captured in battle with impunity.[39] When Native Americans did appear in criminal court, they also could not testify against white people. Immigrants of color and Asian or Latino Americans were similarly barred from testifying against white people.[40] As a result, under American criminal law, for almost all people of color, without the right to testify, the right to be protected from crime was largely meaningless.

In a very real sense then, the U.S. criminal justice system developed for more than two hundred years without concern for millions of Americans commonly targeted for violence and harm. Those who had a right to be protected, to testify, and to seek justice were limited to those with positional power. The hierarchy of harm legally prevented millions of people from having rights to be free from violations, rights to report or testify, and rights to expect accountability or redress.

By severely limiting who has a right to safety or protection, the U.S. justice system, from its earliest origins, increased the vulnerability and likelihood of victimization for millions of unprotected people. The less people are legally protected from crime and violence, the more likely they are to experience harm, because those who would harm them can operate with impunity. Whether or not the justice system recognizes the right to protection affects the safety of individual people. This sinister contradiction was built into the bones of the justice system: denying protection to common victims made them more vulnerable to becoming victims. Again and again.

From Emancipation to Civil Rights: A Solemn Farce

The origins of severely limiting which victims matter to the justice system were not easily erased. The end of slavery in 1865 briefly brought substantial changes in the operation of criminal law, with Black Americans beginning to serve on juries, becoming police officers and court officials, and finally being granted the right to testify as witnesses in court, a crucial right for the legal protection of crime victims.

In the South, however, those rights were short-lived, as the emergence of Jim Crow segregation laws after Reconstruction ended in 1877 once again stripped Black Americans of many of those opportunities for protection and participation. New rules prevented Black people from eligibility to serve in official criminal justice positions, and judges began systematically excluding Black citizens from juries.[41] Black Americans found themselves once again without any meaningful protection from crime and violence. As historian Leon Litwack describes in *Trouble in Mind: Black Southerners in the Age of Jim Crow*, "The courts granted virtual immunity to whites accused of crimes against black men and women."[42] Instances of attacks and killings of Black Americans who did testify in criminal court left many thousands extremely reluctant to participate in criminal trials at all. Not surprisingly then, few prosecutions of white Americans who committed crimes against Black Americans were pursued.

Those cases that were pursued only very infrequently led to conviction. White juries habitually refused to find white defendants guilty of crimes committed against Black Americans, no matter how clear-cut the case against the perpetrator was. As Litwack describes, even conscientious justice officials could not influence criminal court outcomes toward fairness or protection for Black citizens. In reacting to an all-white jury acquittal of a white man facing murder charges for killing a Black American, with overwhelming evidence of guilt, Georgia judge Henry Hammond remarked in 1907 that the criminal legal proceeding was a "solemn farce."[43]

Beyond the routine impunity of white people for crimes committed against Black Americans, criminal justice officials also frequently failed to pursue justice in any crime involving a Black victim when the perpetrator was also Black, so long as the crime did not affect white neighborhoods. These were deemed insignificant cases and prosecutors regularly dropped the charges, even in the most serious crimes. In New Orleans, for example, in the 1920s only 6 percent of all homicides of Black citizens resulted in a conviction when the alleged perpetrator was also Black.

Black Americans living in the northern states rarely saw more legal protection or more access to justice than their southern counterparts. They were also systematically excluded from juries and intimidated out of testifying against white defendants.[44] Northern justice officials also often looked the other way instead of prosecuting crimes committed against Black victims.

Black Americans were not the only demographic group to be deemed unworthy of legal protections when victims of an intraracial crime. In northern states, immigrant victims of crime also lacked protection in cases in which they were victimized by other members of their immigrant ethnic group. According to historian Jeffrey Adler, in "Less Crime, More Punishment," prosecutors in jurisdictions with immigrant populations were regularly "anticipating intransigence from foreign-born witnesses, believing such violence inevitable, and hence casually dismissing cases."[45]

The hierarchy of harm had moved from being de jure—actually written into the law through two separate legal systems—to de facto. Justice system officials' discretionary choices showed largely the same disregard that existed under official law and amounted to very little change. The hierarchy of harm was now unofficially operating through daily decisions.

In this era, female victims of domestic violence and sexual assault also fared poorly in criminal court when the accused was white. Even as laws to prohibit violence against women became more commonplace, criminal courts did not take many of these cases seriously. White men rarely faced charges when accused of domestic violence or sexual assault crimes against white women, and for those who did become defendants, juries frequently acquitted them even when the evidence was unambiguous.[46] The cultural notion that it is important to protect white men's rights to "manliness" led judges and juries regularly to excuse white male aggression.

White men faced even fewer criminal consequences when the female victim was Black. As described by Danielle McGuire in *At the Dark End of the Street: Black Women, Rape, and Resistance*, the sexual assault of Black women by white men was a rampant feature of life in the era of Jim Crow in the South, and it occurred with near-total impunity.[47] As McGuire put it, "White men were raised to believe that they could do whatever they wanted to do to black women and there would be no punishment."[48] In the very rare instance in which there was a conviction, some were still relieved of accountability through pardons. As Litwack noted, South Carolina governor Cole Blease pardoned both Black and white men convicted of raping Black women, because he had "very serious doubt as to whether the crime of rape can be committed upon a Negro."[49]

While the actual rape of white women by white men was largely discounted by criminal courts and rarely led to sanctions, in stark contrast, even the slightest allegation, however lacking in evidence or even outlandish, of a rape of a white woman by a Black man led to extreme and often legally sanctioned violence against the alleged attacker and a decades-long reign of lynch-mob terror.

Black Americans faced lynching death for nearly anything, from asserting political rights, to defending themselves against violent attacks, to committing extremely minor perceived slights, to having committed no perceived transgression at all. And vigilante terrorism was known to grow even more fierce and sadistic when the accusation included rape of a white woman. The notion that white women were regularly targeted for sexual harm by Black men was based in myth. Still, the justice system did virtually nothing to protect Black Americans from these vicious and savage attacks, and often outright supported or even facilitated lynching, torture, and mob violence. From 1877 to 1950, more than 4,000 lynchings occurred, with few participants ever facing arrest or prosecution.[50] Despite intense efforts by antilynching activists and lawyers, less than one percent of lynchings after 1900 resulted in a conviction, and those that did were usually for public order offenses, not homicide.[51]

The legal sanctioning of extrajudicial violence against Black Americans in the South was so rampant that it essentially operated as an adjunct of the official justice system. As Litwack noted, "The differences between the lynch mob and the courtroom were not always clear . . . nor were there discernible differences between a speedy trial and mob justice, between lawless lynchers and lawless judges, sheriffs, constables, policemen, wardens and prison guards."[52] For nearly one hundred years after slavery ended, the original construct of two legal systems that embedded a hierarchy of harm, defining which victims mattered and which did not, remained largely intact. Black Americans still lived without legal protection against crime and violence while they also lived under the control of American criminal law—and the savage vigilante justice it endorsed.

4

A Tale of Two Cities

The 1921 massacre in Tulsa, Oklahoma, was one of the most violent acts of domestic terrorism in U.S. history. It is also one of the most shocking examples of how control under the law without protection of the law has operated for Black victims of crime. After more than seventy years of disregard, the horrors of this event have slowly gained long overdue attention in American consciousness. In the first decade of the 2000s, the story of the thousands of people subjected to mass violence, people who were never viewed as victims and perpetually denied justice, began receiving official acknowledgment in Oklahoma and beyond. In 2021, on the centennial anniversary, President Joe Biden traveled to Tulsa to commemorate the massacre. He was the first U.S. president in the century since the mass killings to do so.[1]

The nearly one-hundred-year struggle to receive national recognition for the Tulsa victims stands in stark contrast to another domestic terrorist attack that the state of Oklahoma experienced. Seventy-three years after the Tulsa massacre, the Oklahoma City bombing in 1995 killed, injured, or otherwise traumatized thousands of people, most of them middle class and white. However, the response and the legacy could not have been more different. This time, the horrific tragedy led to a near-immediate sea change in criminal procedure on behalf of victims, an immense outpouring of victim assistance and support, and a fueling of the national victims' rights movement calling for sweeping changes to American criminal justice. A comparison of the response to these two crimes demonstrates how the different layers of our world—social, political, and legal—have absorbed and perpetuated the hierarchy of harm so much so that an entire community of terrorism victims was almost erased from history.

The Tulsa Massacre: "Without Parallel in America"

In 1921, Tulsa was home to a thriving "Black Wall Street" community in the Greenwood District. There, Black businesses and families enjoyed greater economic prosperity than any prior generation had—more than just about any other Black community in the nation at the time. But in June of that year, a white mob, aided by justice officials, burned Greenwood to the ground. The precipitating incident was the arrest of a young Black male for allegedly assaulting a white girl, though the truth of that dubious claim was never established. An inflammatory news story ran about his arrest, detention, and imminent lynching, driving a white mob to the jail where the teen was being held. When the mob arrived, they found Black Tulsans standing guard to protect the jail and the young man inside. A fight broke out and shots were fired. Upon learning of the melee, hundreds of white Tulsans descended on Greenwood.[2]

Over the next twenty-four hours, the mob looted Greenwood homes and businesses, set fire to buildings, and indiscriminately shot Black residents. The local police department later "deputized" and armed hundreds of white residents, who went into Greenwood and joined in the mob violence.[3] In the first known incident of a plane dropping a bomb in a U.S. city, privately owned planes flew above Greenwood, and some reportedly dropped incendiaries on the neighborhood.[4] Buildings burned for dozens of city blocks. While the death toll has never been conclusively tallied, most historians estimate that between one hundred and three hundred or more people died and many thousands more were injured. Upward of six hundred Black-owned businesses and churches, the library, and the local hospital (the only hospital serving Black Tulsans in the segregated city) were burned down. More than nine thousand Greenwood residents were left homeless, with their homes and property destroyed in the flames.[5] The NAACP's Walter White, who led the organization's investigations into racial violence incidents across the country, commented after observing the aftermath that the Tulsa massacre "in sheer brutality and willful destruction of life and property stands without parallel in America."[6]

Eventually, after a day and night of violence, the Oklahoma governor called in the National Guard to quell the massacre. The National Guard arrived and initiated mass arrests—of the Black victims, not the white perpetrators. They detained more than six thousand Black Greenwood residents, many of whom were inside their homes at the time. After the residents were forcibly removed by National Guard troops—some were detained for as long as eight days—mobs moved in and set the empty homes and buildings ablaze.[7] Thousands of Black families lost everything—their homes, their livelihoods, and their loved ones. Many were forced to flee the region in the aftermath, never to return.[8]

What had started out as an attempt to protect a teenager from an extrajudicial lynching when the law would not protect him led to the pillage and destruction of the entire Black community. Justice officials did more than look the other way; they aided and abetted the violence, including officially deputizing white vigilantes to burn and to kill. And when the National Guard arrived to quell the violence, they rounded up the *victims* of the massacre—the Black Americans whose homes, property, and lives were under attack—and jailed them. The hierarchy of harm was so embedded in the response that local justice officials, elected officials, and the National Guard could not view the Black citizens of Greenwood as victims at all, even as their loved ones were shot and killed, their businesses destroyed, and their homes burned to the ground.

No one was ever convicted for murder, destruction of property, or inciting mass violence in Tulsa that day.[9] A month after the massacre, a grand jury indicted Tulsa chief of police John Gustafson, and he was prosecuted for failing to quell the violence, as well as numerous other charges of corruption unrelated to the Tulsa massacre. Gustafson was convicted of negligence and dismissed from the police force. He was also sentenced to jail for unrelated corruption practices.[10] The *Chicago Whip* reported that Gustafson "was said to have laughed" as the city's Greenwood district burned.[11] The grand jury indicted about seventy other people, many of whom were Black residents who suffered losses, but none of those indictments resulted in prosecution.

The Red Cross provided humanitarian help with food and emergency medical care for the displaced and injured, but Greenwood residents were never compensated for their victimization and near-total loss of their possessions and property. More than one hundred lawsuits were filed seeking compensation for losses sustained in the mob violence, against the city of Tulsa as well as insurance companies, but none of these suits was successful.[12] Tulsa victims also filed claims totaling over $1.8 million dollars with the Tulsa Real Estate Commission, but nearly all these claims were disallowed, except for a claim filed by a white business owner whose guns were stolen from his store.[13] The modern-day equivalent of property damages incurred is estimated at more than $25 million.[14] That does not include the immense toll arising from the deaths of family members or lasting injuries, including financial, physical, and emotional.

Until the first decade of the 2000s, most Americans had never heard of this domestic terrorist attack. It wasn't until the year 2001, eighty years after the fact, that the state of Oklahoma took official action to acknowledge the crime, following decades of advocacy by survivors and allies. Finally, that year, the state of Oklahoma established a commission to study the events of 1921. Reviewing thousands of pages of documentation, interviews, and evidence, its members found that public officials in Tulsa had contributed to the mass violence against Black Tulsans and, despite the initial national news coverage of the violence, local and state officials had sought to prevent continuing public awareness or education about the massacre and had refused to publicly acknowledge what had happened in Greenwood. After intensive review, the commission recommended a series of actions, including memorial recognition and reparations for survivors and their descendants. Astoundingly, however, Oklahoma leaders rejected the recommendation for reparations, and as a result, no survivors have ever received victim compensation.[15] The hierarchy of harm meant that these atrocious acts were not treated as crimes. Victims were not given voice. Redress and accountability were a far cry from the official response. And victims who sought protection were instead blamed and criminalized. A full accounting has never been made of the harm caused to generations of Black Tulsans.

Oklahoma City: "But a Little Lower Than Angels"

Nearly seventy-four years later, mass violence again wreaked havoc in Oklahoma. On the morning of April 19, 1995, a massive bomb exploded just as people were starting their workday at the busy federal building in downtown Oklahoma City. The explosion was so powerful that hundreds of surrounding buildings and businesses were also damaged. One hundred and sixty-eight people died in the blast, including nineteen children who had just been dropped off that morning in the federal building's day care center, and over four hundred more people were violently injured. Horrifying images of the shocking crime, featuring destroyed buildings and bloodied bodies, played constantly on television screens across the country. The devastating scenes looked like a war zone. Most of the victims of this horrific mass violence were federal workers who worked and lived in Oklahoma City; they were predominately middle class and white. It was characterized at the time as the worst act of violence ever carried out by a "homegrown terrorist" in U.S. history.[16]

Federal law enforcement agencies quickly deployed thousands of agents to find and arrest the perpetrator. Twenty-seven-year-old

Gulf War veteran Timothy McVeigh was arrested within days. He reported being motivated to carry out this extreme act of mass violence because of his outrage about an event in Waco, Texas, two years earlier, in which federal agents bombed and besieged the compound of a religious cult called the Branch Davidians, which was being investigated for illegal activity and child endangerment.[17] Eighty people died in the disastrous Waco raid, including twenty-seven children. Two years later, McVeigh amassed weapons and built the bomb he set off in Oklahoma City, in apparent hopes of inspiring more attacks on a government he viewed as tyrannical.

The investigation and prosecution of Timothy McVeigh was "one of the most exhaustive" federal law enforcement efforts in U.S. history.[18] No stone was left unturned to make sure "every clue was found and all the culprits identified."[19] The FBI conducted more than 28,000 interviews and "amassed three-and-a-half tons of evidence" in building the case to prosecute him.[20]

The criminal trial captured the news media's attention for weeks. And the actions prosecutors took to protect victims' interests in the court process were unprecedented. In response to two different pre-trial rulings that limited victim participation in the trial, prosecutors twice enrolled support from public officials to change federal law and override the court rulings, within a matter of days both times. First, when the judge moved the trial venue to Denver from Oklahoma to ensure an impartial jury, Congress quickly passed legislation to authorize cameras in the courtroom and require officials to provide remote viewing to victims in an auditorium in Oklahoma.[21] Then, when the judge later ruled that victims who watched the guilt or innocence phase of the trial would not be permitted to provide "victim impact statements" during the sentencing phase (as it may influence their subsequent testimony), prosecutors maligned the judge and argued that all of the victims had the right to be heard. They argued that describing the debilitating effects of this mass violence on victims' lives was an important part of what the survivors needed to further the recovery process. Congress again took swift action. Within eight days, Congress enacted the Victims' Rights Clarification Act, requiring courts to allow victims both to attend the trial phase of criminal proceedings and also to provide victim impact statements at the sentencing phase.[22] As law professor Paul Cassell, who represented some of the surviving families of bombing victims, told the *New Yorker*, "When you have the Oklahoma bombing victims as your illustration, you have access to Congress."[23]

This perceived disregard for the victims' voices in the prosecution of Timothy McVeigh became a turning point in the growth of the increasingly visible victims' rights movement. It led many states to add victims' rights amendments to their state constitutions and bolstered calls for a federal constitutional amendment. Growing courtroom rights and the expanded use of victim impact statements became a mechanism by which victim visibility in the justice process grew, above and beyond acting as a witness for the prosecution, the main role of victims in court. While victims are still not a party to the case and have no independent representation, after Oklahoma City, speaking in court through statements at sentencing flourished. Today, these impact statements typically happen after the conviction and before sentencing.

Because of their place in the hierarchy of harm, the victims of the Oklahoma City bombing spurred unprecedented activism for victim visibility. The result transformed criminal court procedures across the country. Bearing witness to harm caused by violent crime has helped many victims heal. Whether in court or other forums, this kind of recognition can play a critical role for survivors' healing as well as for the broader public's awareness of and sensitivity to the impact of violence suffered. In 2018, for example, the long line of female gymnasts who provided victim impact statements in the trial against athlete doctor Larry Nassar, who was convicted of sexual abuse, brought unprecedented attention to an epidemic, child sexual exploitation in sports, and thousands of victims who had suffered in silence found recognition and repair in listening to the women athletes testify.[24]

Beyond fueling a national call for victim visibility in criminal courts, overwhelming concern for the Oklahoma City bombing victims also transformed the provision of victim services around the country. Outpourings of support flooded Oklahoma City. Many thousands of people donated to support the victims with services and financial aid. The state of Iowa gave $100,000 from its own victim compensation fund to the victims and to Oklahoma City.[25] Children from around the world participated in sending artwork and messages of support for the impacted families. Denver residents opened their homes to bombing victims who wanted to attend the trial in person—and the federal government paid for their flights and transportation. Oklahoma City collected millions in charitable donations to cover expenses and other support and the federal government provided benefits estimated at $100,000 per surviving spouse.[26]

The Office for Victims of Crime, established in 1984 to channel federal dollars to states for victim services, also took unprecedented measures. Victim services providers engaged in an intense effort to reach, communicate with, and support surviving family members and persons injured in the attack. Phone calls, mental health counseling, financial loss recovery, medical bills, employment leave assistance, funeral expenses, peer support groups—the effort to listen to, support, and offer help in recovery to these survivors was historically unparalleled.[27]

The Office for Victims of Crime documented the full-scale response, and it became a model that the organization then utilized to prepare local and state officials for managing the aftermath of mass violence. In a report published five years after the tragedy, in October 2000, the Office for Victims of Crime described the details of the effort: ensuring that every victim received compensation, launching a new organization to provide ongoing mental health support, and establishing another organization to provide ongoing therapeutic debriefing sessions to victims.[28] This massive effort to fully address victims' needs was a national first.

Concern for the victims of the Oklahoma City bombing changed criminal court procedures, the provision of victim assistance, and the future of American criminal justice. When victims of mass violence rank high in the hierarchy of harm, American political and criminal justice systems take unparalleled steps to seek justice and repair. That kind of aggressive government action to offer immediate financial and emotional support to terrorism victims grew to even greater heights after Oklahoma City. Six years later, when the World Trade Center in New York City was destroyed in the 9/11 terrorist attacks, the U.S. government response went even further. As part of the US Patriot Act, Congress amended the Victims of Crime Act to authorize private donations into the federal compensation fund for the first time since establishment of the fund. Hundreds of thousands of dollars in private donations were deposited into the fund and redistributed to surviving families.[29] The federal government also provided a travel agency to handle travel accommodations to survivors for criminal proceedings, funerals, and other needs. In the two decades since, more than $1.6 billion in aid was amassed. It is estimated that the federal government awarded more than $1 million to each of the surviving families of the three thousand people killed, dwarfing the amounts provided to Oklahoma City survivors—and leaving some to speculate that a class hierarchy was at play—were Wall Street workers conceived of as valued even more than federal employees in Oklahoma?[30]

While the response in support of the victims of the Oklahoma City bombing—and later the 9/11 victims—was unprecedented, the profound impacts of these atrocities still have ripple effects for thousands. More can and should be done to foster recovery efforts for these survivors. And the widespread concern and assertive action taken represent a strong example of what government officials are capable of doing—that is, when the political will exists.

If we are looking at our history honestly, we must acknowledge that the Oklahoma City bombing was not the first act of domestic terrorism on Oklahoma soil to have killed hundreds and hurt thousands. It was just the first one with victims who were widely recognized as innocent and thus deserving of strong government action. One year after the bombing, Attorney General Janet Reno, in a speech honoring the work of the National Organization for Victim Assistance in supporting Oklahoma City victims—at a conference held in *Tulsa*—remarked, "On my table in my office is the picture of a little one-year-old child who was killed in the blast. She is my symbol of victims everywhere and what we need to do to make sure that they are protected. . . . I draw the most strength from the victims. You are but little lower than the angels."[31]

The worlds of 1921 Oklahoma and 1995 Oklahoma were very different, to be sure. Concepts such as victim compensation and victim impact statements had not yet made their way into criminal law vernacular in 1921, and federal law enforcement and victims' aid programs did not exist at the level they did by 1995. But the calls for justice for the Tulsa massacre victims have been ongoing up to the present day. The unrelenting efforts to secure justice and compensation for those victims are the only reason many Americans today are aware of what happened, and why history books have at long last been rewritten and memorials finally built.

The collective official unwillingness to mandate a comprehensive recovery for Tulsa victims, even today, is symbolic of the way the hierarchy of harm operates underneath the surface, even as official harm hierarchies of victim worthiness have been wiped from the law books. The modern-day concepts of victim compensation and victims' rights in court proceedings could still be utilized to heal the lasting effects of unacknowledged trauma for victims of mass violence from the prior generation, especially when the impacted community has been urging compensatory action for decades. What was operating in these polar-opposite responses from the justice system was the hierarchy of harm. It was obvious to the justice system, media, and politicians that the people harmed by the Oklahoma City bombing were innocent victims who deserved support, up to and including transforming criminal court proceedings across the country on their behalf. But the residents of Greenwood and their offspring were at the wrong end of a justice system and a political infrastructure that refused to see them as victims, and instead aggressively fueled traumatic stress and continually denied accountability, no matter the lasting harm.

Few crimes have the power to capture widespread public attention, mobilize the legal system, and catalyze political change like domestic terrorism. These are the types of public safety crises that cause ripple effects in society for decades to come. If any type of crime could level the hierarchy of harm, a mass casualty event would surely be it—a moment when every victim, caught at the wrong time in the wrong place, is viewed as innocent. And yet, these two events in American history, in the same state, debunk that notion, illustrating the hierarchy of harm's formidable nature and perpetual grip on systems of power.

These opposing examples from Oklahoma of immediate recognition versus deep and lasting disregard are also emblematic of the experiences of everyday victims in the justice system today. True, over the last century the legal system has been transformed. Discriminatory laws that legalized violence and prohibited court participation have been outlawed. All victims can testify and now have additional legal rights to compensation and impact statements. Rampant and savage extrajudicial violence sanctioned by justice system officials has been quelled, and popular awareness of the racial trauma caused by centuries of a lack of protection from harm is increasing. An entirely new field, the field of victim assistance financed by the government, now exists. As evidenced by the government aid that was quickly sent to help Oklahoma City survivors, modern-day support for victims can be robust. The development of this new field, and the delineation of new government obligations, is a crowning achievement of the victims' rights movement. Yet for all that has changed, too much has stayed the same. Both inside and outside the courtroom, the harm hierarchy continues to determine who has victim visibility, who gets fair treatment in courtrooms, in the media, and in the political arena, and who gets access to the new victim assistance infrastructure.

5

Good Victims, Bad Victims

"When I used to be a prosecutor, I didn't think you could be a victim unless there was a prosecution," Pete Baroni remembers thinking.[1] The former prosecutor from DuPage County, Illinois, prosecuted everything from misdemeanors to serious felony crimes, a job he held for ten years before becoming a public safety consultant for the Illinois state legislature. "If you didn't come forward, didn't cooperate, or walked away, you were not a victim. It was time to move on to the next investigation."[2] In the day-to-day workings of packed criminal court dockets, that sentiment is not all that unusual. Victims are supposed to be the people who work with the prosecutors to secure a conviction. They return phone calls, attend court appearances, and help prosecutors seek justice. If there is some reason you don't make the cut, through the lens of the court process, you don't really exist.

It is not hard to imagine how this kind of thinking develops. In the adversarial justice system, the worth of the case rules supreme. Criminal court is a contest between the state and the defendant. If the system is working as it is designed to, each party pursues that goal—a conviction if you're the prosecutor or an acquittal if you represent the defendant—sometimes by any means necessary. The value of a victim can boil down to how she or he either helps or hurts that goal. Law enforcement investigates the case, prosecuting attorneys pursue proof and conviction, and defense attorneys pursue doubt and dismissal. Investigators interview victims and assess what they can identify, say, and prove or not prove. Whether the case ends in a plea deal, which happens in the vast majority of cases, or in a trial, what a victim offers in the pursuit of a conviction plays a crucial role in determining case outcomes. If victims aren't a part of that, they end up as trees falling in the forest of justice that no one hears. For those who do participate in the criminal court process, there is yet another hurdle to being seen as a worthy victim: How good of a witness are you?

Hierarchy Inside the Courtroom: Bad Victims

A prosecutor from the time she graduated from law school, Suzy Loftus worked in some of the hardest divisions in the San Francisco District Attorney's Office, from domestic violence to elder abuse. Just after returning to the office from maternity leave in 2006, she was assigned a new case in the general felonies unit. The defendant had shot a woman whom he saw leaving his clothing store, because he thought she had stolen clothes. The victim, Debbie Smith, was driving away from the store when the defendant shot into her car, hitting her in the neck, with bullet fragments just missing her carotid artery. But for the near miss, the shot would have been fatal. A Black woman from the neighborhood, Smith had a criminal record that included prior theft crimes. The store was located on Third Street, in San Francisco's Bayview neighborhood, an area with higher rates of crime than that of the surrounding neighborhoods.[3]

After meeting with Smith, Suzy was shocked that the store owner had nearly killed her over an alleged theft of a pair of jeans (which were not found). But the prosecutor's unit manager thought it wasn't a winnable prosecution, given the profile of the victim compared with the defendant's, who had no prior record and was not from Bayview. Suzy pursued the case anyway and went to trial. By legal standards, it should have been open and shut. The victim walked into the store and then left, and after she got into her car, the store owner walked outside and shot into the car—at the very minimum, a clear case of reckless disregard for human life. It was a miracle that Ms. Smith was alive. Still, after hearing from the defendant and the victim, the jury returned a verdict of not guilty on all counts. Jurors clapped as the defendant left the courtroom. "The jury didn't like the victim," Suzy summarized. "This kind of bias happens often. Others said, 'drop the case,' but what he did was extremely dangerous. What if he killed her or what if someone else had been walking by at that moment? This shouldn't have been about evaluating *her* worth; she was the victim. They are all worthy, isn't that the point?"[4]

Unfortunately, for too many victims in criminal court, feeling worthy is laughably far from the reality of their experience. In the world of criminal prosecutions, lawyers will readily admit that there is a lens through which victims are seen. There are good victims and bad victims. Does the victim have a prior criminal record? That's a bad victim because it means they are less believable on the witness stand or are not even a good enough witness to call to the stand. Was the victim under the influence of drugs or alcohol at the time of the crime? That is a bad victim because their memory is not considered reliable, so their credibility is in question. Is the victim perceived of as "gender-nonconforming," or a person who is homeless or even a person who is seen as "unattractive" or "unlikable"?

These are the often unspoken but crude and dehumanizing evaluations attorneys make all the time, assessing characteristics or circumstances that could affect judges' or juries' capacity to sympathize. Do the victim and defendant know each other? That could taint the motivations of the witness and limit their reliability. Was the victim engaged in risky behavior and therefore contributing to their own victimization? Then the victim is to blame for what happened and won't be viewed sympathetically. And then there's the perpetual elephant in the room: both explicit and implicit racial bias, which exists in criminal court at pervasive levels, as researchers have demonstrated time and again. This bias means that judges and juries, consciously or not, believe the testimony of white victims more than they believe the testimony of victims of color. Middle-class and elite victims are also perceived as being more reliable than poor victims.

The evaluation of victims as good or bad is a hierarchy enforcer, and it leaves the majority of everyday crime survivors out. After all, the reality is that most crime happens between people who know each other. And crime is more likely to happen when people are compromised; being under the influence of drugs or alcohol or having a prior record, for example, makes a person a more vulnerable target for crimes like robbery or theft. So, there's a way in which the very things that make people more vulnerable to being victims—familiarity with someone, being under the influence, engaging in risky behavior, or having a prior record—make them less-good victim witnesses in court and less likely to find justice.

Still other victims are treated with even less regard than those who simply would not be very helpful to a prosecution. These victims are the ones being prosecuted. The right to act in self-defense is not universally respected and depends largely on where a person sits in the hierarchy of harm. Across the United States, many thousands of women, the vast majority of whom are low-income women of color, are serving sentences for crimes they committed in response to severe abuse. A 1991 review concluded that more than two thousand women at that time were serving sentences for defending themselves against domestic abuse.[5] Another review a year later found that 90 percent of women in prison for killing men had been abused by the men they killed.[6]

These women pulled a trigger or fought back out of desperation while facing unrelenting harm. And now they are in court as defendants, facing time for the crimes they committed to protect their own lives. While many men, particularly white men, receive lesser sentences or no sentence at all for perpetuating domestic abuse or even intimate partner homicide, the women who fight back, especially women of color and low-income women, cannot effectively mount a claim of self-defense in the face of extreme victimization.

This is how the justice system continues to enforce the hierarchy of harm. The people who are more vulnerable to attack and have experienced extreme victimization are convicted and jailed. The people who cause the abuse are likely to garner more sympathy and to receive less time than the women who fight back.

To have a crime against you prosecuted in a court of law, you must be reliable and sympathetic, you must refrain from contributing to your own victimization and from defending yourself even in severe and life-threatening situations, and you must be filtered through racial, class, and gendered narratives about your worthiness to be a good, innocent victim. Even if you can make it through these cruel screenings to be considered a potentially good victim at the outset, defense lawyers, in doing their job to protect their clients and to prevent a conviction, will often search for ways to undermine your credibility.

Victims commonly report feeling as if they were the ones being investigated and accused of wrongdoing. The determination of the defendant's innocence or guilt can turn on the perceived innocence or guilt of the victim. Under an adversarial regime that rests on a generations-old, ingrained hierarchy of harm, victim credibility assessment is both a fair legal strategy and a deeply harmful and discriminatory game. The impact of these continual victim assessments is worse than victims simply experiencing frustration or intimidation in criminal court. The impact is a reinforcement of the hierarchy of harm itself, limiting access to justice to the small number who qualify for the top of the harm hierarchy, and perpetuating the dangerous notion that people perceived of as bad victims are ultimately not really victims at all.

Hierarchy Outside the Courtroom: Missing White Woman Syndrome

On the morning of May 5, 2002, carrying her pink Barbie book bag and wearing her sunflower rhinestone earrings, seven-year-old Milwaukee resident Alexis Patterson walked one block from her home to her school, where she greeted her friends on the playground. But when the bell rang for the school day to begin, she didn't make it to her class. The school did not report her absence to her parents, so it was not until Alexis didn't come home from school eight hours later that her disappearance was reported. After twenty years, she has still not been found.[7]

One month after the disappearance of Alexis in Wisconsin, on June 5, 2002, fourteen-year-old Elizabeth Smart was abducted from her home in Salt Lake City, Utah. She was missing for nine months, during which time she suffered extreme sexual abuse, physical torture, and deprivation. Local, state, and national media covered her disappearance extensively, and her eventual miraculous rescue has been attributed to the scale of media attention. News reporters released a sketch of the alleged captor, which led to Elizabeth's discovery, alive, in Sandy, Utah. The harrowing ordeal generated even more coverage after her rescue, including national shows such as *Dateline, Today, Oprah Winfrey*, and *Nancy Grace*. A made-for-television film about the crime was produced and released just eight months after Elizabeth was found. The attention to her story is also credited for the swift adoption of federal legislation establishing AMBER alert systems to improve public notification of missing children.

News stories about Alexis, by contrast, while extensive in Milwaukee, were sparse at the national level. The story of missing Alexis, an African American girl, generated sixty-seven media mentions within six weeks of her disappearance, while the story of Elizabeth, a white teenager, was covered over four hundred times within the first week.[8]

The stark difference in media coverage of crime victims depending on race has been evidenced and criticized for decades. Media research studies in 2005, 2010, and 2015 all revealed the same pattern.[9] Cases of missing white girls and women generated significantly more coverage, and the intensity of the repetition of that coverage was far greater than was that of similar stories of missing girls and women of color.[10] This disparity in media coverage has been so persistent in its imbalance that renowned American journalist and author Gwen Ifill referred to the phenomenon as Missing White Woman Syndrome.[11]

The amount of media coverage is even more wildly disproportionate when considering the actual rate at which white girls and women go missing compared with women and girls of color, as well as with boys and men of color. The 2018 statistics from the National Crime Information Center found that while Black children represent about 14 percent of the total child population in the United States, they constitute about a third of all missing children. In other words, Black children are dramatically overrepresented as victims yet underrepresented in the media stories about missing children.[12] In the 2015 study, for example, Black children accounted for 35 percent of all missing children in the country that year but for only 7 percent of the media stories about missing children.[13] Commenting on the disparity in coverage, National Center for Missing and Exploited Children vice president Robert Lowry told CNN in 2019, "I think there's a false belief that white children make up the biggest number of missing children when in fact (proportionally) it's just the opposite."[14]

The problem of discrimination in coverage is not limited to victims of abduction or kidnapping. Victims of color who die by homicide are also covered unequally by the media. In *You're Dead, So What?*, author Cheryl Neely reveals that while Black women are nearly two and a half times more likely to die by homicide compared with their white counterparts, their deaths are far less likely to generate as much media coverage as the deaths of white women, and when their homicides are covered, "many reporters provide negative background details about the victim, implying that she was somehow culpable, particularly if there was a history of substance abuse, prostitution, or sexual promiscuity."[15]

Similar trends exist for male victims of homicide. The coverage of men of color is not proportionate to their significantly higher rates of vulnerability, and the coverage that does happen is less likely to describe the victims sympathetically or may even provide details that essentially blame the victim for the outcome, even when those details have nothing to do with the circumstances in which they were killed.[16]

Considering the extremely unequal rates of death by gun violence for men of color in the United States, this media indifference is nearly as shocking as the disparities in loss of life. Findings from the National Victimization Survey of 2019 reveal that, while Black Americans make up 13 percent of the U.S. population, they comprise 51 percent of homicide victims. Homicide is the leading cause of death for Black males ages fifteen to thirty-four—and they are dying by homicide at a rate that is *twenty times higher* than white males of that age range. Homicide is the second leading cause of death for Latino males. In analyzing the 2019 victimization data, researchers Heather Warnken and Janet Lauritsen concluded, "Looking at risk on a continuum from highest to lowest, black males under the age of 35 living in urban households with incomes under $25,000 have a risk for serious violent victimization nearly *15 times greater* [emphasis added] than that of females age 55 or older living in nonurban households with income $75,000 and greater." One would never know this appalling difference in vulnerability by looking at media coverage.

Other demographic groups who also experience victimization at proportionally higher rates similarly experience devaluation in the media. Unfair media coverage has been demonstrated when the victims are immigrants, people who are lesbian, gay, or transgender, or people with disabilities. A 2019 analysis of media stories about immigration and crime in the most circulated newspapers in the United States found that between 1990 and 2013, the percentage of those stories in which immigrants were portrayed as victims of crime decreased significantly, while the percentage of stories portraying immigration as causing crime or immigrants as criminals increased significantly.[17] This is despite countless studies showing that immigrant communities have no effect, or a negative effect, on crime rates, and immigrants are less likely, or no more likely, than U.S.-born individuals to commit crimes.[18] A 2016 analysis of local media coverage about homicides of transgender women of color found that the murders were commonly described in trivializing ways and the victims were often misgendered.[19] Another 2016 report looking at media reports about disabled people killed by a parent or caregiver found a significant number of articles focused on speculating on the reasons the caregiver killed and describing the murders as a result of the hardship the caregiver or guardian faced caring for the disabled person, or as "mercy killings."[20]

Media hierarchies of harm are reinforced in the political arena. Megan's law. Chelsea's law. Marsy's law. Amber's law. Pamela's law. Caylee's law. . . . The list of laws named after white-girl victims of crime goes on. In 2019, the Associated Press released an analysis of namesake criminal justice laws and found that since 1990, more than eight in ten of these laws were named after white victims or honored groups of victims that included a white person. Only 6 percent of these laws honored the namesake of a Black victim.[21] All these victims were undoubtedly worthy of concern and response. But the conception of innocent victims in media and politics focuses on white women and girls, despite the fact that this demographic is far less vulnerable to becoming victimized by the very crimes these laws set out to address, creating both an erasure and a public safety problem. Resources flow where media attention flows, and the media know what will grab eyeballs: perceived vulnerability, defined along the hierarchy of harm, quickly triggers concern and attentiveness among everyday people. So, even if police resources are more greatly needed elsewhere, any public outcry for action that is stoked by media puts political pressure on the criminal justice apparatus—forcing it to act. In other words, the crimes that saturate media stories, the nervous public, and local police departments eager to stamp out a publicity crisis are all influenced by the hierarchy of harm. Their actions are too often compelled by the spotlighting of specific cases that fit the narrow bill of innocent victim.

One of the most sweeping examples of the lengths to which politicians will go in response to the abduction and death of a white girl happened in 1994 in New Jersey. Jesse Timmendequas, the neighbor of seven-year-old Megan Kanka, kidnapped Megan as she rode her bike around in her own driveway, then raped and killed her in a gruesome and monstrous act of violence that shocked the nation. Mr. Timmendequas had two prior convictions for sexual molestation of children. Megan's shattered parents criticized sex offender registry laws in New Jersey for failing to notify the public of where he lived and of his dangerousness.[22] Public officials took swift action in response to the outcry. Within ninety days of Megan's death, the New Jersey legislature passed a package of seven bills that expanded mandatory registration requirements for every person convicted of a sex offense, required public notification about all registered persons in New Jersey, and mandated a life sentence without the possibility of parole for anyone convicted of a second sexual offense.[23]

The New Jersey General Assembly introduced and passed the bills all within a month of Megan's death, without the normal committee hearings or other procedural steps that happen before proposed legislation is typically presented for a full vote on the floor. A handful of legislators commented on the rushed process and worried that the bills were hastily crafted with little consideration for the constitutionality or potential effectiveness of their broad requirements. Other legislators dismissed these concerns and painted those questioning the process as more concerned about pedophiles than about children. After New Jersey took quick action, state after state, and the federal government, passed similar laws in the subsequent years to strengthen sex offense registry requirements and to mandate public notification.

The unprecedentedly fast response and sweeping action of state and national government leaders to this sickening crime is both inspirational and crushing. When called to action to protect those who are recognized as innocent victims deserving of protection, no rules are unbendable. State leaders sought to direct every state resource toward preventing a similar catastrophe from ever happening again. That level of responsiveness to tragedy is meaningful. Megan's surviving family mattered to those in charge, as they should. But it is also a tragic reminder of how hierarchies of harm work and how deeply entrenched they are, not only in our institutions but in the psyches of those in power, of those who set government priorities.

For generations, the violent and horrific deaths of many thousands of children who do not neatly fit into the hierarchy of harm, who are not viewed as being worthy of protection or as likely to drive political agendas, rarely resulted in new criminal justice laws or unprecedented state action. No emergency legislative sessions were called for Alexis in Milwaukee, or thousands like her. No sweeping bills were introduced that sought to drastically change a justice system that clearly did not protect these victims from harm. There were few press releases or races among elected officials trying to appear to be the most committed to ensuring the safety of these victims. Seeing the response to victims at the top of the hierarchy, most often white and middle-class, is among the strongest indicators of the extreme lack of response or concern that too frequently exists for just about everyone else.

The Hierarchy of Help

Beyond media and political bias, harm hierarchies outside the courtroom also influence access to victim assistance and compensation. Congress passed the Victims of Crime Act (VOCA) in 1984, lauded as a breakthrough in recognizing the needs of crime survivors. Signed into law by Ronald Reagan, the legislation was part of the major changes he ushered in that focused media and political attention on the plight of victims of crime. VOCA operates the Crime Victims Fund and distributes the money in that fund to all fifty states.

The funds are used for two main programs: victim compensation and grants for victim assistance organizations. Funds are collected from fines and fees assessed against people convicted of federal crimes. White-collar prosecutions in particular can generate enormous sums of money for this fund. Every year, millions of dollars are deposited and then redistributed to the states. States then operate their own compensation programs and grants to victim assistance providers. Individual victims can access help by applying for victim compensation and by seeking support from a victim assistance organization. The compensation is available to cover medical bills, lost wages, and funeral or burial costs. The victim assistance programs typically include counseling, emergency shelter, and support navigating the justice system.

Victim compensation and victim assistance are key mechanisms to help people in crisis stabilize. Without access to this kind of support, victimization debt can devastate victims and drive them into deep and lasting poverty, poor health, and early death. The rapid expansion of the availability of these publicly funded programs across the nation represents one of the most successful modern efforts to expand a public assistance program in the last two generations. But there's a catch: for the most vulnerable and chronically victimized Americans, compensation and assistance programs are not really an option at all.

Ray Winans, of Detroit, Michigan, knows all too well the gap between the established victim assistance programs and the unmet needs of most victims of crime. The co-founder and former executive director of D-LIVE, a hospital-based violence prevention program, and now the CEO of Detroit Friends and Family, a community-based violence prevention program, Winans has been working for more than a decade to improve safety in Detroit neighborhoods struggling with high poverty and concentrated violence.

Winans has seen too many lives cut short or permanently altered because of violence. But what he hasn't seen are a lot of victims successfully attaining victim compensation. Nearly all the victims he helps did not know about victim compensation or victim assistance until they met Winans. That is not unique to Detroit. In Chicago, from 2015 to 2021, only one out of every fifty victims of violent crime in the city applied for victim compensation.[24] In Los Angeles, 61 percent of victims of violent crime reported having never received information about victim compensation.[25]

Then, for those who do learn about it and apply, many are denied. "The public systems that interact with gunshot victims blame them for their own victimization," said Winans. "There is a near-constant assumption that they have been doing wrong and that's why they are hurt. These public systems never see them as victims or offer help."[26]

The majority are low-income victims of color suffering from gun violence and facing life-altering injuries. Mostly uninsured, they face huge medical bills—the ambulance, the emergency room surgery, follow-up surgeries, physical therapy, wheelchairs and other physical support devices, and pain management medication. One national estimate concluded that, on average, one emergency room visit costs a shooting victim $5,254, and if they're admitted to the hospital—which is common for shooting victims—it costs $95,887—nearly *100,000 dollars*.

For far too many, that's immediate and insurmountable victimization debt. According to 2017 data, less than one-fourth of all gunshot wound victims have private insurance coverage. While some are covered by government insurance like Medicare and Medicaid, nearly *one-third* have no health insurance whatsoever.[27]

While the costs of physical rehabilitation mount quickly, so do the costs of mental health recovery and survival needs. Even basic survival expenses, including housing and food, become harder

and harder to afford. Those whose loved ones have died from violence also face costly expenses, such as dealing with the deceased's
medical bills, other debts, funeral expenses, finding mental health
support, or suddenly grappling with untenable living costs if a
breadwinner is killed.

Most of the time, no matter how hard Winans and his colleagues
work to help victims fill out compensation applications, tracking down frequently extensive backup documentation or records
requirement, the victims' applications are denied. *No verification of
employment.* Even if the reason they cannot work is the injury they
sustained. *No verification of home address.* Even if they were homeless at the time of injury. *No telephone.* Even if they cannot afford a
phone. *Noncooperation with police.* Even if they tried to cooperate.
They are denied for a myriad of reasons, none of which seems to
reflect the actual circumstances of their lives.

At least 80 percent of the people Winans has helped apply
for compensation in the last five years have been denied. In the
year 2020, only two of the sixty-three people D-LIVE helped
apply for compensation were approved. And the denials have dire
consequences.

"Without financial help, what are victims to do? They cannot pay their bills, they cannot pay for school supplies for their
child, they cannot pay for food," Winans reports.[28] People are left
to adopt desperate means. One young man, Eric, was shot and
paralyzed with hospital bills piling up but could not continue to
work because of his paralyzing injury. He was denied compensation despite multiple attempts. Eric "became so desperate that he
began selling the pain pills he was prescribed for injury pain management," according to Winans.[29] He was then arrested for selling drugs. This was not someone who had ever sold drugs before
being injured. But he could not see another way out. He suffered
in pain and limited his own physical recovery just to have money
for survival. Eric went from being a "victim of one public health
crisis, gun violence in the community, to contributing to another
public health crisis in our community," Winans reflected. And now

Eric has more than a permanent physical injury; he has a criminal record and an even deeper hole of poverty out of which to climb. This is what it means when compensation applications are chronically denied.[30]

A lack of help has ripple effects on families, too. Winans has seen the tension in families grow because the financial burdens of care and lack of support are too great to manage. "One sixteen-year-old was shot, and his mother was so angry. The teen could not understand why his mother was so mad when he had been a victim." But the mother knew all too well how the local police department and public services systems would see it. She had three other young children in the house and did not want them removed by Child Protective Services. "Even though her son was a victim of crime, she knew that the police would think it was his fault and she would also be blamed," Winans recalled. She was so scared to acknowledge her son's injury that she would not apply for compensation. She worried it would trigger a protective services investigation. "She distanced herself from him so that she would not lose the custody of her other children."[31]

It is impossible to calculate the devastating multigenerational toll on individuals, families, and communities of blaming victims for their own victimization and then denying them access to compensation. Particularly considering the concentrated and unequal impact of violence in the United States, the failure of these resources to support stability and recovery for the most harmed and least helped is a tragedy of epic proportions.

The strongest predictor of future victimization is having been a victim in the past. Victims of violent crime are four times as likely as non-victims to become a victim again. But helping people recover can reduce that likelihood. So, a failure to get timely help to those in post-victimization crisis is shocking government indifference and a setup for future harm. If victim assistance and compensation programs were geared toward helping the population most frequently violently victimized, they would operate quite differently. Public systems would recognize the overlap between extreme poverty and vulnerability to violent victimization. Yet as it stands, the system is not designed to support these survivors.

Despite increasing numbers of criminal justice agency regulations that require notification to victims about victim compensation, many victims remain unaware of it as an option. Most victims report that they have never heard of compensation and were not aware that it, or other victim assistance programs, existed.

Even for victims who do hear about these programs, discriminatory practices prevent many survivors, especially working-class or poor victims and victims of color, from receiving compensation. The rules prohibit a lot of people from being eligible. Most states require reporting within seventy-two hours or less. Nearly every state requires a police report and evidence of cooperation with law enforcement for victims to be eligible. While that may seem logical—police and prosecutors can secure more convictions with victim cooperation—it is not realistic or informed by the realities that many survivors face. Because of the hierarchy of harm, the justice system is not safe for many victims, so cooperating with law enforcement to attain services becomes an avenue that is cut off. For many, it feels more dangerous to report than not to report.

"Being under the influence" is another reason for many to be deemed ineligible. In a 2019 mass shooting in Dayton, Ohio, a gunman fired forty-one rounds into a crowded bar late at night, injuring twenty-seven people, nine of whom died. Surviving victims and co-victims were in shock and needed aid. Nineteen of those who applied for victim compensation assistance were refused help. The *Dayton Daily News* uncovered the denied applications and learned that some applications for assistance were denied because the victims were "under the influence" at the time they were killed.

"Contributing to your own victimization," incomplete or inaccurate applications, failing to cooperate are also the basis for denial of compensation, as well as the legal status of the applicant. In five states, having a prior criminal record, and in two other states, being on probation or parole, are also reasons for denial of eligibility.[32] Until 2021, Ohio even excluded people who were merely *suspected* of having committed a crime.

While these reasons are race neutral on their face, in practice they function as another discriminatory filter that aligns with the hierarchy of harm. People of color are more likely to have criminal records and are more likely to be deemed to have contributed to their own victimization or are suspected to have been involved in crime. In Florida, Black people made up 30 percent of victim compensation applicants but 61 percent of those denied based on a legal record.[33] In Ohio, 42 percent of survivors who applied were Black, but 61 percent of those denied based on a record were Black.[34] An Alameda County, California, grand jury found that Black applicants were about twice as likely as white applicants to be denied for alleged "involvement" in their own victimization or for perceived lack of cooperativeness. The investigation concluded that higher denial rates for Black victims were driven by law enforcement opinion, which is vulnerable to racial bias.[35]

Barriers to compensation and discrimination in victim assistance also impact immigrant victims; lesbian, gay, bisexual, and transgender victims; and victims with disabilities. Though few states bar noncitizens from compensation outright, nearly every state asks for a social security number on the application form, a requirement that discourages immigrant victim applicants.[36] In a survey of victim services providers, respondents most frequently listed immigrants, refugees, and individuals with limited English proficiency as underserved communities.[37] LGBT survivors regularly report largely negative experiences when reporting crime and seeking victim services. One national study found that, of LGBT and HIV-affected victims of interpersonal violence who tried to access emergency shelter, more than four in ten were turned away, most commonly for reasons related to gender identity.[38] In another national survey, six in ten trans people who had interacted with law enforcement reported experiencing mistreatment.[39] Disabled survivors of violence also report difficulty accessing victim assistance. For example, Deaf people experience higher rates of domestic and sexual violence victimization but less support, including barriers such as phone-only emergency hotlines.[40] In a survey of victims in Illinois, 24 percent of victims of violent crime reported that one of the reasons they didn't receive needed services was that services were inaccessible due to a disability.[41]

Even for those victims approved for compensation, actual payment is hard to attain. A 2022 hearing on California's compensation program, for example, revealed that even among those *approved* to receive victim compensation, most never successfully submit a bill for reimbursement.[42] It can take months, or longer, to hear back about a decision on a claim. The average wait time is more than two months, but sometimes it takes much longer. Kentucky reports that it takes an average of nearly three years—1,080 days—from the time the state gets an application before it makes a decision.[43] Worse, once a decision had been made, for those approved, most claim payments are reimbursement-based, meaning even after approval survivors have to pay for costs up-front before they receive financial assistance, and then wait many more months for reimbursement.

Despite significant annual growth in available public resources for compensation and assistance, the number of crime victims who receive support in the aftermath of violence remains abysmally low. For every one hundred victims of violent crime in 2019, for example, only about eight applications for compensation were submitted, and only *six* were approved.[44]

Beyond limited access to compensation, many victims also face barriers accessing victim assistance programs. Of the money that is distributed to victim assistance programs, over 71 percent goes toward serving female crime victims. And of those dollars, the majority serve white females.[45]

*   *   *

Without government assistance available, Winans did what so many grassroots violence prevention service providers do—he built his own programs to help people recover. Without a lot of resources, but with unrelenting commitment, neighborhood-based organizations across the country are helping people adjust to life after violent injury, including helping people find places to live, get to and from hospital appointments, manage debt, or simply meet other survivors and connect with people who care. Winans changed his work schedule to be available to talk with people in the wee hours of the night. He stays up late to be there for them when no one else can. With post-traumatic stress disorder and anxiety, many violent injury survivors harbor debilitating feelings of isolation and chronically struggle to sleep. "Everyone has forgotten about me because I am a burden now," one survivor told him.[46] Winans started visiting people in the hospital around three in the morning, while they lay awake. He brought cards, Monopoly, and Connect Four and sat with them. Other survivors started coming with him, back to the hospital from which they were discharged, to play the games and chat with Winans and the other survivors. Being there for them in these ways has been a lifeline.

At every step of the process—from which victims get thrown in jail by prosecutors and which victims are featured on the nightly news, to which victims have laws named after them and which victims receive compensation—the hierarchy of harm determines whose humanity is recognized and whose is erased.

The Innocence Paradox

Forty-two-year-old Tinisch Hollins knows the reality of the hierarchy of harm that victims face both inside and outside the courtroom very well. A San Franciscan going back three generations, Tinisch was born in the city's Bayview–Hunters Point, a small, predominantly African American community that doesn't always show up on tourist maps. The eldest of six children, she grew up living with her parents, siblings, aunt, and cousins. Her mother passed away from a rare genetic disease when Tinisch was fourteen. From that day, Tinisch became the other maternal figure in the household and, as crime and fear mounted in her neighborhood, she also became the confidant whom other neighborhood kids relied on for advice and help, the proverbial big sister for just about everyone in her community.

Looking out for her younger siblings and other children in the community was a lot like swimming upstream. The residents of San Francisco's Bayview community faced an unjust contradiction: one of the Golden State's most notable centers of wealth and business regularly disregarded the well-being of its Bayview citizens, many of whom were living in generations-old dilapidated public housing projects, originally built as temporary military barracks in the 1930s, right next to a superfund site of toxic waste left over from navy operations decades earlier.

And the environmental conditions were only part of the disregard. Starting at eleven years old, Tinisch became surrounded by continual violence. Police shot and killed a mentally disabled boy who lived next door to her maternal grandmother while he played outside by himself, mistaking his toy for a gun. The crime scene tape that outlined the boy's body remained visible for two years after the incident. Months later, Tinisch's "protector" in the family, Deontay, a thirteen-year-old foster child who lived with her paternal grandmother, was shot and killed in a drive-by shooting.

In the subsequent years, Tinisch lost dozens more loved ones and neighbors to gun violence. Instead of providing safety or support, local public systems responded with surveillance and crackdowns. More police patrols, surveillance, and arrests. And it was not just the public safety systems that toughened up. New public housing eviction rules for people with records. More restrictions on eligibility for public assistance. More school suspensions. The tough-on-crime era was expressed through every public system, not just the criminal justice system. It was more of a tough-on-people era. And still the violence continued.

Young Tinisch was constantly worried about her younger siblings having to contend with so much traumatic loss. She volunteered at youth centers and started dance crews—anything to help the kids get away from the violence. But try as she might, it was nearly impossible to protect them. Mitchell and James, her two younger brothers closest to her in age, both started having problems in the crowded classrooms of their elementary school. School troubles evolved into police troubles. By the time each of them was in middle school, they were on probation. It was easy to get on probation as a teen in Bayview but, with constant surveillance, much harder to get off. Any new mistake and it was back on probation. Tinisch does not remember a time after middle school in which they were *not* on probation.

While she struggled to keep her little brothers out of trouble, the young victims of violence Tinisch knew in the neighborhood experienced a justice system just as suspicious of them as of the people who committed crime. No matter how tragic or random the instances of violent loss of life or injury were, Tinisch doesn't remember a lot of expressions of concern for the victims, only intimidation, threats, accusations. Many survivors felt almost as terrified of interacting with police, prosecutors, and criminal courts as they were of the violence itself. "When the justice system got involved, a lot of times it endangered people's lives even more," Tinisch recalled. Police would pick up kids from the neighborhood and drive them around in the back of the police car. "Just trying to make it look like these kids were cooperating with police to start the rumor mill." Presumably this tactic was used to persuade confessions, but it risked lives. "I've literally buried loved ones because of law enforcement actions investigating cases."

But no matter the risk to her own safety, Tinisch never gave up trying to keep her loved ones safe. She came to know the local public systems very well: the housing authority, the Medicaid system, the school system, the human services agency. She became expert at navigating these systems for the stability of her family and friends. Eventually she took a job in the mayor's office and other government agency positions.

Over the years, her nonstop systems navigation meant she built a reputation in the community as the person to turn to in a crisis. She'd know what to do—until, when the unthinkable came to pass, she didn't. In 2013, her younger brother James was shot and killed. Just four years later, in 2017, Mitchell was killed too. Tinisch, the rock for so many, went from helping other people out of crisis to being in crisis herself: stonewalled trying to get information; struggling to find resources for her brothers' burials; trying to find therapeutic support for her distraught aunt and other siblings. No assistance, no courtroom statements, none of the things the victims' rights movement had enshrined into law seemed to exist for her as these tragedies unfolded around her.

Both of Tinisch's brothers had been on probation at the time they were killed. Neither were individuals the hierarchy of harm easily recognized as worthy of protection or safety. James was killed committing a crime to support his addiction. Mitchell was robbed and killed. But to many people Tinisch interacted with, because of their records, neither brother was a real victim. Yet, as Tinisch recounts, "They were murdered, and the trauma we experienced was no less real just because they had records."

The ripple effects on her family were deep. "These public systems harmed my family long before gun violence took my brothers," she said. "These systems created more stress, more barriers, and that leaves people with more trauma." The public safety systems failed to offer real protection. Instead, the justice system saw the entire community as suspect. "No one in my community gets to be a victim of crime," Tinisch said. "Being recognized as a victim when you're hurt by violence, that's a privilege."

*   *   *

The political action to advance victims' rights in the name of law and order did not seek to advance rights for all victims. It was the "innocent" victims who concerned President Reagan, President Clinton, media pundits, politicians, law enforcement groups, and more. This idea of innocence, however benign sounding, has perpetuated a three-hundred-year-old hierarchy of harm through a linguistically new, but emotionally ancient, mechanism of exclusion.

At its core, the hierarchy of harm presents an innocence paradox: you can secure justice only if you are perceived of as innocent, a perception that falls along racial, class, and gender lines. If you are not innocent in the eyes of the courts, the media, or the politicians, you are not protected from harm. You are not seen as a victim; instead, too often, worse than ignored, you are actually criminalized. Paradoxically, those the media, politicians, and court officials view as most innocent are, statistically speaking, often the *least* vulnerable, and those who are disregarded, blamed, or criminalized are the *most* vulnerable. By refraining from challenging the harm hierarchy, the law-and-order victims' rights movement further cemented it, leaving millions invisible, and making us all pay the public safety cost.

PART III

Poisonous Priorities

6

Up Is Down and Down Is Up

In the spring of 2015, Shakyra Diaz walked into the Fifth District police station in her hometown of Cleveland, Ohio, to file a police report after her home was burglarized. As she entered the small storefront lobby, she saw a dazed-looking teen sitting at a table with a police officer. The girl looked to be about sixteen years old, with decorated fingernails and baggy clothes. She sat with her mother, who was holding a baby and speaking to her in Spanish, urging her daughter to talk to the officer sitting in front of them. As Shakyra filled out paperwork, she overheard the girl slowly describe a horrific crime. Hesitant and trying to speak softly, the teen took a while to get out what she was trying to report. She told the officer that an older male acquaintance had forcibly taken her to a nearby hotel, trapped her in a room, and sexually assaulted her for three days until she escaped.[1]

Shakyra was shocked at what she was hearing, and even more shocked when she witnessed the officer's response. The officer began pressing the teenager for details with rapid-fire questions, and as the girl struggled to respond, he got increasingly frustrated. He slammed his hand on the table and screamed, "Do you want him to get away with this?" The rattled girl shut down even more. She stopped talking, sunk into her chair, and put her head down on the table. When the officer kept pressing, the girl turned to her mother and begged to be allowed to leave. "I don't want to be here," she said.

Alarmed, Shakyra walked over to talk to the officer. She suggested he seek out a female officer to help or, at the very least, continue taking the girl's statement in a private room. The teen-age girl looked up at her and mouthed "thank you." Surprised by Shakyra's interruption, the officer responded that there were no female officers there.[2]

At the time, Shakyra was working as the policy director of Ohio's American Civil Liberties Union and had a rolodex that included many local officials. Unsatisfied with the officer's response, she contacted Cleveland mayor Frank Jackson to tell him what she witnessed. The mayor asked his public safety director to investigate. Local officials had reason to be responsive to Shakyra's concerns. For the last few years, the city had been reeling from an alarming media discovery: the majority of rape cases, hundreds reported each year, sat in file folders uninvestigated, with no testing of forensic evidence, no follow-up interviews, no arrests—nothing. "Disregard for this exact crime that this girl was reporting that day—that was a major issue that had been driving news headlines in Cleveland," Shakyra recalled.[3]

Public attention to local justice officials' disregard for rape victims had begun to ramp up about five years prior to Shakyra walking into the police precinct. In 2009, Rachel Dissell and Leila Atassi, two investigative reporters with the *Cleveland Plain Dealer,* had uncovered more than four thousand rape kits sitting in boxes at the police department, untested, dating all the way back to 1993. Kits like these hold the evidence that medical examiners collect and preserve immediately after a sexual assault—biologic swabs for possible DNA or physical injury documentation that can be analyzed by a forensic lab. The kits are crucial to most rape investigations. For months, Cleveland police representatives had stonewalled the reporters' inquiries about sexual assault investigation statistics, saying they didn't have enough personnel to review case files. The reporters persisted, and eventually police granted them permission to review the files themselves. After sifting through box after box, they found the thousands of untested kits and learned that only 27 percent of all reported rapes in Cleveland ever made it from the police department's files to the prosecutor's office. Of those 27 percent, few were ever charged by prosecutors. The reporters homed in on the scandal, writing about the topic nonstop and producing more than 150 stories over the course of the next few years. Their stories got attention. Local leaders set up a task force, the state attorney general offered help to expedite rape kit testing, state legislation was introduced, and cold case investigations finally started to move.[4]

And still, after all this, Shakyra Diaz found a child, the victim of a brutal assault, being callously interrogated in the public lobby of her local police station. Per the mayor's request, the city's public safety director investigated the police station incident. After watching police lobby video recordings, he validated what Shakyra witnessed, and the officer was reprimanded. But Shakyra felt that officials were missing the bigger point. "This kind of intimidation and disregard has long-term consequences. This girl isn't going to report again. That mentality this officer demonstrated, it was pervasive," she explained.[5]

The policy director's dismay emanated not just from witnessing this disturbing incident but also from her deep familiarity with Cleveland's other justice system priorities. At the ACLU, she had devoted hundreds of hours to pushing city officials to address an entirely different problem—police and prosecutors had been arresting growing numbers of Black Clevelanders for possession of drug paraphernalia, specifically crack pipes, and charging these cases as felonies. The Cleveland Police Department had a policy in place to send confiscated drug paraphernalia to the laboratory to test it for traces of drugs so that prosecutors could then pursue felony drug possession charges against those arrested with crack pipes (paraphernalia is a misdemeanor, whereas possession is a felony and is eligible for prison).[6]

Crack pipe felony convictions were driving Black Clevelanders into state prison at alarming rates. For years, while the number of white arrestees for possession dropped, the number of Black arrestees rose, with 80 percent of those arrested for possession being people of color, despite similarities in drug use rates across racial demographic groups.[7] And for years, judges and grand jury officials had raised alarm bells about the disparities. Shakyra and a coalition of organizations had protested the practice and eventually called for an independent expert to review the data, a review that revealed that white defendants in the surrounding suburbs were charged with misdemeanors and diverted away from incarceration to treatment or community service, while Black Clevelanders caught with crack pipes were sent to prison. In response to the outcry and mounting evidence, the *Cleveland Plain Dealer* conducted its own analysis, uncovering and publicizing the same trend of high drug arrest rates and deep racial disparities.[8]

With a front-row seat to the intricacies of how law enforcement handled both sexual assault cases and drug charges, Shakyra was struck by this completely upside-down set of public safety priorities. "The justice system had all the time in the world to pursue these simple possession cases, using crime lab resources to test crack pipes and incarcerate people. Meanwhile rape kits were sitting untested as officers belittled victims," she recalled.[9]

While extreme, Cleveland's misplaced safety priorities were not unique. At the same time Cleveland officials were ignoring people facing real danger while driving crack pipe possessors into state prison, other cities across the country were showing similar patterns. In 2008, Los Angeles, California, had a backlog of more than six thousand untested rape kits going back more than ten years. Over the course of that same decade, the number of drug arrests had climbed steadily each year, so much so that by 2008, drug offenses accounted for the largest percentage of felony arrests in the city. Just as in Cleveland, rape kits sat on shelves while police handcuffed drug users in ever-increasing droves.[10]

In neighboring Orange County, California, law enforcement took actions beyond simply increasing drug arrests: officials began manufacturing *their own drugs* to sell. In the 1990s, the Orange County Sheriff's Department built its own crack manufacturing lab, made crack, and then supplied it to undercover police officers in Santa Ana, one of Orange County's largest cities. The officers posed as drug dealers, sold it, and arrested the buyers for possession of crack. They orchestrated these "reverse sting" operations—where police pretended to be sellers instead of buyers—down the street from a middle school. "Undercover officers have tried to avoid sales to juveniles," the Santa Ana police chief told the *Los Angeles Times* in a 1994 exposé on the scandalous practice.[11] More than four hundred people were arrested during the eighteen-month-long operation before a judge ordered an end to the program.[12] Meanwhile, those same local officials struggled to address serious violent crime: less than 25 percent of homicide cases in Santa Ana resulted in an arrest or prosecution during the same time police were manufacturing crack, a tragic fact considering that the rate of homicide in Santa Ana was higher than the statewide or national average for much of the 1990s and the first decade of the 2000s.[13] Despite the homicide crisis, the investigation of these murder cases chronically failed.[14]

Santa Ana police were not the only ones selling cop-made crack while violent crime grew. On the other side of the country, the sheriff's department in Broward County, Florida (home of Fort Lauderdale), was sued for doing the same thing: manufacturing and selling crack to arrest people for possession. After the lawsuit reached the Florida Supreme Court, the court prohibited the "outrageous law enforcement conduct," with Judge Harding noting that "it is incredible that law enforcement's manufacture of an inherently dangerous controlled substance . . . can ever be for public safety."[15] Meanwhile, Fort Lauderdale has had homicide rates nearly double the national average for more than thirty years and has struggled with an inability to successfully investigate or prosecute homicides, with less than 30 percent of homicide investigations resulting in arrest on a consistent annual basis.[16]

In cities like Cleveland, Los Angeles, Santa Ana, and Fort Lauderdale, how could *these* be the public safety priorities? How could crack pipes ever be ahead of rape kits in the line for forensic review, or the arrest of people buying sheriff-manufactured drugs ever trump murder investigations? If concern for victims of violent crimes truly determined public safety priorities, vulnerable community members would not be ignored while aggressive enforcement of petty crimes soared. But for decades, these upside-down priorities persisted.

These priorities emerged for two main reasons: money and politics. First, the calls for law and order and victims' rights were heeded through a massive transfer of cash to a justice system that has been better at declaring wars against phantom enemies than at identifying who is vulnerable to being hurt. As money increasingly flowed to criminal justice, allocation of the money focused attention on the wrong crimes, the wrong enemies, and the wrong approach. Justice agencies largely received financing for strategies that captured large numbers of people for low-level crimes—money was designated for surveillance and patrol rather than for complex investigations or community engagement for prevention.

Second, while surveillance budgets grew and focused a lot of law enforcement energy on petty arrests, political rhetoric was turning would-be victims into would-be criminals. Politicians glommed onto racialized stereotypes about who commits crimes and won votes by framing millions of people, many of whom were living in unsafe environments and vulnerable to being harmed, as people to be afraid *of,* instead of afraid *for.*

That left most victims, invisible under the hierarchy of harm, more likely to be targeted for arrest than protected from danger. In Cleveland, most of the rape kits that sat untested on shelves for years belonged to women of color, mostly low income—the very people who have been chronically disregarded as victims for generations. Black and Brown women in Cleveland were more likely to be among those targeted for drug possession arrests than to be treated with concern when reporting sexual assault. In Santa Ana, many of the people killed by gun violence each year were Latino youths suspected of being in gangs, a group of youth that, despite being vulnerable, were never perceived as real victims. "Most of those who commit drive-by shootings know who they are shooting at," the mayor of Santa Ana remarked, in an effort to reduce public concern about climbing homicides at the time.[17] If the person reporting rape or being shot can be dismissed as not really a victim because they may be using drugs or may be in a gang, the horrific crimes committed against them don't have to be taken as seriously.

Prioritizing crack pipes over rape kits is emblematic of what goes wrong when the call for protecting victims and improving safety is resolved by expanding the money and power of a justice system poisoned by the hierarchy of harm. Focusing on crack pipes over rape kits reflects a set of financial and political decisions that beefed up the presence of the justice system, mostly in urban communities, but treated entire communities as if they were only communities of suspects, not communities with victims deserving dignity and protection.

Money for Surveillance and Arrest in Communities of Color

In 1990, Los Angeles mayor Tom Bradley said, "Through the use of mobile booking units, horse-mounted police officers and other high-profile deployment strategies, the police are waging an all-out war on crime. I want to give them the personnel to escalate our attack. . . . The city has made our blue-uniformed officers the number-one priority."[18] As anyone familiar with police procedurals would notice, the "blue-uniformed officers" contrast with the white-shirted officers or civilian-clothed detectives in that the blue uniforms are the police's muscle—not their investigators. Bradley's priorities were a sign of the times. Beginning with significant increases in federal dollars to cities and states earmarked to expand law enforcement, the expansion represented a shift from the "old-fashioned" kind of police work required to solve crimes—interviews, research, patience—to the warlike mentality focused on driving arrests up, no matter what those arrests are for.[19]

Bradley was not the only law enforcement leader aggressively building up blue uniform patrols. Chicago had begun implementing similar strategies two decades earlier with Chief Orlando Wilson advocating for "constant surveillance of every corner of the city."[20] And police agencies also implemented arrest quotas that rewarded officers for making arrests—no matter how trivial.[21] One New York City police officer captured the policing mentality of the era: "We own the block. . . . They might live there but we own the block."[22]

This shift in law enforcement strategies was not coincidental. It was fueled by politicians driving major federal investments. As historian Elizabeth Hinton meticulously documents in *From the War on Poverty to the War on Crime*, in the second half of the twentieth century, every presidential administration from Kennedy to Reagan transferred significant federal money to local and state justice agencies primarily geared toward building out their capacity to surveil and arrest, almost exclusively in urban communities of color.[23] John F. Kennedy funded "anti-delinquency" efforts that focused local justice agencies on monitoring urban Black youth, whom the administration portrayed as potential future criminals.[24] Lyndon Johnson launched a War on Crime that, for the first time in U.S. history, invested substantial federal dollars in local police budgets and began militarizing police, especially in urban communities. Johnson's centerpiece, the Safe Streets Act of 1968, as Hinton describes, provided the present-day equivalent of roughly $15 billion to local police over a fifteen-year time span.[25] After Johnson, Richard Nixon continued the trend with more federal investments in law-and-order policing, grants for state prison expansion, and proposals to ratchet up sentencing.[26] After Nixon, Gerald Ford increased funding for juvenile incarceration, and Jimmy Carter expanded surveillance in public housing projects.[27]

This political strategy grew exponentially under Reagan, the president who fueled the law-and-order victims' rights movement. While his National Commission on Victims of Crime advocated for expanded powers for justice agencies, Reagan's overlapping War on Drugs expended billions of dollars to provide justice agencies with equipment, grants, and incentives to focus local justice systems on arresting and punishing drug crimes, primarily in communities of color.[28] Upon the signing of the sweeping Anti-Drug Abuse Act of 1986, which the *New York Times* reported would funnel money to law enforcement for "new boats, planes and weapons, more drug law-enforcement agents . . . and new jail cells,"[29] Reagan pronounced, "[T]oday marks . . . a victory for safer neighborhoods, a victory for the protection of the American family."[30]

Justice agencies became adept at pursuing drug-related crimes in urban communities because that's what they received money for. The Law Enforcement Assistance Administration, and later the Local Law Enforcement Block Grants Program, covered 90 percent of the cost of weapons and technologies, spurring a buying spree for cameras, wiretaps, patrol officers, undercover officers, and informants.[31] In Shakyra Diaz's home city of Cleveland, for example, justice agencies received more than $32 million in federal grants from the U.S. Department of Justice from 1998 to 2006, most of which was earmarked for drug war–related expenditures, such as regional narcotics task forces focused on low-level drug arrests and purchases of drug war–related equipment and supplies. Meanwhile, the federal dollars Cleveland received for tackling violence against women paled in comparison: about 5 percent of the Justice Department funding to Cleveland during that same time period went to addressing violence against women.[32]

After Reagan, George H.W. Bush's administration kept the same federal spending priorities, and political analysts described

Bill Clinton as the Democratic politician who took the crime issue back from Republicans by fully embracing a tough-on-crime stance and funding even greater growth in justice bureaucracies.[33] He pledged to add one hundred thousand more police to cities across the country and greatly expanded federal incentives for prison building, among other criminal justice expenditures.

Administration after administration invested federal dollars in building up justice agencies' presence, but comparatively fewer resources were focused on developing those agencies' sophistication in solving difficult serious crimes including murder, sexual assault, and child abuse, or developing their capacity to support victims or partner with communities to build strong crime prevention strategies.[34] It was a lot of money to contain perceived threats: the Black Clevelander using drugs who might go on to commit another, more heinous, crime; the Latino Santa Ana youth stealing a phone who might be part of a gang that might in the future commit a more serious crime all while *actual* crimes against vulnerable populations went mostly unsolved. Whether these expenditures came in the form of the War on Crime, or War on Drugs, or the tough-on-crime movement, they were perceived as pro-victim and pro–public safety. But the biggest winners were the politicians and the justice system, not the communities living under a constant threat of arrest without access to very much real help.

Money for Surveillance Contributed to More Focus on Petty Crime Versus Serious Crime

In 2011, single mother and Los Angeles native Ingrid Archie was barely able to survive on $300 a month when she was convicted of petty theft and placed on probation. She had been struggling to find stable work and care for her family. Ingrid had been raised in the foster care system from the time she was six years old, after being removed from her abusive family home. Her life in foster care was tumultuous, and she had an old criminal record from those years that prevented her, now an adult and a mother, from being eligible for most jobs. She was enrolled in college and took whatever part-time work she could qualify for, but it was impossible to make ends meet. Every time she received a job offer, the background check would rescind it. Her prior record and new three-year probation term also prohibited her eligibility for child-care assistance.

In 2014, her circumstances shattered even more when she became a victim of domestic violence after her live-in boyfriend assaulted her. Ingrid took her two children and moved into a domestic violence shelter. Now living in fear and traumatic stress, in a moment of desperation, she stole diapers from a convenience store while her children waited in the car. She was arrested. That conviction, combined with her status on probation and her prior record, resulted in a sentence of three years in state prison—and another felony on her record. Once she was incarcerated, she lost custody of her children, who were then placed in foster care.[35]

Ingrid's experience is not isolated or unique. As federal money flowed to local criminal justice for surveillance and incarceration, millions of people were arrested and incarcerated. Many were incarcerated for low-level offenses like petty theft that hardly seem worth the lifelong effects of imprisonment, family disruption, and felony records. But that is what happened to millions of people and their children, primarily people like Ingrid—people of color from low-income communities, many of whom were invisible victims long before ever committing crime.

In *Victims in the War on Crime*, criminologist Markus Dirk Dubber described the practical implications of a law-and-order movement created in the name of victims but executed through the tactics of surveillance and mass incarceration: a campaign of "mass incapacitation for possession offenses"[36]—having an outlawed item in your possession, which is an arrestable offense. While possession of illegal contraband—guns, drugs, stolen property—can be dangerous, these types of crimes became a major focus of local justice systems in part because so much money was earmarked for them, and in part because they are easier to prove in court than are more complicated, and often more dangerous, crimes like actual robberies, rapes, shootings, or trafficking. With federal money, police and prosecutors convicted people for drug possession, gun possession, burglary tools, drug sales instruments, stolen property possession, you name it. Arrests went up, the federal money was deemed effective based on that metric, and more money flowed. As Dubber pointed out, however, these are also often offenses for which there is no victim. "The war on crime, though ostensibly waged on behalf of crime victims, has been first and foremost a war on victimless crime," he wrote in 2002.[37]

Justice officials in cities like Cleveland became expert drug offense chasers, without effectively addressing crimes more difficult to stamp out. In 1991, law enforcement in California made one and a quarter million arrests for misdemeanors, but solved fewer than half of all reported violent crimes.[38] This divergence points to the perverse financial incentives that affected law enforcement bureaucracies and individual officers. Mona Lynch, the criminology professor who analyzed grand jury reports on the Cleveland crack pipe scandal, found that police officers' overtime pay for making court appearances in felony crack pipe cases provided motivation for officers to make those arrests. They were paid automatic overtime hours for court appearances on felony arrests but not for misdemeanor arrests. The more felony drug arrests, the more money officers made.[39] And government criminal justice grant programs have often measured success in terms of numbers of arrests, incentivizing a focus on low-level arrests for entire departments.[40]

One historian estimated that only three out of every two hundred people who encounter the criminal justice system are arrested for violent crimes.[41] And a lot of victims were swept up in all those other police stops. A 1991 independent commission that reviewed the Los Angeles Police Department's shifting tactics warned, "LAPD officers are trained . . . to seek out potential criminals before they commit crimes. . . . [This] creates a potentially grave problem . . . in some cases it seems to become an attack on [racial and ethnic minority] communities at large. The communities, and *all within them* [emphasis added], become painted with the brush of latent criminality."[42]

Law-and-order politics had spawned a justice system that prioritized a "widespread assault on anyone and anything the state perceives as a threat" and the victims' rights movement ended up providing political cover for this war. Meanwhile, people like Ingrid lacked safety, or a lifeline to recover, both before and after incarceration.[43]

Rhetoric Cast Vulnerable People as Predators and Justified the Surveillance Approach

While successions of presidential administrations were transferring federal dollars to state and local justice systems for surveillance and patrol, the political rhetoric justifying these aggressive investments included fear-mongering narratives about the scourge of drugs, gangs, and urban crime. Perhaps the most extreme example came on the scene in the 1990s, with jarring news headlines about youth: "Teenage Time Bombs: Violent Juvenile Crime is Soaring, and It Is Going to Get Worse"; "Teenage Violence: Wild in the Streets"; "Heartbreaking Crimes: Kids Without a Conscience"; "Children Without Pity"; "'Superpredators' Arrive: Should We Cage a New Breed of Vicious Kids?"[44]

Sensational stories about an ostensible generation of uncontrolled violent youth, coupled with racialized imagery of youth of color, ran in newspapers and magazines and on cable and broadcast television news. These headlines drove politicians to tout even tougher new policies. In the span of a few years, politicians changed hundreds of laws related to perceived juvenile delinquency: from transferring juveniles into the adult justice system to toughening school discipline policies, increasing police in schools, and preventing the sealing of juvenile records. Between 1991 and 1999, the number of children in youth prisons increased 41 percent, and the number of youths held in adult jails quadrupled.[45]

As political and media attention to the alleged depraved youth problem gained steam, in 1995, Princeton University professor John DiIulio coined the term *superpredator* to describe what he predicted was going to be a growing wave of morally corrupt teen criminals born into families that cultivated criminality. His primary data point for this assertion was the increased number of Black and Latino children from low-income families born in that era. "On the horizon . . . are tens of thousands of severely morally impoverished juvenile super-predators. They are perfectly capable of committing the most heinous acts of physical violence for the most trivial reasons," DiIulio wrote in the *Weekly Standard*. "They fear neither the stigma of arrest nor the pain of imprisonment. So, for as long as their youthful energies hold out, they will do what comes 'naturally': murder, rape, rob, assault, burglarize, deal deadly drugs, and get high."[46] The *superpredator* phrase spread among media outlets and politicians alike. In just five years after DiIulio coined it, *superpredator* appeared nearly three hundred times across forty major media outlets, representing extraordinary repetition in an era before social media and digital news.[47]

Politicians of both parties cited the "coming superpredator" epidemic in support of a tough-on-crime policy agenda. In 1996, then first lady Hillary Clinton famously said, "[T]hey are not just gangs of kids anymore. They are often the kinds of kids that are called super-predators—no conscience, no empathy. We can talk about why they ended up that way, but first, we have to bring them to heel."[48] Republican presidential candidate Bob Dole echoed the same sentiment: "Unless something is done soon, some of today's newborns will become tomorrow's super-predators—merciless criminals capable of committing the most vicious of acts for the most trivial of reasons."[49]

Victims' rights groups were a part of the superpredator bandwagon. Oregon's Crime Victims United group, for example, placed a ballot initiative, Measure 11, dubbed Oregon's One Strike and You're Out law, on the state's 1994 ballot to enact mandatory minimums and to require juveniles over fifteen years old to be charged as adults. Crime Victims United in Oregon later said Measure 11 has "not only protected innocent people from violent criminals, and given victims real justice, but has also given people considering committing serious crimes something to think about."[50] Likewise, Crime Victims United in California joined with then governor Pete Wilson, the California District Attorneys Association, the California Police Chiefs Association, and the California Correctional Peace Officers Association to promote Proposition 21, a 2000 California ballot initiative that toughened penalties for youth gang crime and expanded transfers of youth into the adult justice system. "Proposition 21 . . . will toughen the law to safeguard you and your family," they wrote. "California['s] juvenile population will increase by more than 33% over the next fifteen years, leading to predictions of a juvenile crime wave."[51]

The political rhetoric was successful at toughening laws and further beefing up justice budgets, but as a prediction it was wrong. There was no juvenile crime wave. In fact, when DiIulio coined the policy-driving phrase, juvenile crime had already been on the decline for the preceding four years. But the notion that youths of color were dangerous and predatory was so easily accepted by media and politicians that the facts mattered little. The wheels of the justice system expansion were already in motion, and thousands upon thousands of youths, mostly of color and low income, were surveilled, arrested, and incarcerated. The fact that many of these youths were vulnerable to victimization in unsafe environments was of no importance.

The developments of the 1980s and 1990s, where money and politics led to upside-down public safety priorities, were consistent with the way justice system deployment decisions had been developing for generations. In *The Condemnation of Blackness*, historian Khalil Gibran Muhammad documents the way in which, in the early part of the twentieth century, social science research created a myth of the inherent criminality of Black Americans and how that myth justified increased arrests in Black communities, while political responses to crime in low-income white immigrant communities were quite the opposite.[52] Muhammad chronicles these differences in cities such as Philadelphia, where responses to crime problems in low-income white communities amounted to a series of "progressive reforms," such as investing in family services, after-school programs, employment development, and education.[53] The political leaders at the time "wanted to work with white moral reformers to save whites from becoming criminals," a prevention strategy that identified the cause of crime as not the fault of the residents but as an outgrowth of environmental conditions.[54]

Meanwhile, policing became more aggressive in Black communities experiencing the same environmental challenges. And those distinct responses of prevention versus arrests and surveillance *decreased* the safety of Black victims.[55] When white Philadelphians committed crimes against Black Philadelphians, police and prosecutors rarely acted and in some instances even arrested and incarcerated Black victims who sought to protect themselves when the justice system would not. The hierarchy of harm repeated over and over again—defining both who gets the privilege of being recognized as a victim and who is perceived as a threat, regardless of circumstances: permanent criminals in one community and permanent victims in another.

The Life and Death Impact of Upside-Down Safety Priorities

Despite the law-and-order victims' rights rhetoric, the significant expansion of federal money and incentives to strengthen local justice systems did not improve those systems' responsiveness to many vulnerable victims. Instead, the bulk of that transfer of cash and power focused on giving law enforcement tools and authority to surveil and incarcerate "would-be criminals," defined along race and class lines, in larger and larger numbers. It did not matter if many of those targeted as latent suspects were actually survivors of crime—people overcoming traumatic violence without support, and potentially holding key information to tackle a real instance of violent crime. All this built up a justice system not very good at distinguishing between vulnerability and dangerousness.

The consequences of this public safety strategy are literally a matter of life and death. The invisibility of many victims living in communities targeted for mass surveillance increased their vulnerability—vulnerability to being aggressively prosecuted for minor infractions and vulnerability to being disregarded when they were harmed by violence, viewed as part of the neighborhood crime problem, not as a victim. Majority white, middle-class, and suburban communities have been largely spared from the sweeping crackdown approach to public safety. The notion that too many innocent people might get swept up in that kind of aggressive safety strategy is accepted in the halls of political power and restrains deployment, arrest, and prosecution decisions in many majority-white communities. But somehow that same consideration, a recognition that all these aggressive tactics might sweep up too many good people, including victims themselves, has eluded decision-makers for decades when the communities in question are predominantly low-income communities of color. And the consequences have been dire.

The reason *Cleveland Plain Dealer* reporters Rachel Dissell and Leila Atassi began asking local police and prosecutors about unsolved rape crimes in 2009 is that a horrific crime discovery had been made, causing shocking national headlines. During the same time that Cleveland police and prosecutors chased down people with crack pipes, low-income Black women in Cleveland were being targeted by an extremely violent serial killer who lured women into his home, then raped and murdered them. These horrifying murders were uncovered when police found eleven bodies buried in Cleveland resident Anthony Sowell's house in 2009. Neighbors had complained of an odor emanating from the area, and long after the first complaint, the home was finally investigated, with the bodies of the deceased victims uncovered throughout the house.[56]

At least one victim, Vanessa Gay, was able to escape before being killed. Extremely traumatized by the violent attack—and having witnessed a decapitated body in Sowell's house after he sexually assaulted her—Vanessa called the police after she miraculously got away.[57] Incredibly, the call operator told her she was required to report the crime in person at a police station; the call operator could not take the report over the phone. Injured and in shock, Vanessa did not have a safe way to get to a police station.

Traumatized by both the assault and the astonishing lack of concern when she called police, Vanessa sank further into drug addiction. Not until nearly a year and half later, and months after police had finally discovered the bodies of eleven women hidden in Sowell's home, did anyone in the justice system take note of Vanessa's survival of the horrifying attack. Vanessa was in court, having been accused of a probation violation. She realized a court reporter was taking down all that she said when she was brought before the judge in her own case. This was her chance to document her horrific story with officials. She described what happened and told the judge that she had tried to tell police about what had happened twice, once by phone on the night of the crime and then again when police arrested her some months after the attack for having an open container of alcohol in public. She testified that the police officers arresting her laughed and ridiculed her when she described the assault and then arrested her for alcohol possession.[58]

Over the same period that Anthony Sowell was on the loose in Cleveland—specifically targeting low-income Black women with a history of drug addiction—*thousands* of Black Clevelanders were sent to state prison for felony drug convictions arising from trace amounts of drugs on paraphernalia. While the justice system was churning out these drug convictions at lightning speed, Black women in Cleveland were facing life-threatening danger and extreme disregard.

The generations-old hierarchy of harm means it's all but certain that had Vanessa been white and middle-class, she would have been taken much more seriously as a victim and treated much less harshly as a defendant. And the racialized disregard of Vanessa and Anthony Sowell's other victims was also blatant: some of the families of the disappeared reported they had to make their own missing person posters when police refused to take their missing person reports. This so shocked area residents that wealthy white women from the nearby Rocky River suburb, after learning about the lackluster police response through the media, called into local radio stations to react to the unfairness, saying this would never have happened to them in their suburban community.[59]

Vanessa was punished as a user while completely ignored as a survivor, because the hierarchy of harm biased the justice officials against her and because the local justice system was literally funded and designed to pay more attention to drug possessors than to rape survivors in communities of color. After years of intense investigative reporting on the disregard of rape victims in Cleveland, reporter Rachel Dissell concluded that "the rapists were smarter than the police because they knew exactly who the police would not care about. They knew how to target vulnerable victims, people whose credibility would be questioned, people who the justice system didn't protect."[60]

7

The Public Safety Myth

Tom Hoffman was a police officer for thirty years. So that meant most of his adult life was spent immersed in the patrol and surveillance priorities that ballooned justice budgets across the United States. In 1974, the twenty-one-year-old from the San Fernando Valley became an officer in Los Angeles, California, where he patrolled the streets of South Los Angeles, climbed through the ranks to captain, and then became the assistant police chief in West Sacramento twenty years later. Over those two decades, policing changed drastically. Police forces grew, military equipment poured in, and the warrior mentality flourished. "Our primary intent was to arrest and incarcerate as many people as we could. And on top of that it was to facilitate prosecutions that would result in the longest incarceration terms possible. We were there to kick ass and take names. The cops most glorified were the most aggressive," Tom recalled. Applicants to the police academy with a military background, particularly war veterans, received ten additional points on their application scoring sheet, seen as already trained for the tasks at hand. "The federal government handed over billions of dollars for this . . . the war on drugs, the war on gangs, the war on parolees, we were at war and that's what public safety was about."[1]

So, in 2006, when he switched out of his career in policing to oversee California state parole operations, he didn't expect much difference. It was still a law enforcement position, after all. What he couldn't have anticipated was just how drastically his view of public safety would change when he went from putting people into jail to overseeing the agency in charge of supervising people leaving incarceration.

"I truly had no idea what happened to people in the system. . . . I don't remember many of us ever thinking about it. We dropped them off at the jail and what happened next was on someone else's watch."[2] Suddenly, as the new head of California parole—the state with the largest parole population in the country at the time— "what happened next" was decidedly on his watch. What he found transformed his perspective. "If you go into this system, you're screwed. In every sense." He found there was very little rehabilitation, and the conditions inside prison mostly prepared people for either more imprisonment or more crime, not safe release. People left unprepared, often with few places to go and no resources. "In many ways it felt like we were putting people back on the streets, by the thousands, and wishing them ill. . . . The only thing we knew how to do was re-arrest them for violations and incarcerate them again."[3]

Tom started reading up on corrections research and analyzing the data he found about which interventions could turn people's lives around and stop recurring engagement in crime. Plenty of studies pinpointed the link between lower recidivism rates and education, workforce training, cognitive behavioral therapy, and supportive family and community connections. Other studies even demonstrated that too much incarceration or parole supervision can make people *more likely* to return to crime instead of less likely. He was slowly realizing there was very little safety in the state's public safety system. "Billions of taxpayer dollars spent every year without anyone giving a damn about any of the science. How is that safe?"[4]

Few public officials understood—or cared—about the data that changed Tom's perspective for a few reasons. The continued political influence of the law-and-order mindset that equates justice system growth with more victim protection led to the lopsided deployment priorities Shakyra experienced. It also led to widespread acceptance of a deeply engrained public safety myth. The myth is that because the justice system has grown, public safety has improved. It is true that over the years that the justice agencies grew and incarceration rates soared, crime declined—a lot. So a powerful myth emerged that the decline was *attributable* to mass incarceration: crime went down because of the increased punitiveness and power of the justice system.

This myth has been frequently accepted as fact, especially among politicians, leaving few reasons to seriously reconsider public safety priorities. Twenty years after President Bill Clinton signed the Violent Crime Control and Law Enforcement Act, creating a federal Three Strikes and You're Out law, for example, Clinton remarked that "because of that bill we had a 25-year low in crime, a 33-year low in the murder rate."[5] While experts have critiqued the comment and pointed to the limited role this specific bill likely had on large crime reductions, many politicians, media pundits, and justice leaders repeat this "more incarceration resulted in less crime" sentiment almost reflexively. In statehouse after statehouse, common wisdom continually holds that, even if there have been some negative societal effects attributable to the growth in incarceration and surveillance, crime went down, so there's no reason to rock the policy boat too much.

While this powerful myth has steered the direction of U.S. crime policy, the data do not support it. A closer look reveals a very different picture: mass incarceration did not slash crime rates. The articulated goal of the buildup of the justice system— improving public safety—has not materialized. And a closer look at some of the core policies adopted during the height of the mass incarceration era, usually enacted in response to horrific cases of high-profile victims—from longer sentencing for people convicted of drugs, gangs, and guns to wide-net mandatory supervision and surveillance—reveals that these specific policies have not achieved their aims. Despite the drive to enact these longer incarceration laws in the name of victims, they have not actually made us safer.

After more than twenty-five years of reduced crime rates from 1993 to 2019, gun violence increased again. In some cities, the sharp increase in homicides between 2019 and 2021 was nothing short of alarming. Americans' fear of crime in 2021 was higher than it had been in more than two decades. Media and political leaders pointed to different reasons for the sudden spike, from the social and economic fallout from the global COVID-19 pandemic to the increased availability of high-powered weaponry. And some blamed the criminal justice reforms enacted between 2015 and 2020 that reduced incarceration as the cause of the increase.

As the political debates swing back and forth with the resurgence of law-and-order rhetoric in 2021 and 2022, it is crucial to take a clear-eyed look at the data. Ignoring what is known and not known about the relationship between justice policy and crime rates is a mistake too costly—in dollars and lives—to repeat.

The "More Incarceration Equals Less Crime" Myth

In the 1950s, right before the law-and-order political agenda took hold of U.S. crime policy and dominated it for four decades, the effectiveness of imprisonment was in question among experts in the field. Costly, ineffective, and inhumane, imprisonment was seen as a form of punishment that would eventually be sharply curtailed or even phased out of modern societies.[6] Instead, the opposite happened. Legislators of all stripes clamored to sponsor bills in support of adding additional criminal statutes to the books, and states across the country enacted federally supported policies that drastically exploded the use of incarceration.

While the solutions proffered were not based on sound science, the political attention given to the issue of crime was warranted. Crime rose sharply from roughly the late 1960s through the early 1990s, the period when many politicians called for more criminal justice resources and power. At the height of crime rate increases in the 1990s, the levels of violence were shocking: roughly 750 violent crimes occurred per 100,000 people in 1993. The drop in crime from the early 1990s was as dramatic. By 2019, crime had dropped to its lowest point since the regular collection of crime data began. From 1993 to 2019, FBI Uniform Crime Reports data showed a decline of more than 50 percent for both violent and property crime. In 2019, fewer than 400 violent crimes occurred per 100,000 people, a nearly 50 percent decline from 1993. Until gun violence surges returned in 2020, the preceding ten years represented the consistently lowest crime rate period since 1960.[7]

These reductions were celebrated, and for good reason. But the reductions also became the go-to measuring stick for championing the effectiveness of the justice system—even though data tell a more complex story about what causes crime declines or increases, one in which the justice system is not necessarily the main driver.

In 2014, the National Research Council of the National Academy of Sciences published the most thorough and comprehensive scientific analysis to date of the impact of incarceration. More than thirty of the top social scientists, historians, lawyers, and other experts in the nation worked together to conduct and review the more than four-hundred-page-long study.

The Growth of Incarceration in the United States: Exploring Causes and Consequences concluded that any positive impact of incarceration increases on reduced crime was limited at best and quickly had diminishing returns. In other words, as incarceration rates grew, initial positive crime-reducing impacts became statistically immaterial and ultimately harmful. The graph of the positive impact of incarceration on crime went up briefly, and then sharply turned negative as incarceration rates rose. And those negative effects of harsh penal policies fell "most heavily on blacks and Hispanics, especially the poorest." The report concluded that the sentencing policies that drove increases in incarceration are "ineffective as a crime control measure."[8]

While mass incarceration is not responsible for the dramatic crime reductions between the early 1990s and 2019, there is evidence that policing did affect crime rates. The most notable is the link between police responsiveness to concentrated violence out-breaks and lowered crime in the immediate aftermath. Unlike the mentality of the 1980s and 1990s of perpetually stopping and frisking entire communities, more nuanced and informed polic-ing focused on increased presence in "hot spots" for limited time periods—in small areas experiencing spikes—has been evidenced to help reduce crime.[9] Importantly, however, like the overwhelm-ing negative social impacts of mass incarceration, borne unevenly by communities of color, policing also has collateral consequenc-es. In his book *Uneasy Peace*, Princeton professor Patrick Sharkey describes the diminution of trust between aggressively policed communities and police as a ticking time bomb. Even when cer-tain policing strategies work in the short term, the long-term cost can be significant.[10]

Even the impact of American policing improvements, shifting from mass surveillance to more narrowly tailored hot spot polic-ing, is not a conclusive cause of the national downward shifts in crime from 1993 to 2020. Numerous experts have pointed out that crime rates similarly declined internationally over the same period that the United States experienced a dramatic crime decline, with no parallel mass incarceration policy shift afoot in comparative nations.[11]

To understand more about why American punitiveness has not been reliable as the primary vehicle for driving crime trends, it is important to consider the fact that much of crime and violence is not known to the justice system, and there are other societal factors that likely have more influence than the justice system.

Most Crime Is Not Reported

While it may be surprising to people unfamiliar with criminal jus-tice, most crime and violence is not reported to law enforcement. Despite the major growth in justice system budgets and power, less than half of all crime happening across the country is report-ed. According to the National Crime Victimization Survey, conducted annually by the U.S. Department of Justice, 46 percent of all violent crimes each year are reported.[12] Other research suggests that, of the violent crime that is reported, bystanders, relatives, or acquaintances—not victims—report a substantial portion of it. People are even less likely to report property crimes such as car break-ins, burglary, or theft. Nationally, 37 percent, a little more than one-third, of all property crimes are reported to law enforcement.[13]

The fact that most crime is not reported to the justice system provides two critical insights: most victims do not rely on the justice system to address the problems they face, and the justice system is neither recording nor resolving much of the crime communities endure.

People do not report crime to the justice system for many reasons. Some victims are simply not physically able to report. Child abuse reports to law enforcement, for example, dropped substantially across the country in 2020 during the COVID-19 pandemic, a reflection of the fact that the most common reporters of these crimes are teachers. Nationwide, school closures meant children were not in school. Few would conclude that low reporting in this period meant actual abuse declined. In fact, it's more likely that actual abuse increased with so many children required to stay home around the clock. It's just that fewer teachers could report, so the number of incidents reported to law enforcement did not match the likely reality.

As it relates to adult victims, a national victim survey conducted in 2016 found repeated themes as to why adults do not report: a lack of trust in the justice system, a belief that criminal justice officials would not be able to do anything to help, a relationship with the perpetrator, or fear of retaliation if the reporting is uncovered.[14] Many victims do not trust the system or do not trust that interacting with it will help.

The belief that ultimately drives victim silence—that the justice system may not resolve the crime—aligns with the data about what happens after reporting. Less than half of crimes reported to law enforcement are solved. Reported violent and serious crimes have a solve rate of about 60 percent, with wide variations locally, and reported property crimes have a solve rate of less than 20 percent, again with wide variations.

Kansas City, Missouri, for example, once designated the fifth most dangerous city in the United States, struggles with more homicides and shootings per capita than most of the nation does. And yet, few of those violent gun injuries result in convictions. In fact, most have not been prosecuted at all. When Jean Peters Baker became the top prosecutor in Jackson County (Kansas City's county home) in 2011, she initially didn't realize how few shootings resulted in justice system action. She started reviewing clearance rate data, which is the rate at which a reported crime is closed at the law enforcement level (either because an arrest has been made and a prosecution initiated or because the suspect has died). She uncovered that fewer than one in five nonfatal shootings in her jurisdiction were cleared. She was shocked. Her office was not even investigating most of the violent crime in her community, violence that was happening at alarming rates. She'd been to enough community meetings to imagine the reasons. "The trust is not always there," she said. "I see a lot of public officials pointing fingers and blaming the community for not coming forward. But if we cannot genuinely offer protection to people that do come forward, why would it make sense for them to do that?"[15]

Kansas City is not alone in this reality. In many of the jurisdictions where concentrated violence persists, low reporting and low prosecution rates are a consistent problem. In Detroit, around the same time Peters Baker was uncovering the gap in Kansas City, the case closure rate for nonfatal shootings was also roughly 20 percent, and in Houston it was about 35 percent. In 2019, the national case closure rate for aggravated assaults involving a firearm was just 31 percent, and the rate was just 22 percent for robberies involving a firearm.[16] So few nonfatal shootings were reported in some cities that law enforcement agencies installed ShotSpotter technology, sound recording devices that can detect gunshots and report them to police, because otherwise most shootings would not be reported. In Oakland, California, ShotSpotter technology recorded more than 6,000 instances of gunshots in 2020, and of those, 5,500 were not otherwise reported to police—that's 91 percent.[17] Looking at city after city experiencing low levels of reporting and even lower levels of formal response to violence, the notion that justice system actions are the main driver of crime trends starts to ring hollow.

Other Societal Factors Affect Crime Trends

In addition to the fact that most crime is not reported to law enforcement, there are factors that influence trends in crime more than the actions taken (or not taken) by the justice system. While experts express a range of theories on what affects crime trends, most agree there are numerous, complex factors, many of which are unrelated to criminal justice. Examples include the shrinking percentage of the population that is male and between sixteen and twenty-five years old. This has been theorized as possibly the biggest contributing factor to less crime because most people who engage in crime fall in this demographic.[18] Additionally, alcohol consumption has fallen since the 1980s.[19] Alcohol is more correlated with violence than many illicit drugs, so less alcohol consumption leads to less alcohol-induced crime.[20]

Economic changes affect crime, and economic mobility usually correlates with less crime.[21] "Nothing stops a bullet like a job," according to Father Greg Boyle, the renowned founder of Homeboy Industries, a reentry job training program for people exiting the justice system in Los Angeles. Along that line, Patrick Sharkey pointed out in *Uneasy Peace* that nonprofit community-based organizations can impact crime by strengthening what he and other sociologists refer to as informal social control, social cohesiveness that prevents people from becoming disconnected.[22]

And then there's the elimination in 1978 of lead-based paint, which is known to cause cognitive problems in brain development, including aggressive behavior, leading some to theorize that its elimination contributed to crime reductions.[23] Changes in the use of technology and media can also affect crime trends. When the COVID-19 pandemic forced most people indoors and online to an unprecedented degree, the number of cybercrimes exploded.[24] Even access to health care affects crime: experts estimate that the expansion of Medicaid in the 2010s drove crime rates downward.[25] Our physical environments also affect crime. Planting gardens in vacant lots has been linked to reduced crime.[26] Anything that affects human relationships—the economy, the environment, even the weather—can also affect crime.[27]

These are just a few examples of factors influencing crime trends that are beyond the control of the justice system. But what about the aspects that the justice system does control? Criminal justice agencies do control what happens after someone is convicted of committing a crime, so what do the data tell us about how well the sentencing and management of people postconviction improves public safety?

Tom Hoffman's sobering realization that people exiting the justice system face tough odds of staying away from crime is consistent with the data. Despite the call for tough sentencing and harsh incarceration to improve public safety, these policy choices do not have a track record of generating behavior change for the better or stopping repeat crime. While time and again, high-profile victims have rallied politicians, led to new sentencing penalties, and emboldened the power of the justice system, these measures have not actually achieved public safety.

The Tough-Drug-Sentencing Myth

On June 19, 1986, Len Bias, one of the most talented and celebrated college basketball stars ever to play the game, died of a drug overdose, just two days after being drafted by the Boston Celtics, the top professional basketball team in the nation at the time. His tragic death, which came at a time when President Reagan and other politicians were advancing a tough-on-drugs stance, especially related to crack cocaine, dominated news coverage and riled politicians. Within weeks, the U.S. Congress drafted, and President Reagan signed, the Anti-Drug Abuse and Law Enforcement Act of 1986. Eric Sterling, who served as assistant counsel to the House Judiciary Committee at the time, described the hasty hysteria that drove the bill process: "It became the sole focus of legislative activity. . . . Literally every committee, from the Committee on Agriculture to the Committee on Merchant Marine and Fisheries, were somehow getting involved. . . . People were shouting about how crack cocaine was the most addictive or dangerous substance to ever exist, and one lawmaker was calling for the death penalty for some drug-related offenses. It was hyperbole piled on top of exaggeration."[28]

Even though Len Bias suffered a seizure after ingesting *powder* cocaine, the legislation enacted a mandatory 100-to-1 sentence-length ratio for *crack* cocaine compared with powder and enacted dozens of other stringent mandates for drug crimes. Statehouses across the country followed suit, passing similar tough drug sentencing laws. Within twenty-five years, the federal prison population grew more than seven times larger, with more than half of the inmates incarcerated for drug crimes.

While the Reagan-initiated War on Drugs, which continued for nearly forty years, fueled immense growth in arrests and incarceration, there is no evidence it had an impact on drug use. In fact, more Americans died from opioid-related overdose deaths from 2000 to 2020 than have died from drug overdoses for all other drugs combined, since the Centers for Disease Control and Prevention began tracking overdose deaths in 1968.[29] The U.S. drug addiction crisis was at an all-time high in 2021.[30] The typical reasons people become dependent on drugs have not been linked to criminal law penalties. The reasons commonly have to do with circumstances such as anxiety, stress, family disruption, mental health disorders, trauma, or weak social connections.[31] Despite the billions spent on enforcement and incarceration, harsh drug sentencing laws have failed. Experts have opined that these sentencing laws have instead worsened the drug crisis. Harsh penalties prevent people from seeking help for themselves or for loved ones and do more to hide harmful drug use than to address it. Because harsh punishments cause social isolation, they inadvertently *increase* drug use.[32]

The federal government signed the first mandatory drug sentencing laws in 1951, in response to a concern that young people were becoming addicted to drugs in greater and greater numbers. In the subsequent twenty years, however, drug use skyrocketed. Federal legislators were so frustrated with the nonexistent impact of these mandatory sentencing laws on drug use that in 1970 they voted to repeal the 1951 mandatory minimum drug laws.[33] The bipartisan group of legislators recognized that it was a failed experiment, that threatening tough incarceration to stop drug use does not work.

That rational and evidence-based conclusion did not last long. The growing law-and-order movement, reaching its pinnacle under Reagan's War on Drugs, turned the nation's approach to drug sentencing upside down. A mere fifteen years after bipartisan legislators repealed mandatory minimum drug sentences, the federal government again passed harsh mandatory incarceration laws. Once again, those mandatory minimums were ineffective, and once again, people across the political spectrum sought to undo them. In 1991, elected and criminal justice officials called for the repeal of tough drug sentencing laws.[34] Repeal advocates failed, and in the subsequent decades, the number of tough drug sentencing laws only grew.

The Tough-Gang-Sentencing Myth

On January 30, 1988, college student Karen Toshima went out to dinner in the Westwood area of Los Angeles—a predominantly white neighborhood at the time, with movie theaters, upscale restaurants, and window shopping—to celebrate a recent promotion at work. After dinner, she crossed the street to head back home and was struck in the head by a stray bullet. She died the next day. A dispute between rival gang members had broken out nearby, and when someone pulled out a gun to shoot a rival, Karen lost her life in the crossfire.

Since it happened in a middle-class neighborhood to a person who was not from the poor neighborhoods in which gang violence is typically concentrated, the tragic homicide inspired widespread public outcry and media attention. Within a few days of Karen's death, law enforcement organized a "gang summit," where more than a dozen local law enforcement agencies planned together and declared 1988 "The Year of the Gang." State legislators introduced new anti-gang legislation, and a Westwood official offered a $25,000 reward for information related to the case.[35]

While nearly four hundred people were killed by growing gang violence in Los Angeles in the year prior to Karen's death, virtually all the victims were Black or Latino Angelenos living in low-income neighborhoods. Just a few months prior to Karen's death, a nine-year-old African American boy was shot and killed while swinging on a swing in his neighborhood playground in South Los Angeles, and in the same area, a sixty-seven-year-old African American woman, Alma Lee Washington, was killed as she sat in her wheelchair in the doorway of her home. No rewards or state legislation emerged after those deaths.[36] As the hierarchy of harm would predict, despite the shocking loss of life from violence facing Black and Latino families, Karen's homicide was the one that fueled quick action.[37] And the change that emerged in response to Karen's death was as familiar as the disregard for the boy on the swing and the grandmother in the wheelchair: more power and more money for the criminal justice system.

Within eight months, in September 1988, California governor George Deukmejian signed into law the Street Terrorism Enforcement and Prevention (STEP) Act to enact the toughest gang criminal law penalties in the nation at the time. "As long as some of our young people are involved in drugs and gang activities there can be no positive future for them or their victims," Deukmejian remarked at the bill signing.[38] The STEP Act established being in a gang as a crime and created sentencing enhancements for any crime committed in furtherance of a gang.

After the STEP Act passed, California's legislature and voters further toughened criminal penalties for gang involvement, and California courts interpreted the laws in ways that gave broad discretion to local criminal justice agencies in going after gangs. Like so many other tough sentencing penalties initiated in California, the STEP Act inspired other states to follow suit. By 2000, nearly every state in the nation, as well as the federal government, had laws mandating longer sentences for people in gangs and authorizing broad surveillance strategies to stop gangs. These strategies include things like gang databases to register gang members with law enforcement and authorize searches when police encounter someone in the database.

To be sure, the severity of gang violence was something public officials would have been negligent to ignore. But tough sentencing penalties and widespread surveillance did not work. California gang membership skyrocketed after the laws passed, and the number of gang-related homicides in Los Angeles doubled within the next decade, rising to more than eight hundred annually by 1998. Southern California law enforcement agencies racked up more than $25 billion in spending on a "war on gangs" from 1980 to 2010 but ended up with higher rates of gang violence than before.[39] And that war mentality flourished to unthinkable real-world impacts. In 2021, researchers at Loyola Law School exposed gang activity operating *within* the ranks of the Los Angeles County Sheriff's Department. Deputies formed groups with gang names, got matching tattoos, used gang monikers and hand signals, wore gang colors while off duty, and even harassed "perceived enemies and critics in a manner that most would consider gang-like."[40]

Eighteen different gangs operated within the sheriff's department, severely undermining system legitimacy and costing millions in lawsuit settlements.

The war on gangs through tough criminal penalties has not been evidenced to work for many of the same reasons other tough mandatory sentencing schemes don't work: tough criminal law penalties have less influence on people's decision-making than other factors, including extremely unsafe environments or difficult personal vulnerabilities people face.

In the case of gangs, there's an additional reason tough penalties backfired. The more people who entered prison, the stronger and larger prison gangs became. This was especially true in the states with the largest prison systems, including California and Texas. The prisons became places where gang membership grew and gang violence intensified.[41] In this sense, the STEP Act, and other laws like it, actually expanded gangs.

Beyond the failure of this crackdown to stop the proliferation of gangs, the laws severely worsened racial disparities in the justice system. For example, as of 2019, 92 percent of all adults in California prisons with a sentence lengthened by a gang enhancement law were Black or Latino.[42] Gang surveillance also drastically increased the number of youths of color *without* any ties to gangs who were entered into police gang databases, with the only evidence being their zip code and the color of their skin.

In 2002, in Union City, California, the principal and administrators at Logan High School rounded up nearly sixty students—all Black and Latino—and detained them in two empty classrooms in the middle of the school day. Staff ordered Black students into one classroom and Latino students into another. Local police then fingerprinted the teenagers, collected their personal information, name, home address, and phone number, and photographed them. Police told the kids they would be entered into the statewide gang database. The kids were terrified, and their parents, who were not notified about the incident, were appalled. The school had no evidence that these kids were in gangs. The administrators said they were trying to send a tough message. With help from the Ella Baker Center for Human Rights and the Youth Law Center, the parents and kids protested, publicized the incident, and found lawyers. The ACLU took the case and the school agreed to reverse course.[43]

However, for thousands of other profiled youths of color, that kind of retraction never happened. In his book *Punished: Policing the Lives of Black and Latino Boys*, sociologist Victor Rios documented cases of youth *victims* of gang violence, unaffiliated with gangs when they were hurt, being entered into gang databases. In one case, this led to police following the youth, school administrators monitoring him, and store owners surveilling him. Rios noted this was "not an isolated case . . . there was a recurring pattern of criminalizing the victim." The young man said he "might as well" engage in violence, since the officers that profiled him left him with "nothing to lose."[44]

The Tough-Gun-Sentencing Myth

In 2017, Chicago police superintendent Eddie Johnson, speaking at a legislative hearing in support of a state senate bill to lengthen sentences for gun possession, said gun violence in Illinois would be "reduced by half" if the proposed bill were to become law.[45] That level of impact would be very welcome in a state that had been reeling from an intractable epidemic of gun violence, especially in Chicago, for many years.

On its face, the concept behind mandating lengthy incarceration sentences for illegal guns appears quite rational: give the justice system authority to remove as many people in possession of illegal guns as possible from the community through tough criminal law penalties and incarceration and gun violence will go down. It incapacitates would-be shooters, and it deters others from illegal possession. Certainly, the families that have had to bury loved ones and the thousands left permanently maimed by gun violence deserved strong action.

And yet, following the bill's passage, that prediction of cutting gun violence by half never came to pass. The subsequent year did not see a 50 percent reduction. Nor did the year after that. True, from 2017 to 2018, shootings in Chicago, for example, declined by 14 percent, but that was a smaller decline than the city experienced in the year *before* the bill's passage. From 2016, the year before passage, to 2017, shootings had declined by about 22 percent.[46] Not only did a 50 percent reduction fail to materialize, in 2020, Illinois was again grappling with big increases in gun-related violence, along with many other cities across the country in the midst of the COVID-19 pandemic. Again, forces beyond the control of the justice system, like the pandemic, likely have a bigger impact on behavior than stringent penal codes.[47]

Why doesn't mandating longer sentences for illegal gun possession slash illegal gun possession or gun violence? Research in Illinois and beyond has raised a lot of questions as to the effectiveness of sentencing to enact behavior change. For example, the state's independent data agency, the Illinois Sentencing and Policy Council, analyzed the gun sentencing laws enacted in the year 2000 and found no difference in gun violence rates before or after the laws were put in place.[48]

Another study on Chicago neighborhood-by-neighborhood data went further and concluded that some rates of gun violence in Illinois *worsened* after gun sentencing enhancement laws were enacted, despite the best of intentions behind many champions of these various bills.[49] The National Academy of Sciences systematically reviewed U.S. sentencing enhancements for illegal guns in 2005 and concluded that "available research evidence on the effects of policing and sentencing enhancements on firearm crime is limited and mixed."[50] The research that has emerged in the nearly two decades since would not change the National Academy's conclusions.[51] Meanwhile, public health approaches to reduce gun violence show immense promise and efficacy.[52] Public health approaches include common-sense gun safety regulations such as better background checks or "smart guns" that cannot fire without the owner's fingerprint, as well as community-based conflict mediation and neighborhood-led safety programs.

Experts have noted that harsh sentencing laws likely have limited impact in part because the demand for guns at the neighborhood level outweighs the threat of lengthy criminal law sentences. Unsafe environmental conditions or individual circumstances have been reported to supersede penal codes in people's reasoning for carrying illegal guns. If people do not feel safe without guns, even if they see many others incarcerated for illegally possessing them, some will still choose to do the same if they see it not as a choice but as a necessity.[53]

Grade school kids help paint a picture of how unsafe environmental conditions can drive dangerous decision-making. In 2014, Chicago school administrators found and confiscated a handgun from the backpack of a twelve-year-old.[54] That same year, a nine-year-old in Manassas, Virginia, brought a handgun to school in his backpack.[55] In 2017, a nine-year-old in Middleton, Ohio, did the same thing,[56] and in 2018, in Lauderhill, Florida, a nine-year-old brought a gun to his school and then pointed it at three classmates.[57] In 2021, school staff found a gun on an eleven-year-old in North Naples, Florida.[58] When these children in different schools, cities, and states were asked why they took a gun to their elementary schools, each of them had the same answer: they wanted protection from bullies. They were all being bullied at the time, they all feared for their safety, and they all wanted the bullying to stop. The fact that a child would feel so unsafe on an elementary school campus that they would bring a gun to school should be a wake-up call for school administrators everywhere.

And this is not a phenomenon isolated to elementary school kids. In 2017, a *Journal of Pediatrics* study analyzed Centers for Disease

Control and Prevention national data on teenagers, finding that high school students suffering from bullying were more likely to carry weapons to school than were teens who were not bullied. And the number of teenagers with these experiences is not small: that same study found that one in every eighteen high school students carries a gun to school.[59]

If many thousands of people—from children and teens bullied on school campuses to adults living in communities with recurring violence—harbor so much fear about their immediate surroundings that carrying an illegal gun becomes a choice, then what the penal code has to say is probably not as urgent as the present danger. When we do not protect people, the after-the-fact condemnation of the choices they make to feel safer, however dangerous those choices may be, is an insincere and ineffective approach to public safety.

Shockingly, all those bullied nine-, ten-, and twelve-year-olds caught with guns in elementary schools were *arrested and criminally charged* for illegal gun possession rather than viewed as children sending an unambiguous message that they were unsafe and unprotected. They were sending signals of significant distress. They got handcuffs in response.

Mandatory Arrest, Supervision, and Surveillance Myths

Even for gut-wrenching crimes of interpersonal violence, including sex offenses and domestic violence, tougher criminal law punishments have not significantly affected outcomes. The supervision and restrictions placed on people convicted of sex offenses is another example of good intentions paving a road to failure. The horrifying deaths of children, particularly white children, at the hands of child sexual predators has repeatedly driven lawmakers to urgent action, leading to changes in criminal laws across the country. From Jacob's law to Megan's law to Jessica's law, and many others, states and the federal government adopted sex offense registry systems for tracking by both law enforcement and the public.

In 1989, Patty Wetterling's eleven-year-old son was abducted at gunpoint by a stranger and never found. She found the strength to channel her pain into helping others and started working on behalf of other missing and exploited children. Her determination to prevent this kind of tragedy from happening to anyone else led her to advocate for sexual offender registry laws. President Clinton signed into law the first federal registry in 1994, the Jacob Wetterling Act, named after Patty's son. Since then, every state in the nation has adopted a mandatory registry, and hundreds of subsequent laws have been passed to make the surveillance and restrictions greater and greater. Today, the registry contains about nine hundred thousand names, including many juveniles, who face lifetime restrictions on nearly every aspect of their lives.

Few things are more unimaginably horrifying than the violent sexual abuse of children. Unfortunately, the criminal justice system's implementation of mandatory registries has led to widespread concerns about their effectiveness. The crimes that are included as registerable offenses are very wide ranging, and many fall far outside the realm of violent abuse of children, such as public urination, consensual sex between teenagers, and indecent exposure. Beyond the overly broad range of offenses, people on the registry face a near-impossible web of restrictions, including where to live (not near a school, bus stop, church, day care center, or anywhere children gather, for example) and with whom and how they can earn a living. The requirements are so onerous that many people cannot find places to live or work for years at a time, or for an entire lifetime.[60]

In certain cities, mapping out the restrictions reveals that nowhere within city limits is eligible for people on the registry. In 2005, Miami-Dade County, for example, passed a local ordinance more stringent than the state's residency prohibition of anywhere that is 1,000 feet or closer to schools and bus stops, and so on, making it a 2,500-foot restriction. The probation department, responsible for determining what areas of the county are eligible for residency, concluded that an old warehouse with no running water or sewage was the only place that met the restrictions. Soon, more than 250 people on the registry lived there, in tents outdoors on concrete, with no bathrooms or electricity.[61]

These kinds of policies are so impossible that many people abscond or end up homeless, making it *more* difficult to track them through the registry. What's more, because a small percentage of the people on the registries committed violence against children, clogging the registries with so many additional names has meant it is not easy to discern who is an actual potential danger and who is not.[62] And, once again, we see excessively harsh punishments having the opposite intended effect on victims. Many victims have revealed that they are *less* likely to report abuse because they are related to the abuser and do not want the person to be permanently ostracized through being on the registry.[63]

Decades after the abduction of her son, Patty Wetterling, after studying more and more about child abuse prevention and the gross overreach of sex offense registries, began to publicly question the laws, saying they had gone too far. "The solution that's been sold over the years is lock 'em up and throw away the key. But we've caught a lot of people in the net who could have been helped. . . . We've been elevating sex offender registration and community notification and punishment for 20-some years, and a wise and prudent thing would be to take a look at what's working. Instead, we let our anger drive us."[64]

Mandatory domestic violence arrest laws face similar scrutiny for ineffectiveness, even if the initial reason for their emergence was based on a desire to force the justice system to take the crime of domestic violence seriously when it had been ignored for so long. The long-standing hierarchy of harm had, for many generations, excluded many women and child victims of family violence from protection. The historical law of coverture, allowing men to dominate their homes as they desire, means that justice agencies perpetually turned a blind eye to family violence. The battered women's movement that emerged in the 1960s developed divergent views on how to address domestic violence, with many activists preferring expansion of shelters and civil protection over criminal law solutions. Nonetheless, some leaders called for mandatory arrest policies, and the federal government endorsed them. The federal Violence Against Women Act authorized grants to states that enacted mandatory arrest policies, which required that an arrest be made in every domestic violence call to the police. More than twenty states enacted these policies. Arrests for domestic violence shot up. Years later, however, research has demonstrated that these laws cause more harm than good. States with mandatory arrest laws have higher rates of domestic violence homicides than do states that do not, fully 60 percent higher.[65] Victims in mandatory arrest states also appear to be less likely to report domestic violence, with some desiring a resolution other than automatic arrest. And, as the hierarchy of harm continues to dominate criminal justice mentality, women of color victims in mandatory arrest states frequently report being arrested as the *aggressor* or as a *mutual combatant*, even in scenarios where there is ample evidence to the contrary.[66]

Many of the supervision and surveillance practices of people on probation and parole have also not proven beneficial to public safety. In 2018, the Brookings Institution reviewed five major studies on the impact of parole supervision and found that, across the board, the *less* supervision, the better the person on parole succeeded at reintegrating into a law-abiding life.[67] More than 4 million Americans are under some form of correctional supervision in the United States, and, just as Tom Hoffman found in California, the majority will return to incarceration for technical violations of the rules of their supervision. But if there is no public safety benefit to all those returns to incarceration, why put so many supervision restrictions on millions of people?

Libraries are full of books about the perils of mass incarceration policies and how the policies have destroyed communities. The failed policies highlighted in this chapter are but a snapshot of that reality from a public safety policy perspective. The public safety crisis of the 1980s and 1990s was real and *did* call for action. But the actions taken in response, and often in rushed reaction to devastating crimes involving high-profile victims, did not make us safer.

The argument in defense of those actions has been that victims would have been worse off if the criminal justice system *hadn't* intervened in such a drastic way—that the violence that plagued the 1980s and 1990s would have been worse. Maybe, but that presumes there wasn't a second path, or a third. What if policy makers had sought to solve the problem of crime by first talking to those most affected by it? What does a violence reduction strategy look like if you ask the people being hurt what they need to be safe?

The environmental conditions that continually create unsafe circumstances for far too many would be prevented and the community would be a full partner in devising solutions. Instead, the law-and-order politics that dominated the development of public safety systems for decades did the opposite: expanded money and power for the justice system to engage in mass surveillance in communities deemed a threat and mete out ever-longer sentences. Yet, despite this approach being in the name of victims, these policy priorities, more often than not, further victimized millions of vulnerable people, failed to address most survivors' needs, and, despite all the hype, did not improve safety.

If we want to disrupt the hierarchy of harm and truly understand the trade-offs we are making with the current approach to public safety, we must confront the circumstances facing the very people these bureaucracies are supposed to protect. Until then, the poisonous hierarchy of harm will continue to prevent real protection for most. Ironically, the clues to what is driving much of crime and victimization and what might help to alleviate it already reside in the failed system that we have. The justice system falters in protecting victims and preventing crime in a thousand ways, but the silver lining might be that many of these failings point in the same direction—unaddressed trauma.

PART IV

Hurt People and Healed People

8

The Cycle of Trauma

When Aswad returned to Saint Francis Hospital in Hartford, Connecticut, in the spring of 2011, the level one trauma center was averaging at least one gunshot-wound victim per day. Two years earlier, Aswad himself had nearly died in that hospital of a gunshot wound after an attempted robbery. While it was always stress inducing to walk back into the building, this time he was there to finally get the bullets lodged in his back removed, a day he had long anticipated. Aswad warmly greeted Dr. Marshall, the emergency room physician who had saved his life that fateful night and who had monitored his rehabilitation. He had gotten to know the doctor pretty well on his long road to physical recovery.[1]

When it was time to start, Aswad lay facedown on the operating table. Despite the delicacy of this bullet-removing surgery, it required only localized anesthesia, so he was able to stay awake during the operation. As the doctor worked on his back, the two got to talking. Dr. Marshall commented that he had seen so many other victims of rampant gun violence in Hartford over the years. Too many died, he said, but many others survived their injuries, as Aswad had. The doctor described one of the more devastating injuries he had seen, a few years before he met Aswad. Brandon, a fourteen-year-old boy from the North End, the same neighborhood where Aswad lived and was injured, had suffered a gunshot wound to his face. Dr. Marshall did everything he could in the emergency room, but try as he might, he could not save the boy's eye. At the age of fourteen, Brandon had permanently lost an eye to gun violence, as Dr. Marshall told Aswad, and would have to wear an eye patch for the rest of his life.[2]

Forgetting for a moment how still he was supposed to be, Aswad gasped. An image that was burned into his memory from three years earlier popped to the surface. He remembered that one of the two young men who shot him had worn a patch over his eye. Aswad started asking questions about what the teen looked like—his height, build, skin tone—and soon enough, he confirmed his hunch. The doctor was describing one of the two people who had shot Aswad. One of his assailants, Brandon, had been a victim of gun violence four years prior to picking up a gun himself and nearly taking Aswad's life. The tragic irony hit Aswad hard.[3]

As Aswad shared his revelation, Dr. Marshall set his scalpel down on the table, similarly struck by the gravity of what Aswad was telling him. They both sat, silent, deep in thought. Dr. Marshall and his team labored intense hours to save people's lives, but the doctor felt as if they worked in a "revolving-door hospital" for gun violence victims. After a few quiet minutes, Dr. Marshall finished the bullet-removing procedure while Aswad's mind stayed fixed on the kid who had lost an eye to a bullet, only to wound him with a bullet a few years later.[4]

While the public safety policies of the last forty years that emphasized justice agency growth, surveillance, and incarceration failed to improve safety, a profound clue to understanding, and resolving, so many crime cycles has been hiding in plain sight: unaddressed trauma. Once we accept that the policy priorities that have been enacted allegedly for safety fell short, we can inquire about what the real safety priorities should be instead. There is a cycle of unaddressed trauma that is driving much of crime and violence—and it is also interruptible. Understanding this cycle and what to do, and *not* do, in response, holds the key to unlocking a safer future.

Hurt People Hurt People

Trauma is the mental and physical impact of experiencing a life-threatening, deeply distressing, or shocking event, such as being a victim of or witness to violence, unexpectedly losing a loved one, or experiencing a natural disaster. Decades of research demonstrate the deep and lasting effects of trauma. The experience of a drastic break with safety, a sudden loss, or an emotional disturbance that deeply harms the sense of self causes a physiological reaction, beginning with a short-term flood of adrenaline and including longer-term physical and emotional changes. Left unacknowledged or unaddressed, the impact of trauma on the heart, mind, and body can be life altering, ranging from the development of post-traumatic stress disorder (PTSD) to debilitating depression, chronic anxiety, or hypersensitivity, substance use disorder, mental illness, chronic physical illness, and shorter life expectancies.

Among many people working in violence prevention and criminal justice, "hurt people hurt people" is the oft-heard summation of where much of the violence and crime in our society originates. Virtually everyone who works in youth programs or crisis assistance and most people who work in the justice system itself, from court-appointed attorneys to judges, probation officers, and police, recognize this pattern. Many of the people who hurt others were hurt long before, and most of the time, that prior hurt was never adequately addressed.

These lived realities are reflected in the scientific findings on the link between untreated trauma and crime. Like Brandon, many of the people who commit crimes have prior histories of significant and unaddressed trauma. Being previously victimized and suffering from unaddressed trauma is a very common background for the people entering justice systems. Many were victims of or witnesses to violence in their homes or neighborhoods, and their exposure to trauma-causing situations was often repeated. Well before committing crime, their own trauma led to a loss of safety that was never recovered.

Study after study spanning the course of the last thirty-plus years has demonstrated that people in the justice system have among the highest rates of chronic trauma exposure of any group of people. Many incarcerated people—across race, ethnicity, gender, and country of origin—have histories of early-life experiences that involve physical abuse or sexual abuse, violent victimization, witnessing community or family violence, losing a parent or family member, or being maltreated through neglect or extreme poverty at rates notably higher than do people in the general population.[5]

A snapshot of just a few of the studies demonstrates the pattern. In 2012, behavioral psychologists surveyed adult male incarcerated populations in the United States and found that over half of adult incarcerated men had experienced trauma prior to crime involvement.[6] A separate 2014 study described the history of traumatic events incarcerated men have experienced as "violent, interpersonal, sudden and life threatening" and so widespread—with 96 percent reporting some form of prior assault victimization—that prior trauma was "a near universal experience."[7] Researchers have also found that these prior traumas were not isolated incidents: incarcerated men had a history of chronic trauma over the course of many years prior to engagement in crime.[8] Similarly, numerous studies reveal that nearly all women in the justice system have histories of victimization, with most research revealing even higher rates of early-life victimization than was the case for incarcerated men.[9] A 1996 study, for example, found that 70 percent of incarcerated women reported prior experiences of physical violence, and of those, 78 percent had experienced repeated traumatic events that were so extreme as to be a medically recognized source of the onset of post-traumatic stress disorder.[10]

Traumatic experiences in early childhood are particularly impactful. Early trauma has a significant influence on a wide range of life outcomes. Among leaders in health care, the health effects of untreated childhood trauma have become a mainstream topic. Part of the reason for increased attention in health care is the emergence of a concept known as adverse childhood experiences, or ACEs. In the 1990s, Kaiser physicians in San Diego, California, conducted a major research project on ACEs. They sought to assess the long-term health effects of early trauma on adults: How does something traumatic from one's childhood affect a person's propensity to develop a smoking or alcohol addiction as an adult or the likelihood of developing a disease like cancer or diabetes?

The study asked participants to fill out a ten-question survey inquiring about different types of childhood trauma: verbal abuse, physical abuse, sexual abuse, emotional neglect, lacking food or caretaking, witnessing violence, familial substance abuse, parental death or abandonment, parental mental illness, or, notably, parental incarceration.[11] (Parental incarceration was included because the sudden loss of a parent to incarceration is traumatic for children, especially when that sudden loss is combined with other traumatizing events, like a loss of caretaking stability.)[12] The Kaiser researchers then compared those surveys with subsequent histories of behavioral health problems, such as alcoholism, as well as physical health problems such as diabetes, cancer, and heart disease. The results were startling. People with ACE scores of four or more (which equates to four or more adverse childhood experiences) faced higher rates of diseases such as cancer and heart disease and a death rate from the diseases that was twelve times higher than that for people with lower ACE scores.[13] Higher ACE scores also strongly predicted behavioral health issues such as smoking, drinking, and drug dependence.[14] Since that breakthrough study, a large body of additional research has piled up affirming these outcomes.

If early adversity leads to health and behavioral health impairments, does it also precipitate the commission of crimes? In the field of psychology, the notion that traumatic situations in the lives of children can provoke harmful decision-making in adults has long been documented. Renowned social psychologist and criminal justice professor Craig Haney, in his book *Criminality in Context*, summarized the extensive research, noting that "[t]he basic connections between trauma and maltreatment, on the one hand, and subsequent adolescent delinquent and adult criminal behavior, on the other, have been too well established to dispute."[15] In numerous studies since the 1990s, applying the ACEs survey to evaluate behavior outcomes has demonstrated the predictive relationship between experiencing early trauma and later committing violence or crime.

ACEs research has also shown that a person's early victimization is predictive of the likelihood of committing specific types of violence. For example, studies demonstrate that children severely victimized by physical or sexual abuse who do not get recovery support are more likely to commit those same acts as teens or adults. A 2013 study of people convicted of child abuse, domestic violence, stalking, and sex offenses in San Diego, California, found significantly higher levels of ACEs, specifically higher rates of childhood physical and sexual abuse, compared with a normative sample.[16] "Boys were 45 times more likely to have engaged in dating violence in adolescence when they had been molested by a family member and 26 times more likely when they had been molested by a non-family member."[17] The link was so strong that researchers concluded, "Treatment interventions that focus on the outcome variable (crime) without attempting to heal these neurobiologic wounds are *destined to fail* [emphasis added]."[18]

The more chronic and severe the ACEs, the bigger the impact on behavior. A 2015 Florida study that analyzed the life histories of youth entering Florida's juvenile justice system found a much higher rate of ACEs in youths engaged in the most delinquency.[19] The more arrests at an early age, the more chronic trauma that had occurred even earlier in the child's background.[20] The National Child Traumatic Stress Network published a study in 2013 that analyzed data on justice-involved youth from fifty-six sites across the country. It concluded that for justice-involved youths, "trauma typically begins early in life, is often in multiple contexts and persists over time."[21] The study found that nearly two-thirds of justice-involved youths—62 percent—had experienced a trauma within the first five years of their lives, and one-third had experienced repeated traumas *each year of their lives* from early childhood through adolescence.[22]

Experiencing trauma in adulthood matters, too. While unaddressed early-childhood trauma is predictive of later perpetration of crime, adults who experience trauma can have the same outcomes. For example, studies find similar behavioral health patterns among veterans who develop PTSD from war. War veterans with undiagnosed or untreated PTSD have higher rates of crime involvement compared with people without unaddressed PTSD.[23] According to the Bureau of Justice Statistics, half of the 180,000 incarcerated veterans in the United States have mental health diagnoses.[24] The psychological impacts of PTSD, including hyperarousal, impulse control challenges, fear of danger in nondangerous settings, hallucinations, and other mental health issues, can lead people to engage in violent or criminal acts. The first war veteran diagnosed with PTSD after committing murder—he shot two people dead in 1974—suffered such intense unaddressed PTSD that he slept only in foxholes he dug underneath his home.[25]

Both early-childhood and adult trauma are also linked to the onset of behavioral health ailments such as substance use disorder.[26] Importantly, people with substance use disorder are also more likely to be in our juvenile and criminal justice systems.[27] In other words, unaddressed chronic trauma can be predictive of the likelihood of engaging in future law breaking as well as the onset of alcohol and drug addiction, which can also lead to criminal justice involvement.

Why is it that unaddressed trauma would lead a person to commit a crime? It is easy for most people to intuitively understand that trauma can have long-lasting life repercussions and could even lead to future decisions to commit crimes. And few would dispute that being surrounded by chronically traumatic environments with no relief would severely affect anyone's long-term coping mechanisms. What is key here—in thinking about public safety—is to recognize that the physiological and behavioral reactions that most people have to traumatic experiences when they don't get help are *normal*.

What the ACEs study made clear is that trauma works on the brain and body in a way that transcends zip codes. The participants in the original ACEs study were largely from middle-class San Diego. Over 70 percent of the participants were white, and all had health care.[28] So, it's not culture, it's not gender, it's not education level, socioeconomic status, or race. Everyone who experiences trauma without recovery help is emotionally, psychologically, and physically affected in very predictable ways. It is simply about being human. It is about the way an external source of extreme stress works on a biological level to disrupt the healthy functioning of our bodies—no matter *who* that body belongs to or *where* it lives.

We know this from brain science. Increasingly sophisticated biochemical and neurological studies have examined how the body handles stress. These studies have shown that chronic stress induced by trauma changes the brain: the amygdala, which is the fear center in the brain, becomes recurrently overactive, causing hypervigilance; the locus coeruleus, which regulates the release of the brain's version of adrenaline, can get disrupted and start regularly releasing too much of the chemical, resulting in increased anxiety and aggression; the prefrontal cortex, which is responsible for managing decision-making and reason, becomes chronically inhibited, leading to impulsivity, especially when external events cause uncertainty or fear.

Remarkably, a chronic stress response can also work on an epigenetic level, turning on or off particular genes that regulate how a person's brain, hormones, and immune system will respond to stress in the future. If there are no interventions to alleviate the recurring stress or heal that trauma response, those changes typically have lifelong effects. As Professor Haney notes, "Most people engage in troubled, problematic behavior because bad things have happened *to* them and too little has been done in their lives to transform the resulting troubled trajectories in a different direction."[29]

Understanding unaddressed trauma as a predictor of future criminality is critical public safety information. This is not about excuses to absolve wrongdoing, it is about solutions to intervene before harm leads to more harm. If we can understand why a lot of harm happens, we can better prevent it and address it.

Typically, however, mythology drives narratives around why people hurt others. And that mythology blocks reasoned policy. Just as there is a myth that justice system punitiveness drove crime down and that myth has prevented a clear-eyed assessment of incarceration policies, the myths about why people commit crime—or who is predisposed to commit crime—have prevented strong government commitments to effective crime prevention.

The political myths about why people commit crime have ranged from racist pseudoscientific arguments made at the turn of the twentieth century about "Black criminality" to more benign sounding but just as baseless notions that there are just inherently bad people. Professor Craig Haney refers to the mythology that drives much of criminal justice policy making as the "crime master narrative," a narrative that says it is individual traits, not circumstance, that drive criminal involvement.[30] Instead of recognizing the correlation between early victimization—*and the systemic disregard that followed*—and later involvement in crime, the why-people-commit-crimes myths have undergirded the political drive toward mass incarceration.

As the hierarchy of harm would predict, the pervasive myths about the inherently violent nature of people who commit crime have also applied to some people who are hurt by crime. The myths about why people get hurt are just as damaging to building effective safety policy as the myths about why people commit crimes.

The forms of these myths take different shapes, from blaming "violent" culture to blaming communities or families that "accept violence." When Jaslyn Adams, a seven-year-old child, was shot and killed while sitting in a car with her father at a McDonald's drive-through window in Chicago, McDonald's CEO Chris Kempscinzki texted Chicago mayor Lori Lightfoot commenting on Jaslyn's death and that of another child, saying "the parents failed those kids."[31] Many victims report being faulted for getting hurt, from the shooting victim who shouldn't have been out late or on a particular street to the battered woman who should have "just left" her abusive husband.

False Dichotomies

These myths continue because there is a perilous lie underneath them. The lie that underpins both the myths about why some people get hurt and the dangerous rhetoric about why people commit crimes is that innocent victims are wholly separate from people who commit crimes. In this lie, the world is simple: there are innocent victims and then there are bad people who commit crimes. The adversarial justice system and the law-and-order movement have only served to reinforce this false dichotomy, which happens to support a simple and effective political narrative: that the solution to public safety is to lock up the bad guys. While drawing such a hard line between people who commit crimes and victims makes for an easily digestible stump speech, the reality of how victims and people who commit crimes so often intertwine is a much messier truth.

There is an undeniably large overlap in the life circumstances and accumulation of vulnerabilities experienced by most people who are hurt by crime and by most people who commit crime. The backgrounds of many of the people entering emergency rooms with violent injuries or entering police stations in handcuffs are so overlapping they blur together. Childhood exposure to violence, either witnessing it or being victimized by it. Loss of loved ones.

Chronic environmental stressors, often connected to extreme poverty. Discrimination. Disregard. The circumstances are virtually indistinguishable, and a dominant theme that often runs throughout is unaddressed, recurring trauma. Sometimes people are victims and later commit crimes, or sometimes it is vice versa. Often it is a pattern that repeats, especially when unsafe environments remain unchanged. And yet, society very much operates as if you can only be one or the other.

As a result of this tidy yet erroneous lie, fighting crime has meant separating the perpetrators from the innocent, as permanently as possible. But this obscures the truth about crime and victimization: the common circumstances that lead to it, what could work to solve much of it, and what people need to recover from it.

Aqeela Sherrills remembers when as a twelve-year-old he made up excuses to knock on the apartment door of the sweet twelve-year-old girl staying with her grandmother down the street from him in his South Los Angeles neighborhood. The girl's grandmother would let Aqeela say hello through the screen but was careful to never let the girl outside. Their front door had triple bolts and every window had thick iron bars. So Aqeela would sit outside to chat and laugh with the girl through the bars. One afternoon, as he stood outside her window talking away, two men suddenly came running toward him, and before he could figure out what was going on, one shot the other in the back of the head. Shocked, Aqeela jumped and futilely tried to dive into the bar-covered windows. The victim fell to the ground, hitting the concrete no more than ten feet away. A group of neighbors quickly ran up and gathered around the young man as he bled on the sidewalk. Aqeela stood there speechless as he watched the victim take his last breath.[32]

In that instant, everything changed. It was hard to shake the mental image of the horror he witnessed. It was the first time he had personally witnessed gun violence, but it ended up being far from the last. He would later see other people in the neighborhood get shot, stabbed, and beaten. It became shockingly common. He made the choice many youths in similar environments make: at the age of thirteen, he joined a gang. "I joined for protection. It was my surrogate family. It was the only way to feel safe outside."[33] And while it may have aided in his feeling of security, his exposure to shootings and stabbings only grew. "At some point I became desensitized to the violence. That's what happens. Young minds become desensitized. It is a way to cope with chronic trauma."[34]

And for Aqeela, it was more than the recurring trauma of neighborhood violence that drove him to join a gang. An older family member had sexually assaulted him when he was in elementary school. Aqeela struggled with shame, anxiety, and isolation in response. He felt tormented by the devastating experience of childhood abuse. "I was growing up with all this bottled-up pain around this horrific secret, and those bottled-up feelings manifest in other forms: acting out, behavioral problems. Those are all signs of much deeper harms."[35] Aqeela was unprotected from neighborhood violence and unprotected from interpersonal victimization. Like millions, he managed the aftermath of those harms mostly on his own. And, like many other kids in similar circumstances, that meant joining a neighborhood gang for protection.

Research has consistently affirmed that being subjected to chronically stressful circumstances makes people vulnerable to both victimization and crime involvement. In *Surveying Crime in the 21st Century*, a 2007 book on the role of self-reporting surveys in addressing crime, criminologists Janet Lauritsen and John Laub summarized the research that has piled up from the 1940s, revealing what they refer to as the "victim/offender overlap."[36] "Research on the relationship between victimization and offending has consistently shown that one of the strongest correlates of victimization was involvement in deviant or criminal behavior and that victimization was one of the strongest correlates of offending."[37] They noted that "this relationship was found to exist in numerous countries, across various time periods, among adults as well as youths, and for many types of crime ranging from homicide to bicycle theft."[38]

Research also shows that it's mostly kids like young Aqeela who join gangs, youth who were previously hurt by crime and violence. In 1998, one study found that childhood physical and sexual abuse increased by four times the likelihood of gang involvement for kids exposed to gangs.[39] A 2012 study found that "trauma exposure among gang-involved youth began early (on average at age 6) and was pervasive, with participants . . . reporting an average of 10 traumatic events."[40] Comparatively, research on trauma exposure for the general population of youth indicates an average of two or fewer traumatic events by the age of sixteen.[41]

Imagine a Venn diagram with one circle representing victims and one circle representing those who commit crimes: the overlapping middle is the largest area. There is only a sliver of circle on the outside edge of each side that represents people who are *just victims* and people who are *just people who commit crime*. Despite the unequivocal evidence of an overlap, the justice system has instead perpetuated a false dichotomy that shunts people into one category or the other. And what that means in practical terms is that most of the people in the middle, which is most victims, are often erased from being viewed as an innocent victim in need of protection from harm.

Only a narrow slice of the people hurt by crime and violence are visible as victims, typically the least vulnerable. Despite political and media portrayals to the contrary, middle-class and elite white Americans are less exposed to chronically unsafe environments and more frequently connected to accessible help when they do experience many types of victimization. Meanwhile, people who are most commonly vulnerable to being victims are vulnerable because of societal position or chronic exposure to hyper-stressful environments: those who are low income, people of color, youth, LGBT people, immigrants, Indigenous people, people with disabilities— as well as people with records or on criminal justice supervision.

The dangerous lie of the "victim/offender dichotomy" has played out in American politics on a huge scale. From mass surveillance to lengthy sentencing and brutal incarceration environments, these are tactics that the mythology of the false dichotomy justifies. The superpredator jargon that caught on like wildfire in the 1990s typifies how the myth of the dichotomy drove public safety politics. John DiIulio's racialized theories criminalized an entire generation of young people of color. And yet, many of the very people who became targets of these policies were invisible victims long before. The so-called superpredators targeted for containment were often young people of color who had been imperiled by chronically unsafe environments. For too many low-income kids of color who joined gangs or got arrested for committing crimes, like Aqeela, their invisibility as victims was a major contributing factor, if not the *biggest* contributing factor, to their later participation in gangs or crime. But *their* experiences as victims were somehow never the rallying cry for victims' rights.

Surviving in Spite of the Justice System, not Because of It

Not far from Aqeela's South Los Angeles neighborhood, David Guizar grew up in similar circumstances. David's seventeen-year-old brother, Oscar, was shot and killed when David was ten years old. Oscar was, in the eyes of fifth-grader David, everything—his idol, his mentor, the person he looked up to more than anyone else in the world. David, his mother, and three siblings were thrown into a tailspin of despair. No arrests were made and no information about the circumstances surrounding Oscar's death surfaced. About a year later, David and his mother were exiting their apartment building when they saw a neighbor bleeding and stumbling toward the entrance door. The man, who'd been shot, collapsed and eleven-year-old David held him until the ambulance whisked him away. The man died in the ambulance. "I just kept thinking about Oscar. Is that how he died, too?"[42] Most of David's friends started joining gangs. Pretty soon that choice made sense to David, too. He was beaten up at a bowling alley and shot at while riding his bicycle down the street. The drive-bys never really ceased. "How else can I make it through this?" he used to think.[43] With his entrance into gang membership, other challenges piled up, too. He was drinking and smoking and getting arrested and was kicked out of three schools. But those problems felt unavoidable. "I never thought I would live past seventeen years old. In this environment, how could anyone? Oscar didn't."[44]

But David did—with help from a sympathetic school principal and, eventually, Aqeela. He had begun attending a new high school soon after his first child was born, which is where he met Principal Miller. David's new baby, Oscar, named after his brother, had motivated him to change course. At the new school, despite his burgeoning interest in another life, gang conflicts erupted, as was par for the course. Members of the rival gang forewarned him, "We'll wait for you after school."[45] To avoid violence, David skipped out of school early for weeks at a time. Soon Principal Miller called him into her office. He confided in her the vulnerabilities he faced if he were to stay in school all day; he was trying to stay out of trouble for his son. She proposed an agreement. She would get his classwork from the afternoon teachers, and she would not suspend him if he successfully completed the work. She brought him into a peer support group as well. David started seeing a possible new future. He was referred to community-based youth organizations, where he met Aqeela. He started working for Aqeela, and together they operated community development and youth violence prevention programs.[46]

Aqeela saw a bit of himself in David. Only a few years earlier, he had pulled himself out of a similar cycle of trauma. When Aqeela lost his best friend at age sixteen to gang-related homicide, his deep grief drove him to get out of the constant violence. The risks of leaving his neighborhood were great, but the risks of staying felt even greater. He started looking for after-school jobs across town and focusing more on school, anything to get away. Aqeela graduated from high school and enrolled in California State University at Northridge. There he was able to talk about being a victim of childhood sexual assault. Opening up about this experience was a watershed moment. He found support to process the trauma, both the long-standing grief related to the assaults as well as the emotional fallout of so much loss to gun violence. He had a safe situation in which to receive help to process, which opened opportunities for well-being. He started volunteering with youth programs and building violence prevention programs. He met pro-football great and community activist Jim Brown and joined with him to launch Amer-I-Can, a youth development and violence prevention program. At Amer-I-Can, Aqeela offered David a job.[47]

Against the odds, both Aqeela and David survived their unsafe surroundings. Despite sitting in the mushy middle of the Venn diagram where victims don't get to be victims, both men found pathways to safety and healing. *How* exactly they got the help they needed points the way to a more effective approach to safety—one that begins with confronting a key fact: when people are trapped and unsafe, they are vulnerable to either getting hurt or hurting others. Confronting the lack of safety that existed before either outcome emerged means erasing the perceived bright line between people who have been hurt and people who have hurt others. It means recognizing that responding to traumatic stress with indifference or blame makes us *all* less safe.

Healed People Heal People

Understanding that what we experience in response to trauma can change us physiologically may be startling, but it is also the biggest cause for hope. Just as most people readily acknowledge that hurt people hurt people, so it goes that healed people heal people. We know that trauma stresses the body, causing a cascade of chemical reactions, so it makes sense that the opposite of trauma—connection, support, empathy, and safety—also has a biochemical effect. The flexibility of our brains and bodies to respond to our environments, whether those environments are safe or unsafe, provides a key to stopping the cycle of trauma.

Recent neuroscience has shown that the brain's superpower is its plasticity.[48] In other words, its capacity for constant change. This is what allows babies to learn and what helps people navigate and survive the ever-changing world we live in as adults. For years, scientists believed that adults had limited neuroplasticity, but more and more research points to the brain's ability to regroove itself well into late adulthood.[49] In other words, just as the physiological reactions to trauma are to be expected, these physiological disruptions of the brain and body in response to trauma can also be healed, even reversed.[50] So, while our brains and bodies all react to trauma differently, they all react. The meaningful difference is not who becomes a "bad person" and who does not. It is who is afforded the resources for recovery and who is not.

Since his early days building youth programs, Aqeela has become a nationally recognized leader who has brokered gang truces, trained street peacekeepers, and helped thousands of young people heal. Today he is building what he calls community-based public safety initiatives: programs that train community leaders in conflict resolution and mentoring so they can counsel young people and stop conflicts before they escalate to violence.[51] The community members selected to become neighborhood peacekeepers are people who used to be active in gangs, who have lived in the shoes of the young people they're seeking to help. Aqeela and dozens of other leaders in the community-based public safety movement are helping people recover from trauma as part of a strategy to reduce violence. "Nearly 100 percent of the kids who join gangs have histories of trauma. So much of this complex trauma goes untreated," Aqeela reflected.[52] "But if we can create space to address it, we can resolve it."[53] These community-based public safety programs may not be considered victim services but embracing young people who have survived chronically traumatic environments is exactly that.

Addressing trauma is growing in visibility as a safety strategy. Public health successes are emerging every day that show these strategies work—strategies that address immediate financial and safety challenges, help people access mental health counseling, mentoring, or other opportunities for fostering strong and supportive relationships, learning mindfulness, and much more. In the same way that exposure to violence can raise cortisol levels, resources that help people increase surrounding peace and stability can have the equal and opposite effect. In the simplest terms, our brains and bodies are always morphing, whether that means trying to protect us from trauma with a stress response or allowing us to heal in response to the affirming effects of safe environments.

Seeking Safety, a counseling program that has been helping people recover from trauma and addiction since the late 1990s, has seen firsthand, time and again, the power of our brains and bodies to heal.[54] The program provides skills-based training in a safe, confidential setting to teach people struggling with unaddressed trauma and addiction about the physiological effects of trauma. It helps them develop strategies to manage stress so they can make safer choices and find greater safety in relationships. People from a wide range of backgrounds, including people in the criminal justice system, have completed the curriculum and have experienced significant improvements in life outcomes. Seeking Safety is one of the most-studied trauma reduction programs in the nation. It has operated both inside and outside incarceration settings, and across the board, research reveals that participants experience significant reductions in PTSD symptoms and substance use and that those impacts are sustained over time.[55]

TARGET is another psycho-educational program that seeks to reduce the effects of trauma and that has demonstrated positive impacts on children as young as ten years old. The program teaches youth who have experienced chronic victimization and suffer from complex trauma about how the brain adapts to trauma and how those adaptations affect responses to stress.[56] TARGET provides training and skills-development practice to help kids learn emotional regulation and stress management skills. Researchers have studied the impacts of the program and have uncovered strong positive results, including reduced PTSD symptoms, reduced anxiety and depression, expanded capacity for healthy decision-making under stress, and reduced behavioral challenges.[57]

Dozens of innovative programs across the country show strong results and include art therapy and play therapy; eye movement desensitization and reprocessing therapy, which uses repetitive eye movement exercises to process traumatic memories; and individual coaching. California pediatrician and nationally renowned ACEs expert Dr. Nadine Burke Harris, in her work to reduce the adverse effects of chronic stress, collaborated with the Mind Body Awareness Project to bring yoga and meditation into San Francisco's juvenile hall. Burke Harris recruited girls with high ACE scores for a mindfulness and yoga program. Girls reported less stress, improved sleep, better ability to concentrate in an academic setting, and fewer fights.[58]

Problems Versus Symptoms

While Aqeela's community-based public safety initiatives and programs to reverse the impacts of trauma have been gaining steam across the country for the last decade, these efforts remain very small compared with the war mentality that began flourishing in the justice system from the 1980s on. Over the last few decades, one of the biggest barriers to stopping youth violence that Aqeela has seen has been the criminal justice system's response to it. "The kids in gangs are seen as the enemy instead of what so many of them are: traumatized."[59]

Leaders in health care are breaking new ground all the time by looking closer and closer at the causes of physical health ailments—

not just the response. Not only have health researchers found high ACE scores causative of high rates of health ailments in adulthood, but they have found high ACE scores even *more* influential than having a family history of specific diseases.[60] The breakthrough in health care is clear: it is as important, if not more, to screen people for ACEs as a strategy to prevent the development of disease as it is to screen people for the health histories of their parents, siblings, or grandparents.

When it comes to understanding environmental precipitators of crime and violence, and strategies for addressing them, the impact of the ACEs study on the field of public health offers crucial parallel lessons for the field of public safety. In the health context, uncovering the impact of ACEs on long-term health was essentially the discovery of an unaddressed cause of physical ailment that demands new priorities in preventative health care. The same unaddressed early traumas that later cause physical and behavioral health illnesses also lead to preventable crime and violence.

If we looked at much of delinquency or criminality as a symptom of an underlying issue, and more than likely an underlying issue of unaddressed trauma, as opposed to an immutable trait that must be contained, then we would direct a lot of the people arrested for committing crimes into rehabilitative or restorative programs that have the capacity to recognize unaddressed trauma, instead of warehousing them in prison and jail. We would invest more in effective prevention programs. If we could see the trauma of *all victims* as the core reason much of the cycle of crime continues and choose to address *that*, it would become clear that containment is, at best, a limited strategy and one with often far greater negative consequences.

In the short term, removing someone who is violently abusing their family members or shooting at people in the streets stops the immediate traumatic crime incident. And, for the time during which the person is removed, that person will not commit that crime in that home or in that community again. Immediate incapacitation represents a big part of what the justice system can currently do to intervene in violence and crime. But despite the short-term removal, if our public safety systems do nothing else, the long-term outcomes are a failure. That traditional approach to public safety did not change Brandon's life trajectory or decision to later shoot Aswad, and it didn't provide support to Aqeela or David to prevent their later involvement in neighborhood gangs. It was *in spite of* the justice system's impact on their lives, not because of it, that David and Aqeela were able to redirect their lives. In reflecting on the interventions that saved him—his mother who begged him to avoid the fate of his older brother, Oscar; the principal who saw his dignity and the constraints of his circumstances; and the inspiration and encouragement he found in doing community work with Aqeela—David commented, "I was able to walk through it. I received a blessing. The faith in me, the resources and support. That's what safety looks like."[61]

When Aswad walked away from his operating room conversation with Dr. Marshall, he felt overwhelmed by thoughts of Brandon—a fellow victim of gun violence. He thought about what had happened to fourteen-year-old Brandon after being shot, and he had more questions than answers. *Was Brandon scared? Did anyone ever acknowledge his trauma? If he had received any help or support, would he later have shot me?* The nonstop thoughts painted a picture that helped Aswad understand what happened in 2009 in a different way: Brandon's unaddressed trauma led to Aswad's own trauma. A bigger force was at work: Aswad became a victim because of the cycle of trauma that had ensnared Brandon first.[62]

Through his own experience, Aswad knew intimately how much Brandon's injury at age fourteen must have changed things for him, psychologically and physically. And Aswad was also aware that he himself could easily have been pulled into the cycle of violence. He vividly remembered the intense feelings of fear and exasperation that moved through his body as he lay in the hospital bed writing in pain. Afterward, being released from the hospital right back into the North End neighborhood where he had been victimized was terrifying. He developed paranoia, constantly worrying that the young men who shot him would come back to kill him. Being physically immobilized in an unsafe neighborhood made him feel helpless. He became so fearful that he tried never to leave his mother's apartment no matter what.[63]

One major difference between Brandon and Aswad is that Aswad was an adult when he was shot, and he had the support of his family, which he believes kept him from doing anything rash. Walking home from that last surgery in 2011, Aswad wondered how a fourteen-year-old could ever process the fear and pain without help. Aswad had never met Brandon before the day they violently collided, but after he thought about the trauma Brandon must have endured, Aswad started to feel that he understood very well who Brandon was: terrified, unprotected, injured, and likely on his own to grapple with it all.[64]

Police investigators pursued the case investigation for about a year following Aswad's shooting. Eventually, they found their suspects. Brandon, however, was not the same. He had endured a gunshot injury again and suffered from severely debilitating injuries, the kind that require assisted-living quarters and ongoing medical care for the rest of his life. The revolving door had swung again.[65]

Aswad's awakening to the cycle of trauma that trapped Brandon changed the course of his life. From that day forward, Aswad set out on a mission to advocate for more support for victims of violence, especially young men of color. He completed a master of social work degree at the University of Connecticut. He began working inside juvenile halls, mentoring youth. He started a hospital-based violence interruption program to reduce retaliatory violence by helping shooting victims in crisis. And in 2015, he met Robert Rooks, the California justice reform leader who had previously knocked on doors in Aswad's Hartford neighborhood, where he had met Aswad's mother years before, to organize residents and change Connecticut's draconian drug laws. Robert gave a speech at his alma mater in Connecticut about the work in California to organize victims and to advocate for a new approach to public safety. From that day, Aswad joined with Robert to organize survivors across the country.

Interventions that support healing from trauma are an unequivocal societal good. From a financial, physiological, and public safety perspective, there is no downside to investing in that kind of support. Yet despite all the evidence, we continue to uphold a justice system that—far from alleviating trauma—*contributes* to the cycle of trauma more often than it stops it. Whether it is the trauma-inducing ways in which the justice system interacts with, or fails to interact with, so many victims or the trauma that many people convicted of committing crime experience inside the justice system, we have embraced an approach to safety that far too often ignores the facts about unaddressed trauma and instead traumatizes more.

9

The Trauma of the Justice System

While people victimized by crime chronically experience disregard instead of help recovering from trauma, people sentenced for committing crimes chronically experience trauma-causing conditions inside the justice system. The cycle of unaddressed trauma contributes to crime, and in response, many of the justice system's practices when incarcerating both adults and youths cause even more trauma, ironically in the name of safety.

Not far from Aqeela and David's South Los Angeles neighborhood, Jose, a young man convicted of gang-related crime as a teen, was incarcerated in California's notorious youth prisons. He summed up his experience inside simply: "Every day, nothing but violence."[1]

Staff in the Chino prison where he was locked up used to stage Friday night fights in which they pitted youths against each other and wagered to see who would win.[2] When disturbances in the prison broke out, guards would place youths in handcuffs and make them kneel on the gymnasium floor for so long that their legs went numb. Some threw up, and others passed out.[3] When youths refused to leave their cells or follow other instructions, guards sprayed them with mace then held them for hours without allowing them to rinse, leaving burns on their faces and arms.[4]

In 2001, the Prison Law Office, a nonprofit law firm that advocates for the humane treatment of incarcerated people, filed a lawsuit against the California Youth Authority (CYA) for warehousing teenagers in deplorable conditions.[5] In response to that lawsuit, the California Attorney General's Office commissioned a series of expert reports on the conditions inside.[6] The reports' findings were grim: an environment of near-constant violence. Solitary confinement for twenty-three hours per day, for months and even years at a time. Staff overmedicating youth with such heavy drugs that some slept or stared at walls all day. Guards using excessive force. Incidents of sexual assault. At one point, prison staff even installed metal cages with school desks inside them to provide required educational instruction to youth in solitary confinement. The youths would sit in a desk inside a cage for "class" when they were not confined to windowless four-by-seven-foot cells.[7]

The California Youth Authority did not start off as a "gladiator school." It was initially established in the 1940s as a progressive juvenile reformatory for the small percentage of youths entering juvenile courts after arrest who were deemed too troubled to stay in the county juvenile facilities.[8] But as tough-on-crime policies grew in popularity, the CYA population doubled from the mid-1970s to the mid-1990s to more than ten thousand youths; formerly plain-clothes staff began wearing guard uniforms and carrying weapons; and the culture of imprisonment, violent and cruel, was cemented, no matter how young or small the kids entering the facilities were. One outraged teacher who taught inside CYA told the *Los Angeles Times* in 1999 that incarcerated youth "used to leave [CYA] with the means to support themselves and to change. One of the things we find most appalling now is that they are leaving so angry. It's almost a joke among staff: We hope they don't move to our neighborhood."[9]

While CYA conditions were extreme, they were not that different from conditions inside all kinds of incarceration facilities across the United States, for youths and adults alike. They fell along a spectrum of similarly caustic imprisonment practices that have been occurring across the country for at least the last four decades. Under mass incarceration, violence, isolation, and degradation became embedded in nearly every aspect of imprisonment in the

United States, a design feature that is so foundational to how these places operate that it has become synonymous with the public's understanding of what punishment means. Violent and cruel conditions have become as accepted as "just deserts" for committing crimes. People must endure these conditions as the punishment they deserve to teach them a lesson, American cultural thinking goes. But what is happening inside goes far beyond legally prescribed punishment.

Professor Mika'il DeVeaux, who served thirty-two years in New York state prisons, has described the experience of incarceration as continually living with such unconscionable levels of violence and degradation that prison itself is a "site of trauma."[10] In Dr. DeVeaux's article "The Trauma of the Incarceration Experience," he described the prison experience as "traumatic because of the assaults and murders I witnessed . . . because of the constant threat of violence, because of the number of suicides that took place, and because I felt utterly helpless about the degree to which I could protect myself."[11] He witnessed people killed or seriously injured in fights, was attacked himself, and was punished for rule violations through torturous isolation.[12] Years after his release, he described remaining "haunted by the memories and images of violence" that he both suffered and witnessed.[13]

Institutionalizing Trauma

Like Dr. DeVeaux and Jose, hundreds of thousands of incarcerated people are victimized and traumatized in America's correctional institutions on an annual basis. Incidents range from direct physical violence and secondary violence (witnessing violence happening to other people) to extreme isolation and basic-needs deprivation. Researchers have documented that at least 20 percent of incarcerated people report they have been personally victimized by violence, and that this is likely significantly underreported.[14] More than 80 percent of incarcerated people report personally witnessing violence committed against others while incarcerated, with nearly everyone reporting that this is a part of daily life behind bars.[15]

Some people are traumatized by shocking events that leave indelible marks, like witnessing a gruesome murder at close range. Others experience more subtle but also trauma-inducing abuse, like ongoing humiliation from other residents or staff, excessive force from guards, or psychologically devastating punishments received in response to rule violations, such as deprivation of food, water, or sleep.[16] People in prison even report being subject to forms of sensory torture, including containment in cells with constant lights and no outdoor visibility, exposure to nonstop noise, and loss of visiting privileges or contact with people from the outside.[17] Testifying in a 2001 lawsuit against Michigan prisons for unconstitutionally denying prison visitation, for example, psychiatrist Dr. Terry Kupers recounted instances of Michigan prison officials wantonly eliminating visiting privileges for trivial reasons. One woman lost visitation privileges for "hoarding" Motrin in her cell past the expiration date. A man in another Michigan prison lost visitation privileges after being unable to complete the "pee on demand" drug test because of an enlarged prostate.[18]

The most common traumatizing experiences reported relate to the secondary violence that nearly everyone witnesses, often precipitated with little provocation or warning, including individual fights between people, attacks carried out with makeshift weapons, and multi-perpetrator attacks on individuals that end in permanent injury or death. Beyond the psychological impacts of witnessing such horror, incarcerated people report being physically impacted as well, from lockdowns for everyone after violence eruptions, to large groups of people doused with mace or pepper spray to quell the violence, to people being forced to clean up bloodstains.[19] Ohio-based researchers Meghan Novisky and Robert Peralta conducted lengthy interviews with thirty people released from various prisons in Ohio in 2017 and 2018, finding that every person had witnessed violence repeatedly, some reporting that violence occurred every day, if not several times a day, and at times had witnessed severe violence.[20] One interviewee reported not only witnessing one person cut another with a razor so severely that the victim bled to death but also being instructed by prison staff to mop up the pools of the victim's blood after the attack.[21]

Perhaps the most extreme long-term physiological impact is the use of solitary confinement or lockdowns in response to disruptions in the prison environment, ranging from the supermax prison practice of long-term solitary confinement to shorter-term lockdowns during which no person can leave her or his cell for weeks or months at a time. The Correctional Association of New York, a long-standing prison-monitoring organization, has described isolation as causing "such symptoms as perceptual distortions and hallucinations, massive free-floating anxiety, acute confusional states, delusional ideas and violent or self-destructive outbursts, hyperresponsivity to external stimuli, difficulties with thinking, concentration and memory, overt paranoia, and panic attacks."[22]

"Normal Reactions to Pathological Conditions"

Just as traumatic experiences outside imprisonment affect health, repeated violence and cruelty inside prison stimulates the same physiological reactions: hypervigilance, anxiety, PTSD, and diminished physical health. Long before health scientists evidenced the human body's response to traumatic environments, in 1940, prison warden and author Donald Clemmer coined the phrase *prisonization* to describe the behavioral impact of incarceration: people tend to incorporate the destructive norms of the prison environment to survive, including responding aggressively to conflict or confusion and refraining from showing emotions.[23] The 2014 definitive report by the National Research Council on the consequences of mass incarceration elaborated on the characteristics of the prison environment that contribute to prisonization. The constant threat of victimization is key among them. That threat of victimization translates into toxic levels of stress and even proactively assaulting others to minimize the threat.[24] Importantly, Professor Craig Haney points out that these responses are *normal* human responses to extreme environments. As health science demonstrated, everyone's minds and bodies react to toxic stress, and prisons are literally designed to be an excessively stressful environment. "These adaptations are not pathological in nature," Haney wrote. "They are normal reactions to a set of pathological conditions."[25]

The physiological effect of being continually surrounded by trauma-causing events is heightened for people with prior histories of trauma, which is most of the incarcerated population. For people who suffered early-life trauma, the experience of incarceration can be retraumatizing, leading to even greater mental health deterioration and long-term physical and mental health consequences.[26] Worse, some people in prison succumb to the same type of victimization they suffered prior to committing crimes and being sentenced to prison. One study, for example, found that people who had been sexually assaulted as children faced higher rates of sexual assault victimization in prison than those who had not.[27]

Being surrounded by this much violence has long-term traumatizing effects on people who work inside prisons as well as the people who live there. Corrections staff suffer from high rates of substance use disorder, depression, anxiety, and suicide.[28] A 2011 study found that the rate of PTSD among prison guards in the United States is twice the rate of PTSD among military veterans.[29] Another study found that the rate of suicide is twice as high as in the general public.[30] Still other studies reveal high rates of physical illnesses and much shorter life expectancies.[31] Given the pathological conditions in which they work, these awful outcomes should come as no surprise. In 2017, University of California at Berkeley researchers surveyed more than 4,000 correctional officers working in California state prisons about mental health and found that nearly 70 percent had witnessed someone get seriously injured or killed; 60 percent had seen or handled dead bodies; and nearly 50 percent feared on-the-job violent injury.[32]

Compounding the problem, prison staff are often trained in a culture that frowns on acknowledging the signs and symptoms of trauma, leaving many staff to suffer without the ability to speak openly about these issues.[33] A PTSD diagnosis can disqualify someone from working in a prison, leaving prison staff surrounded by violence but unable to admit to the normal physiological impacts this kind of trauma has on everyone.[34] One former corrections officer who worked in a supermax prison in Arizona told the *Denver Post* that he struggled with depression and had witnessed numerous colleagues struggling to cope. "A lot of them are not able to detach. . . . Alcohol problems. Domestic violence. They have a propensity. The very things they are supposed to be against, they end up doing. . . . You can't just wash it off like in a shower."[35]

"No-Frills" Prisons

Just as the conditions in CYA prisons became more crowded and violent in the 1980s and 1990s, similar changes emerged in most youth and adult incarceration facilities across the country in the era of tough-on-crime. The prison environment changed as mass incarceration grew. Significant increases in the number of people incarcerated led to overcrowding, which made living conditions worse and management of prisons harder. The era was also characterized by a major shift in the purpose of imprisonment. As mass incarceration emerged, rehabilitation as a goal of sentencing and corrections was abandoned and replaced with the primary goal of incapacitating convicted people from the rest of society for as long as possible.[36]

But incapacitation was not the only goal that took hold of crime policy. Demands to purposefully make prisons harsher were part of the political calls to action that grew alongside calls for longer prison terms and victims' rights. "Toughening" the prison environment was an intentional, explicit, and popular political strategy. At the federal level, the No Frills Prison Act was introduced in the U.S. Congress seven times from 1995 to 2001, with the goal of stripping everything from television access to in-cell coffee makers.[37]

While the federal bill never made it into law, it influenced political rhetoric and state policy. Congress, for example, enacted regulations to withhold federal funding from any state prison that provided weights, televisions, or unmonitored phone calls to incarcerated people.[38] And several states enacted their own no-frills policies, based on the viewpoint that "homelike" amenities were offensive to victims. In defense of the no-frills approach, Sheriff Andy Lee, of Benton County, Arkansas, penned an article in 2000 noting that "as sheriffs we must show the victims that we put them first."[39] Mississippi Democratic state representative Mack McInnis championed policies to build more prisons and to ban anything conceived of as an amenity, from televisions and radios to air-conditioning and weight-lifting equipment. In 1994, he authored legislation to spend $1 million issuing new striped uniforms for people in prison, with CONVICT imprinted in large lettering on the back.[40] Commenting about the move, he noted, "I know you psychologists and all . . . say 'well, it's humiliating.' That's damn good, I want it to be."[41] Around the same time, William Weld, the Republican governor of Massachusetts, said he wanted prison environments to be "akin to walking through fires of hell."[42]

The Toxic Form of Prisons

The rapid rise in crowding, the decline in regard for the welfare of people in prison, and the no-frills movement to strip prisons of anything hospitable created dangerous conditions and increased the potential for trauma in prisons—while being politically justified as honoring victims. But the notion that the toxic incarceration environment is in the interest of victims could not be further from the truth.

Even before politicians called for no-frills or supermax prisons, experts understood that the incarceration environment was not conducive to positive behavior change. In 1950, Clemmer urged a reconsideration of the penal use of incarceration, noting that "imprisonment, even within progressive institutions and their carefully-developed training programs, frequently increases the criminality of the individuals they hold."[43] That concern has been reiterated time and again: instead of preparing people for law-abiding citizenship, the nature of the prison environment is more likely to have the opposite effect. In *The Modern Prison Paradox*, Professor Amy Lerman argued that the crime control politics of the law-and-order era "have given rise to institutions that arguably recreate the conditions that lead to criminality in the first place, and they do so in a particularly intense and toxic form."[44] Instead of stopping the cycle of crime, the modern culture of violent and cruel prisons may "perpetuate the problems of crime and disorder they are tasked with preventing."[45]

The normal physiological reactions people experience from recurring exposure to traumatic events are usually not compatible with the behavior changes needed to reduce continual crime involvement, such as better judgment, empathy, and self-regulation. The prison environment is not designed to enhance rational thinking, remorse, or reconsideration of unsafe decision-making. To the contrary, the normal reaction most anyone would have to the kind of harsh incarceration conditions that flourished across the country is decreased capacity for reasoned thinking or empathy in the face of stress.[46]

In his TED talk "The Neuroscience of Restorative Justice," health researcher Dan Reisel noted that the amygdala—the part of the brain that ACEs health researchers documented becomes flooded with adrenaline when we are in fight-or-flight mode and can become overstimulated from toxic levels of stress—also regulates empathy and plays an important role in human relationships.[47] Like the brain's overall plasticity, the amygdala is malleable throughout humans' life course. It can either grow, which increases capacity for empathy and connection, or it can shrink such that the ability to connect with other people is diminished.[48] Environmental factors affect the direction. Significant stress suppresses the growth of new cells in this region of the brain, as well as in other regions.[49] "It is ironic that our current solution for people with stressed amygdalas is to place them in environments that actually inhibit . . . further growth," Reisel reflected.[50] The prison in London in which he conducted research had a 70 percent recidivism rate. He urged more rehabilitation and restorative justice with the goal of expanding, rather than diminishing, people's capacity for empathy and human connection.[51] That would be a much safer approach to accountability.

Despite political rhetoric to the contrary, plenty of crime survivors are intimately familiar with the ways in which the hostility of the incarceration experience negatively impacts safety after people are released back into the community. Many people harmed by crime live in proximity to those coming home after the trauma of incarceration. Robert Rooks remembers when his nephew, a survivor of early childhood violence who was incarcerated for two years in Texas for using marijuana while on probation, was released. "He was never the same after that," Robert recalled. "I don't know what happened, but he was never able to really recover. It wasn't long before he was incarcerated again."[52] Tinisch Hollins remembers her little brothers coming home to San Francisco after incarceration stints, struggling to reintegrate. They struggled with school and employment more than before and harbored depression and tension. Things had changed. "The justice system is a one-size fits none," she noted. "This is a system that causes damage to both victims and people incarcerated. There is nothing safe about it."[53]

Time Never Done

The physiological harm caused by incarceration does not stop upon release. Just as the environment inside prisons is essentially designed to cause trauma, many of the laws monitoring the lives of people on probation and parole, and even restricting people who have long since completed their sentences, are also designed to prevent connection and stability. Post-release rules can be so restrictive as to act as invisible bars that restrict people's capacity to effectively engage in society and can even re-traumatize them. Originally conceived of as an alternative to lengthy incarceration, community probation and parole have grown into an enormous set of bureaucracies in which officers supervise millions of people sentenced to long probation or parole terms. Successfully completing community supervision can be extremely difficult. Supervision rules and regulations expanded during the tough-on-crime years along with the growth in prison sentences. Many supervised people face a near-impossible web of restrictions that make maintaining work and accessing housing or treatment difficult. Restrictions on travel, mandated meetings, and other requirements can add up to being trapped without the ability to stabilize.

Not surprisingly, most people on supervision fail the terms of their probation and parole. And the common consequence for breaking a supervision rule? A return to incarceration. Tinisch Hollins's little brothers could never quite keep up with all the probation rules, keeping them in a loop of probation-to-incarceration-and-back for years at a time.[54]

Others are never able to get past their past, no matter how many years have gone by. Of the more than forty thousand post-sentence legal restrictions imposed on people with old criminal records, more than half of the prohibitions are work related, and many of those are lifetime bans.[55] People with records are prohibited from working in health care, firefighting, banking . . . the list of employment-related bans goes on.[56] Still other restrictions apply related to eligibility for housing, including senior housing and other housing for people of limited financial means, personal loans, educational program admission, volunteering at children's schools, adopting children, getting a fishing license, and serving on juries.[57] In two states, voting is permanently prohibited for anyone with a criminal record, no matter how old the record, and about a dozen other states have other restrictions on voting rights.[58]

The collective impact of these restrictions goes beyond the post-conviction poverty they create. "It is a denial of my ability to ever fully be human again," said Jay Jordan on PBS NewsHour in 2021.[59] Ten months after his eighteenth birthday, in 2004, Jay entered the California prison system where he served seven years for robbery. Like so many, for Jay incarceration was an experience of being surrounded by landmine after landmine, all threatening to detonate and all designed to destroy his humanity. And, like so many, the detonations continued after his release.

Young and new to incarceration, Jay adapted to the prison environment quickly. This meant being in near-constant fights, getting stabbed, and racking up disciplinary "points"—the system correctional officers use to determine the level of security needed.[60] Staff placed him in solitary confinement for those points and recommended a transfer to Pelican Bay, California's supermax prison reputed to be "the toughest of the tough." Before he transferred, his pastor father was finally able to visit him—after officials denied his right to visit his son for *three* years due to a "disturbing the peace" conviction from the 1970s. He told his son that Jay was more than his circumstances. After that visit, Jay began meeting with the secure housing unit psychologist. After numerous talks, the psychologist intervened on the transfer recommendation to keep Jay out of Pelican Bay and place him at a facility closer to home.[61] He was transferred to a prison where people with mental illness are housed and—since he did not have a mental illness—staff asked him to help take care of other residents.[62] The need to fight every day to survive lessened, but he was shocked at seeing how people with mental disabilities were housed. It was one thing to be surrounded by violence in the general population and quite another to witness the isolation and degradation that people living with mental illness in prison endure. "It was the first time I didn't have to fight to survive," he recalled. He remained there until his release. His mother sent stacks of books to keep him occupied, and his father visited regularly.[63]

Upon his release nearly eight years later, Jay was overcome with relief to have survived the ordeal. He was determined to return to his hometown of Stockton, California, and give back to his community. Indebted to his parents, without whom he "would have never survived," he set out to earn a good living and to contribute.[64] He tried to become a real estate agent, but he could not because of his record. He tried to sell insurance. Denied. He tried to become a barber. He could not become licensed because his conviction prevented it. He could not have even become a licensed dog walker.

He decided to launch a youth-mentoring program, to at least prevent other young people from going down his life path. The program grew and was so successful that he received support from the mayor, police chief, district attorney, and city council to house it in the local high school. The night before opening day, Jay received a call from the school. He could no longer work with the program because his old record prevented him from being on a school campus.[65] He spent the evening before the on-campus program launch calling all sixty parents, informing them that he could not operate the program he founded. In a world of exclusions, the extreme stress of incarceration doesn't easily stop.

"People without pre-existing mental illness develop psychological impairments in prison—it does something to everyone. I made it out and I was thinking this country was going to say to me, I did my time, so I get a second chance. Instead, I faced constant exclusion and rejections. That also does something to your mental health. What about my humanity? When do I get to become a citizen again? How are we supposed to recover if we can't ever be done with our time?"[66]

The mass incarceration era has created imprisonment conditions that often traumatize the people working and living inside it, which can add to the trauma of the communities and the families to which they return. Essentially, imprisonment functions as a victimizer, paradoxically justified as necessary to protect victims. Even setting aside the profound moral implications of traumatizing millions of people entering U.S. prisons, it is also unfathomable that a public safety justification can be taken seriously when the resulting criminal justice "solutions" *cause* the very mental health conditions that can lead to future criminality. The physical and psychological effects of imprisonment are basically the same as the effects of repeat victimization. And the effects of being trapped in poverty and excluded from society after release contribute to the toxic level of stress that many people with records continually face. By empowering a system that frequently victimizes people in its care, the justice system, in essence, often takes the original trauma and doubles it. It is difficult to see how compounding trauma in response to crime honors victims or makes anyone safer.

Hope—and Challenges—on the Horizon

Media surrounding the shocking reports revealing violence and abuse in California's youth prisons—combined with many years of grassroots organizing by organizations like the Ella Baker Center for Human Rights and the California Alliance for Youth and Community Justice—finally pushed elected officials to condemn CYA practices and introduce reforms. The reforms grew over the years, and the population dropped from more than ten thousand in 1995 to less than one thousand by 2018.[67]

In 2019, California governor Gavin Newsom announced a plan to shutter the state facilities entirely and to return responsibility to the counties to manage adjudicated youth.[68] Within the span of about twenty-five years, California took a 180-degree turn in its approach to youth incarceration. It represents one of the most dramatic shifts in incarceration policy the nation has ever seen.

While changes in California's youth incarceration practices are perhaps the most transformative, they are not the only signs of hope on the horizon. The notion that vengeance and cruelty somehow protect public safety has started to wither on the vine. Remarkable leaders—from formerly incarcerated people to corrections officials and victims themselves—are championing new approaches to safety, approaches that are shifting the culture of corrections and public safety in the United States.

In 2011, Gary Mohr, the head of the Ohio Department of Corrections and Rehabilitation, attended the first national convening of state corrections officials ever held in his thirty-year career, called by the U.S. Department of Justice.[69] Every corrections head from all fifty states participated. For the first time, these officials discussed and agreed on the need to embrace a major shift in the purpose of corrections—from incapacitation to preparation for release.[70] Roughly forty years after rehabilitation was abandoned as a goal, a new attitude surfaced. For the first time, the group adopted a uniform definition of recidivism—the rate at which a person returns to prison after release—and accepted this as the metric by which corrections practices should be measured.[71] "I really felt something different was afoot in that meeting," Mohr recalled. "I have always said, my job is to work myself out of a job. At the meeting, I felt like I wasn't alone in thinking that way."[72]

Across the country, officials have expanded educational programs, employment training, victim awareness, cognitive behavioral therapy, restorative justice, and other training programs that are demonstrating improved outcomes and are reducing the toxic culture. Sam Lewis lived through those positive changes in the twenty years he was incarcerated in California's adult prisons. "When I was first incarcerated, it was violence, all the time," he recalled. "Years later, things started changing. I was able to complete a master's degree. I would have never survived prison, or release from prison, had it not been for those changes."[73] Now the executive director of Anti-Recidivism Coalition, one of the nation's premier reentry programs, Sam continues to advocate for policies that put safety above vengeance.

But many politicians and justice bureaucracy leaders are not willing to part with the trauma-on-top-of-trauma approach to public safety. Not long after Gary Mohr left the invigorating Washington, DC, meeting, Ohio governor John Kasich empaneled a penal code review committee composed of prosecutors, judges, defense attorneys, probation and corrections officers, and police, including Mohr, as well as some reform advocates.[74] The committee met for twelve months to propose improvements to the functioning of Ohio's justice system. While some of the recommendations were to clarify meanings of technical penal code language, several recommendations would reduce incarceration, something Ohio leaders had been persistently reluctant to do.[75]

The report was released and legislators discussed some of the recommendations, but by and large, it mostly sat on a shelf, where reports from prior years collected dust as well. Mohr was not surprised. "We have seen this story play out before. A bunch of meetings, a report is issued, and then that is it."[76] His frustration was well placed. He witnessed the Ohio prison population grow sixfold over the course of his career, even though the overall Ohio population remained steady. The prisons were overfilled with people convicted of drug crimes, the largest driver of increased imprisonment, as well as people serving extremely long sentences who no longer posed a threat to public safety.

After little emerged from the penal code review committee process, a group of frustrated justice reform advocates discussed a potential policy initiative for the Ohio ballot. Reform could become possible if voters enacted it, instead of waiting for unmotivated politicians. Polling results showed strong promise: voters thought the justice system was wasteful, that too many people were incarcerated, and that the crisis of drug addiction sweeping through the state was far more important to address than spending millions on packed prisons.[77]

The initial response of many to Ohio's Issue 1 was that it looked a bit like a no-brainer: the ballot measure sought to reduce penalties for drug possession, expand earned time credit for people participating in rehabilitation in prison, and reallocate money from the state prisons to drug treatment and trauma recovery. Seasoned Republican political operative Matt Carle, former senior aide to Governor Kasich, applauded the effort. Like so many across Ohio, he'd lost acquaintances to opioid overdose. More than 750,000 Ohio voters signed petitions in favor of placing Issue 1 on the ballot. The measure received more signatures than just about any ballot initiative in Ohio history.[78] Voters from every county signed on.

Then came the campaign against it. Police chiefs, sheriffs, judges, and prosecutors—stalwart champions of tough-on-crime—rallied against the measure. The sitting chief justice of the Ohio Supreme Court even hit the campaign trail, alongside political candidates that attacked it to bolster their own campaigns. Describing the measure as a surefire way to drive crime rates up, they lobbied hard to scare voters. Every sheriff in the state held a press conference calling the measure a "crime-spreader" and urging voters to vote no.[79] Uniform opposition from law enforcement drumming up fear about crime sank Issue 1 on Election Day.

The loss was devastating. The lessons underscore the uphill battles facing efforts to reform criminal justice. An ingrained notion that doing the same thing the country has been doing for the last forty years is safer than change is hard to shake in the face of fears about crime.

The political rhetoric that built mass incarceration in the name of victims easily overshadows honest discussions about what works to hold people accountable and stop crime cycles. As violence rates rose in 2020 and 2021, after more than twenty-five years of national lows, familiar tropes resurfaced in media coverage, and the nation faced the risk of a return of tough-on-crime.

But a new safety movement, which has been steadily growing across the country, is providing a political counterbalance and a new perspective. What fearmongering politicians and traditional bureaucrats have to say about safety is no longer gospel. The new safety movement—with diverse survivors driving the charge—is winning changes in laws, budgets, and hearts and minds. The new safety stakeholders have arrived.

PART V

A New Safety Movement

10

A New Victims' Right:
Trauma Recovery for All

D r. Alicia Boccellari did not set out to focus her career on victims of violent crime. A psychologist by training, Dr. B, as colleagues affectionately call her, started out at San Francisco General Hospital, where she assessed the needs of injured people prior to hospital discharge to provide referrals for mental health support. There, she met people who had been hurt by domestic violence, sexual assault, gun violence, and physical assaults. San Francisco General is a public hospital, and most of the patients Dr. B saw were low income and uninsured. She provided them with a list of places for mental health and crisis support services. But soon she noticed a distressing pattern, which changed the course of her career. Many of the victims she met returned to the hospital weeks or months after their first discharge with additional violent injuries or different urgent health issues arising from the prior injury. None of them had accessed the referrals she had previously provided, and in the meantime, they had gotten sicker or had been hurt again.[1]

Alarmed to see so many victims back in the hospital, she conducted a study to track and document the post-release impacts of violent injury. The results were heart wrenching: 75 percent of people leaving the hospital postinjury exhibited significant PTSD symptoms and suffered sustained personal and economic losses. Many lost their jobs or housing, started experiencing chronic physical ailments, self-medicated and became addicted to substances, or were victimized again. All this led to reinjury or illness.[2] Admitted one day with a bullet wound, then admitted months later with another.

Admitted one day with a stab wound, then admitted months later after crashing a car while under the influence of drugs. Admitted one day for sexual assault injuries, admitted a year later for a psychiatric breakdown.

Put simply, referrals were not working. The barriers to accessing help were steep: physiological impacts of trauma, overwhelming challenges to recovery, isolation, and financial ruin. A few phone numbers jotted down on a piece of paper slipped inside patients' bags of medications as they left the hospital was woefully inadequate. The hurdles to stability tore at the fabric of nearly every aspect of victims' lives. And for those who were living paycheck to paycheck before victimization, leaving the hospital with a life-altering injury was akin to walking off a plank.

Dr. B assembled a team to find solutions. In looking for possible financial assistance that they could offer to victims, they discovered the victim compensation fund, something no one on her team or at the hospital knew about. Learning about compensation felt like discovering gold. So many victims needed this kind of assistance, and maybe the referrals she provided could be paid for by the fund. But the minute she sat down with her first application, she realized why she'd never heard about victim compensation before: the application itself was twelve pages long and complicated. It was nearly impossible for anyone *not* suffering from PTSD to correctly fill it out. Nonetheless, little by little, Dr. B and her team carved out time to help hundreds of victims apply.[3]

It was time consuming, but if it helped, it would be worth it. Only it didn't. When she tracked what happened to those applications, she found that out of over one hundred applicants, only eleven were approved for victim compensation funding—roughly 10 percent.[4]

She reviewed the reasons for rejection: incomplete paperwork, no corroborating police report, "contributing to your own victimization," and on and on. For example, a man named Alex, who had had a few drinks at a local bar one Saturday night, was robbed and beaten as he walked home after the bar closed. He suffered substantial injuries, physically and psychologically. The injuries meant he could no longer perform his job. Without employment, he was spiraling into depression from sleeplessness and anxiety. He was living in a neighborhood where being outside now terrified him. With Dr. B's help, he applied for victim compensation, but the application was denied. He had been drunk at the time of the assault, which was considered "contributing to his own victimization." Other victims were denied because they lacked law enforcement documentation. Despite being in a hospital with injuries that could only have been caused by violence, without a police report, they were not real victims in the eyes of compensation administrators. Others were denied for reasons Dr. B could not even discern.[5]

Dr. B and her team's early experiences with compensation denials have been mirrored all over the country for many decades. On paper, victims may have a right to compensation, but accessing that right can be nearly impossible.

Luckily, Dr. B's colleagues at San Francisco General Hospital had connections in Sacramento. They found a champion in San Francisco state senator John Burton, who was concerned about the fact that state compensation funds regularly went unspent. That's when Dr. B started asking, "What if some of those funds could become grants for community-based trauma services?"[6]

The First Trauma Recovery Center

With Senator Burton's help, they received a state grant from unused compensation fund dollars and matched it with philanthropic dollars. In 2001, the San Francisco Trauma Recovery Center (TRC) was born.[7] The mission of the organization is to help people recover from the debilitating impacts of trauma by providing immediate crisis assistance to meet basic needs as well as assistance for longer-term therapeutic support. The model is a combination of practical help and mental health support. It is community-based and requires limited paperwork, and staff conduct home visits and offer flexible services in multiple languages, including mental health and financial recovery assistance, help engaging with employers, landlords, or schools, and help interacting with the justice system.

What the founders of TRC understood was that helping victims was not just about getting a therapist. While important, therapy alone is rarely sufficient for people living with acute stress. Helping victims is also about helping with real-time, urgent needs, the kind that are very difficult to address amid PTSD, upheaval, or depression, such as figuring out how to get to work when you can no longer drive, finding a new job or public assistance, securing housing in a safer location, and discerning the right kind of help for children who were also traumatized. The TRC helps victims meet the pressing needs that are often completely overlooked, and as a result, they provide victims with the means to erect the scaffolding needed to rebuild their lives.

The results have been nothing short of transformative for thousands of victims who would otherwise be left to fend for themselves in the wake of life-altering trauma. Re-hospitalization rates dropped, addiction rates declined, and housing and employment instability declined. Evaluations demonstrate strong mental health improvement, too. Of the sexual assault survivors in the program, 71 percent accessed mental health, compared with only 6 percent of non–Trauma Recovery Center survivors. For victims of other crimes, access to mental health care doubled. Victims also reported experiencing significant life-functioning improvements: 74 percent showed improvements in mental health, 51 percent showed improvements in physical health, and half showed reduction of PTSD and depression.[8]

Remarkably, victims also increased their willingness to interact with law enforcement on case investigations, with 69 percent reporting an increase in cooperation with police investigations.[9] Providing victims of violent crime with meaningful help in recovering from the wide-ranging life effects of trauma renders them more stable, healthier, and safer, as well as more trusting of a justice system that connected them to a center that made sure they did not have to face the justice system alone.

Evaluations of the center's impact have found much higher satisfaction rates among victims assisted through the Trauma Recovery Center compared with those who received traditional victim assistance. Their success wasn't just a lucky strike. As Dr. B noted, the Trauma Recovery Center's success comes from listening first. "Most of what I have achieved has been through making big mistakes and then learning why I made them," she reflected. "Much of how the Trauma Recovery Center operates is based on the wisdom of the victims we have served. This wasn't a model that started off correct."[10]

The original model focused on creating a one-stop community-based center. But barriers to access were piled high: transportation, time, language, and the natural paralysis and fear that prevents many people experiencing acute trauma from feeling safe enough to leave their homes. So Dr. B and her team started doing home visits. The center hired staff who spoke multiple languages, conducted outreach outside of the hospitals and police stations, and created a living room environment to promote feelings of safety and comfort. They learned that victims' use of public services depended on trust—trust that the services were safe and that the people they interacted with understood what the world looked like through their eyes.

To help explain the Trauma Recovery Center model, Dr. B often shares the story of Angela. Angela's adult daughter, in her early thirties and a mother of three grade school children, ages four to nine, was killed in a drive-by shooting while waiting for the bus on her way to work. The loss was too great for Angela to fathom, and so were the changes brought on by the tragedy. Angela went from doting grandmother to custodial parent of three young grandchildren, all of whom were grappling with their own unimaginable grief. Angela didn't have a car to get the children to school. She didn't have space or accommodations in her home for raising young kids. She lived on a fixed income and couldn't afford desperately needed mental health help for herself or the children. In her haze of grief and fear, getting out of bed every day was nearly impossible.[11] While Angela's experience was horrific, these impacts of traumatic loss are not unusual. This is what trauma does. There just wasn't a public system capable of understanding these impacts, until the Trauma Recovery Center.

The local prosecutor referred Angela to the Trauma Recovery Center, and Dr. B called her. Even over the phone, Dr. B could hear the depth of despair. She set up an appointment, but Angela didn't arrive. Rather than close the file and move on, center staff drove to Angela's home and checked in. The chaos of three young children surrounded Angela, who was barely able to greet them. Center staff jumped into action. They arranged to provide the family with meals; signed Angela up for childcare assistance; helped her with applications for compensation, state disability, and Medicaid; and contacted the children's school and helped the children return and get extra help. They also found a business to donate an SUV, found safer housing for the family, and helped them move. Subsequently, they helped Angela secure legal custody of the children, and they also linked her to a church. After about a year, Angela was able to begin working part-time and move out of San Francisco to a home with a backyard for the children. The children also received mental health support to process their grief. Five years later, Angela and her grandchildren continue living stable, healthy lives.[12]

There is "nothing fancy about it," Dr. B reflected. "It's common sense. If your child is murdered and you can't get out of bed, why wouldn't we do everything we can to help?"[13]

Community Leaders Healing Trauma

Despite the common sense, and the immense need, the San Francisco Trauma Recovery Center was an isolated program for years, only able to help between five hundred and seven hundred clients in one city per year. Meanwhile, in communities around the country, heroic crime survivors have been charting their own pathways forward to support people in recovering from trauma, despite government indifference and neglect. These grassroots leaders garner little help from public institutions, and they don't receive the same kind of support and formal training that traditional service providers rely on. Yet in their unrelenting commitments, they become the key to millions of people's road to recovery from crime.

In 2007, South Los Angeles resident Adela Barajas's sister-in-law, Laura, was killed by a stray bullet shortly after she pulled her car up to the driveway of her home. Laura's murder was a tragedy on top of a tragedy—the mother of four had lost her own mother to a stray bullet just nine years prior. In addition to grappling with her own grief, Adela was extremely worried about how her nieces and nephews could possibly cope. One of Laura's children, seventeen-year-old Joey, was getting bags out of the trunk of Laura's car when the bullets started flying. A straight-A honors student at the time, Joey tripped and fell as he ran for cover when the shots rang out. He and his father, who was also there, tried unsuccessfully to revive Laura with CPR. For children to witness this incomprehensible loss and have no ability to stop it is the kind of trauma few can readily overcome. For years after, Joey felt guilt, thinking he should have been the one to die instead of his beloved mother.[14]

Adela had seen the cycle of trauma play out many times before, and she feared the lives of Laura's children would be irreparably torn apart. Within days of the homicide, she organized a peace march for the children in the neighborhood to bring them together and to help them feel connected and seen. She took on helping her brother raise the four children as if they were her own. She contacted their schools. The schools didn't have help available. She searched for therapy. The private therapists they found were financially out of reach. She began advocating for victim compensation for the family and looking for mental health counseling that would be covered by the state program. Phone call after phone call, and she finally secured a little bit of assistance. But in the end, it was woefully inadequate—all they could find were a few sessions with someone who did not have cultural competency or expertise in childhood trauma.[15]

Shocked at how difficult it was to find support for the children, Adela created her own resources. She pushed the city to clean up and rebuild the neighborhood park so children could play somewhere safe. Within a year of Laura's passing, Adela founded a victim support organization, Life After Uncivil Ruthless Acts (LAURA), to provide peer counseling and group activities for people affected by violence. People could participate in support sessions, barbecues, cooking classes, exercise classes, meditation, and nature trips. She learned about the types of activities that reduce stress for people experiencing trauma and, on a shoestring budget, organized those activities on her own.[16]

Adela did everything she could think of to help Laura's children and the other kids in the neighborhood. She wanted to give them places to feel safe and connected and to have options besides joining gangs in the neighborhood. But for Joey, the pain of losing his mother was too great. He went from the top of his high school graduating class to dropping out of college, using drugs, and getting arrested. Adela was terrified that he was fading into the streets like so many traumatized youths around him. She and her brother were not going to let that happen without a fight. After his last stint in jail, Adela paid for him to receive deeper therapy than was available at the time of Laura's passing. She and her other family members helped him enroll in a vocational college and get certified as a mechanic. He got a good job. And he started to walk in the door at Adela's house telling her about his day, smiling and engaging in ways she had not seen in years. She could see the presence in his eyes again.[17]

Joey's younger brother, Brian, was five years old when his mother died, and Adela was just as committed to helping him find hope and security. She got him into sports, which he was uniquely talented in. At six years old, he said, "When I run, I feel like I can see my mother."[18] Adela helped get him into track, basketball—just about any sport available. She also brought him to LAURA events and to counseling.[19] There were plenty of ups and downs. Slowly but surely, however, Adela and the organization she created were saving lives. "Every kid has to have something to connect them out of the darkness," she said.[20]

Adela knew what the children would face the day Laura died. And she also knew their fate was not sealed. The school system, the health care system, the justice system—none of the public systems interacting with them seemed to understand what Adela knew intuitively. Through sheer force of will, she kept the children connected, listened to, and finding reasons for hope.

Grassroots community leaders like Adela are saving lives all over the country. But too often the public systems around them are more of a barrier than a vehicle for help.

A Legal Right to Trauma Recovery

Expanding trauma recovery services, whether that is a trauma recovery center or a grassroots peer-based support program, should be considered foundational to achieving public safety. Given the links between unaddressed trauma and repeat victimization or future engagement in criminal activity, public safety requires us to ensure that as many victims as possible get real help—comprehensive support from trusted sources—regardless of the circumstances in which they are harmed. To prevent violent injury from spiraling into more loss, which the health care and criminal justice systems will surely end up paying for, *everyone* harmed should receive crisis assistance and trauma recovery help.

And public systems need to take a lot more responsibility for ensuring that help is provided. In 2015, Public Counsel, the nation's largest pro bono law firm, filed a lawsuit against Compton Unified

School District on behalf of students and teachers, demanding that the district address the barriers to learning that students face because of trauma. Compton Unified is a district whose student body is disproportionately affected by toxic environmental stressors, including extreme poverty, chronic exposure to violence, and racism. The trauma that students experience significantly affects their ability to concentrate and learn in school, and many kids struggle with both academic and behavioral challenges.[21]

The first lawsuit of its kind, the claim argued that neuroscience is clear: without intervention, trauma can disrupt children's ability to focus on school and to effectively learn, especially in crowded classroom environments. In much the same way the necessity of accommodations for people with physical disabilities have been acknowledged, so must the school district, the lawyers argued, address the needs of a disproportionate portion of the student body that was experiencing chronic exposure to violence and environmental stress that prevented them from safe learning. As a result of stress and trauma, most students were struggling, failing, or dropping out. And, the lawsuit argued, it did not have to be this way. Turning a blind eye to these students' needs was akin to refusing to provide wheelchair ramps or accessible bathrooms. But beyond the failure to accommodate, the lawsuit alleged that the district's reaction to students experiencing trauma hurt more than helped, from suspensions and expulsions to being shipped off to other schools. The suit argued that schools should be required to make accommodations for students experiencing trauma to help them stay on track and to succeed instead of failing or getting kicked out.[22]

After initially seeking to have the lawsuit dismissed, the school district eventually entered settlement negotiations with Public Counsel, and nearly six years after the lawsuit was filed, the parties came to a resolution. Compton Unified agreed to create a range of trauma-informed school practices. Working with some of the nation's leading trauma experts, the school developed a wellness initiative that includes Positive Behavior Intervention Strategies (PBIS) and restorative practices to prevent suspension or expulsion and to keep students in school when behavior challenges arise.[23] The initiative also includes school-based wellness centers that provide mental health and counseling services, training in trauma-informed practices for staff, and a curriculum to teach students anxiety-management skills.[24] Since implementation, the program has already improved student outcomes, including academic performance. "The resolution reached here is a template for schools everywhere. . . . A school that is not trauma sensitive is a school in name only, no more able to educate than if it lacked teachers and books," said the lead plaintiffs' attorney, Mark Rosenbaum, of Public Counsel.[25]

The victims' rights movement accomplished unprecedented achievements in law and policy change, ushering in new court procedures and new money for services. Every state in the nation now has victims' rights laws, and most of these rights are enshrined in state constitutions. The federal government has also enumerated victims' statutory rights and authorized continual federal funding for victim assistance and compensation. But the main rights victims currently have are mostly focused on the justice process. Victims have rights to be informed of and to attend criminal justice proceedings and to speak at those proceedings. They have rights to restitution and to apply for compensation. These were important changes. But a failure to focus on victims' crisis assistance needs, along with decades of disregard and invisibility for most victims, shows us that these rights are far from adequate.

It is time for a different kind of victims' right. Not just rights that are attached to a broken criminal justice process or a right to apply to a highly restricted compensation program that is unlikely to yield meaningful financial or emotional support. Victims across the country are urging a right to recover from trauma, including a right to attain emergency help when it's needed and long-term recovery support, too. That would mean a right to accessible, culturally competent mental health and trauma recovery care, a right to eviction protection, a right to employment leave, a right to reasonable accommodations at work and school while recovering from trauma, a right to credit repair and debt forgiveness for unpaid medical bills arising from victimization, and a right to crisis assistance support. These are the kinds of rights that would have helped Adela more readily access support for families and neighbors. These are the kinds of rights that invite the establishment of trauma recovery centers in neighborhoods across the country. These are the kinds of rights that would help stop the cycle of trauma and make us all safer.

From One to Forty-One

In December 2012, Robert Rooks hosted a meeting in Oakland, California, with a diverse group of survivors from across the state. David Guizar, Aqeela Sherrills, and Adela Barajas attended, along with about a dozen other people who, like them, had survived neighborhood or personal violence and had expertise in restorative justice, victims' rights, and violence prevention. Together, they constituted Crime Survivors for Safety and Justice, a nascent program of Californians for Safety and Justice. Robert directed it and had brought the group together to talk about advocating for a new approach to public safety.

"When it comes to supporting survivors, what matters most? What would have made the most difference for you?" Robert asked the group.

For David Guizar, the question touched on his immediate circumstances as much as what would have made a difference for his family after his brother Oscar was murdered decades ago, when David was ten years old. Just months before the 2012 meeting, he lost a second brother, Gilbert, again to senseless to gun violence, when Gilbert attempted to prevent a stranger from entering a wedding party. The grip of grief with no support that his family faced years ago was playing out all over again.

Everyone scribbled on sticky notes and stuck their answers to the wall. The group sat silent for a few minutes as their eyes scanned the wall of multicolored papers. It wasn't long before Robert noticed one priority that stood out, variations on a single theme:

"Healing trauma." "Addressing trauma." "Support survivors to recover from trauma."

Forty years ago, victims' rights advocates posed a similar question: How can we help victims? The answers were different back then, in part because of who asked and who had the largest microphone to amplify the answers. Not a lot of youths. Not many victims of color. Not many poor folks. Not a lot of people who were not at the top of the hierarchy of harm. In some cases, the people who gave answers weren't victims at all—they were the law-and-order politicians, justice officials, and lobbyists who usurped the cause for helping victims to expand the power and reach of American criminal justice.

Robert and the group gathered in Oakland were more representative of most victims in the country, and they were determined not to repeat the mistakes of an earlier generation. What they knew, experientially and collectively, was that a lot of victims' voices were ignored the first time around, and it was time to build a new safety movement in a new set of names. One of the key answers that day for how to help was clear: help people recover from trauma.

The group started throwing out ideas. When the Trauma Recovery Center in San Francisco came up, everyone sat up a little straighter. The model of helping victims get through crises and recover from trauma resonated with the group as a potentially scalable solution. By the time they left, the group had an action item on their list: visit the Trauma Recovery Center and see for themselves.

When they visited a few weeks later, what they found exceeded their expectations. David Guizar saw an altar when he first walked in. He listened to stories about healing and help, unlike anything he had heard about. "I felt the connection. I felt grounded there. It was inspiring." While the possibilities were immense, they also learned how little support the program received. At the time of their visit, the first and only trauma recovery center in the country was facing budget cuts and struggling to stay afloat.

The original state grant was expiring, and state legislative leaders were having a tough time renewing state support. When the center's leaders called California state senator Mark Leno, chair of the state senate Public Safety Committee, to champion the program and help save the funds, Senator Leno was eager to help. Just a few years prior, he had called for an audit of the victim compensation program in 2009 and uncovered that most applications statewide were being denied. Millions of dollars, earmarked to help victims, sat untouched year after year. The state had the money to help, the money just never reached a lot of people in need. Still, despite the availability of ample state funds, when he sought to capture some for the trauma recovery center, he ran into roadblock after roadblock. He found out that administrators did not support the TRC because it didn't adhere to the fund's narrow individual victim reimbursement model.

As Senator Leno put it, the state victim compensation program "expected victims to, in a state of trauma, grief and mourning, determine all of their emotional, and psychological, and physical needs for themselves and their family, and then determine what services are needed and where to find those services, and then have money in their pocket to pay for those services, and then go get them, save receipts, and then submit them to the state for reimbursement. It's just a tragic joke."[26]

The joke was compounded by the fact that the amount of money available in the fund had grown significantly. Compensation dollars are collected from two sources: contributions from the federal Victims of Crime Act fund and fines and fees collected from people convicted of crimes. As mass incarceration grew, the fines levied against people with convictions grew. So, for decades, the funds entering the compensation program went up and up, while the amount paid out to victims went down. As Leno puts it, "We were keeping people [convicted of crime] in poverty to fill the coffers of the fund. And it'd be one thing if they were getting to the victims, but they weren't. The line of administrative costs was going straight up, and the funds going to victims was going straight down. I was outraged."[27]

By 2014, the victim compensation fund had a surplus of $80 million. Meanwhile, only about 11 percent of receipts submitted by victims to the compensation board for reimbursement were paid out. So, Senator Leno, joined by his Republican co-chair, introduced legislation to provide a million dollars to the Trauma Recovery Center. The fund's administrators aggressively opposed it, but Senator Leno secured enough support to get the bill to the governor's desk. Governor Schwarzenegger vetoed the bill, having been lobbied by administrators to protect the reimbursement-based model as the only legitimate use of the fund. Schwarzenegger noted in his veto message that "this is not what compensation funds are intended for."[28]

Senator Leno introduced the bill again the following year, and it failed again. By the third try, the nascent Crime Survivors for Safety and Justice team began advocating for the legislation. Survivors traveled to Sacramento to meet with legislators, the governor's representatives, and compensation administrators to advocate for the bill, to share how impactful this model would have been for them, and to urge support.

Finally, in 2013 the proposal passed into law. The TRC avoided budget cuts, and the next year, Senator Leno and Crime Survivors for Safety and Justice were able to secure one-time additional funding to replicate the model in two Southern California cities. In the third year, they secured a permanent line item in the state budget for replication. The fourth year, they secured funding to quadruple the amount of money available for replication. Within a few years, California had opened twelve trauma recovery centers across the state.

Crime Survivors for Safety and Justice grew alongside the advocacy for trauma recovery centers. What started out as a meeting of about a dozen people soon ballooned into a statewide network of thousands. Members joined to meet other like-minded survivors, to learn about assistance programs, and to advocate for new safety policies.

In 2015, the program branched out beyond California. That same year, after meeting Robert Rooks in Connecticut and learning about the growing impact of the work in California, Aswad Thomas joined as the first national staff person for Crime Survivors for Safety and Justice. His first day on the job, August 24, fell on the six-year anniversary of the day he had been shot in Hartford. His healing journey took on a new form. Now, he was organizing survivors just like him to change safety policy across the country.

The following year, Shakyra Diaz, in Ohio, joined the team. Together, Aswad, Robert, Shakyra, Dr. B, and others began traveling the country, conducting outreach to victim service organizations and survivors to learn about the hurdles victims in different states must jump. The trauma recovery center model sparked interest everywhere the team went. The team has educated policy makers in Illinois, Florida, Michigan, New Jersey, Texas, and other states; advanced legislative and administrative reforms to replicate the trauma recovery model; trained victim compensation administrators; and organized educational trips of elected and justice officials from around the country to tour the TRC and develop the model in their respective home states. Dr. B launched a national technical and training assistance program to help develop trauma recovery centers across the country. In nine years, from 2013 to 2022, the number of trauma recovery centers grew from just one to forty-one centers across the nation.

The rapid expansion of trauma recovery centers has been championed across partisan lines. In Ohio, Shakyra, Robert, and others brought a group of survivors to meet with then state attorney general Mike DeWine. He sat with a mother whose son had been killed by gun violence. She had been denied compensation and did not have help for recovery, in part because her son had an old conviction from nine years prior to being killed in a random act of violence. Attorney General DeWine, whose own daughter had been killed by a drunk driver, related to her loss and responded to her grief. Through that shared empathy, trauma recovery centers in Ohio were born.

And this growth has happened with very little money, compared with the hundreds of millions set aside for victims each year and the millions that continue to pile up, often unspent. The bureaucratically imposed restrictions on who can access those funds, firmly rooted in the hierarchy of harm, keep immense resources out of reach for most survivors of crime in nearly every state in the nation. The money for trauma recovery centers is often discretionary pilot money, or it comes in the form of a special grant program to "test it out," and is rarely permanently dedicated or guaranteed. Instead, these centers typically cobble together their operating budgets through a patchwork of grants that come with numerous restrictions, and their resources grow or shrink depending on the generosity of those providing the grant.

After learning of the model, Alyson Simmons left a twenty-year career in state government to launch the Central Iowa Trauma Recovery Center, which has been helping hundreds of survivors each year, with limited resources and red-tape-covered barriers at every turn. "As a survivor, the trauma recovery center spoke to my soul. It is how survivors should be treated, just from a moral perspective, they deserve this elevated level of care," Simmons reflected. The De Moines–based center is a grassroots community-based program designed to reach the most underserved victims. "I call what we do 'care coordination,' not case management. These are people, not cases."[29] With a shoestring budget, Simmons has achieved a 56 percent reduction in PTSD symptoms among her clientele and sharp increases in household stability. By conducting interval assessments to measure the health of people served over the course of involvement with the Iowa center, she has seen reduced depression and anxiety, increased housing stability, and increased employment.[30]

Despite the power that trauma recovery centers provide, Simmons pieces together support though restrictive funding streams. Some staff are funded through one funding stream, while others cannot be. Some purchases for victims may be approved expenditures, while others may not be, no matter how great the need. Each state uses federal Victims of Crime Act dollars differently and places different restrictions on their use. A strong emphasis is often placed on compensation reimbursement instead of on holistic and flexible care. The sharp lines that exist in federal and state funding for victims' programs are very difficult to work around, and center leaders end up having to be very creative to make things work.

Stephen Massey, director of the Springfield, Ohio, Trauma Recovery Center, needs flexible funds to engage in real-time safety planning for survivors. One family he encountered needed to move to get out of a dangerous situation, but they had no phone. He had to pore over the restrictions on funding he received to determine whether he was able to purchase this family a phone. "These kinds of barriers happen all the time," Massey noted.[31] Yet without trauma recovery support, most victims face extreme risk of falling through the cracks economically, becoming dependent on drugs or alcohol to cope, losing housing, losing children to the foster care system, and being unable to help children recover from severe emotional stress.

Instead of hamstringing innovators who are building trauma recovery centers and peer-based trauma support programs across the country, states and the federal government should empower them to help more and more people. Compensation and victim assistance programs are long overdue for a complete overhaul.

Still, advocates keep pushing for more funding, more flexibility, and more support for survivors to recover from trauma. They have testified at congressional briefings, met with federal administrators, and educated elected officials across the country. Simmons is confident their work will pay off. "This model has the potential for generational impact."[32]

One such person who became a champion of the trauma recovery center model was Vanessa Gay, who survived an attack from serial killer Anthony Sowell in Cleveland, Ohio. Vanessa met Shakyra Diaz through a mutual colleague. Shakyra had learned of the horrific crime Vanessa had endured, so when she met Vanessa, she asked her if she wanted to join Crime Survivors for Safety and Justice to advocate for trauma recovery centers in Ohio. Together, Shakyra and Vanessa, and dozens of other leaders in Ohio, successfully advocated for the creation of a trauma recovery center grant program in nine different locations in Ohio, including Cleveland. The day the Cleveland Trauma Recovery Center opened, Shakyra wanted Vanessa to be there, to show her what her courage had inspired. "This is what you did," she told her. Vanessa was brought to tears.[33] This is what healing looks like.

11

A New Lens:
Crime Survivors Speak

Around eight o'clock in the morning on April 22, 2013, a warm spring day in Sacramento, California, four buses pulled up in front of the Sterling Hotel, just a few blocks from the California State Capitol Building. People from Los Angeles, San Diego, and the San Francisco Bay Area slowly poured out of the buses, tired and hungry from the long overnight journey. Robert Rooks hopped off one of the buses arriving from Los Angeles and raced in to start welcoming everyone inside the hotel's ballroom, where breakfast and dining tables were waiting. The weary crowd of more than three hundred people did not know exactly what to expect. Some of the bus drivers had arrived late, and the overnight journey was exhausting. The heater on one bus did not work, and another bus broke down on the freeway in the wee hours of the night. A replacement bus had to be summoned. When the organizers looked at the tired faces, they felt the pressure mount—they wanted the event to be worth the trip.

Billed as A Day of Healing, April 22 was the first day of National Crime Victims' Rights Week, the annual national observance in honor of victims of crime, initiated by President Ronald Reagan in 1981, when his law-and-order brand of victims' rights advocacy began gaining steam.

Just one year prior, in 2012, Robert witnessed the real-world impact of that expression of victims' rights in a California hearing room when the victims' political action groups opposed a bill that would authorize release of terminally ill incarcerated people. Not long after that jarring day, Robert joined Californians for Safety and Justice and started reaching out to victims up and down the state who are not typically included in National Crime Victims' Rights Week. He sat with leaders like Aqeela Sherrills, David Guizar, and Adela Barajas, who for years had been advancing peace in Los Angeles. Together with other leaders, including sujatha baliga and sonya shah, nationally renowned experts in restorative justice and healing practices, they started to develop Crime Survivors for Safety and Justice to help activate a new safety movement.

That Day of Healing in April 2013 was their first big event.

After everyone recuperated, the group left the hotel at around ten in the morning to begin marching. Wearing T-shirts that read "Support Victims, Heal Communities," participants started clapping and walking arm in arm. One organizer chanted, "What do we want? Healing! When do we want it? Now!" Others joined in. They reached the capitol lawn, smiling, chanting, and singing. It was the first time many of the participants had ever been to the state capitol. Together, they formed a massive "healing circle." Aqeela Sherrills grabbed the bullhorn. Standing in the center of the circle, he talked about why they gathered. It was a new day for the voice of victims in safety policy, a voice calling for prevention first, not prisons first; a voice demanding that government leaders see communities as partners in stopping crime, not as problems to be controlled or deployed against.

Holding hands in the circle, attendees called out the names, one by one, of loved ones lost to violence and passed around a large ribbon that everyone held on to at the same time. Some people teared up. Others hugged. They laid the ribbon on the ground, making it into the shape of a giant heart. Reporters watched the event with surprise. In the state that launched the law-and-order brand of victims' rights advocacy that spread across the nation decades earlier, this was not the message they were used to hearing.

Groups of survivors went inside the state capitol building to meet with legislators. Most of the meetings began in a similar fashion. Busy legislators and staffers looked rushed and distracted, glancing at their phones and taking the meeting begrudgingly as part of their official duties. Then participants started talking. "We are survivors of crime, and we want less incarceration, not more. Please stop building prisons and calling it public safety. We need prevention and healing." Most of the rooms fell quiet after that. This was not something elected officials and their staff were used to hearing—no matter which side of the aisle they sat on. One legislator looked up from the papers on his desk. He paused in thought as he glanced at the people sitting in his office, then he spoke: "Where have you been for the last thirty years?"

Listening to Survivors

During the tough-on-crime era, criminal justice agencies like law enforcement, sheriffs, prosecutors, and more became the go-to public safety stakeholders in debates about crime policy. Most of the time, when state legislators or governors consider law or budgetary changes related to safety and justice, these stakeholders are the most powerful voices. That power comes, in part, from political influence: many criminal justice associations make donations to or endorse various elected officials, and some associations also have aggressive lobbyists who walk the halls of state capitols protecting their clients' interests. But even more so, these stakeholders' influence comes from a powerful media and cultural narrative about whom they represent. These agencies are considered public safety experts—safety leaders who represent the interests of crime victims—and according to them, victims want tough punishments.

There is just one problem with that story: most victims of crime do not actually agree with it.

Beginning in 2013 in California, and continuing nationally, Crime Survivors for Safety and Justice has commissioned numerous research studies to better understand survivors' experiences with, and opinions about, criminal justice. From small focus groups with victims from different demographics to representative public opinion research surveys of hundreds of victims each, the group has interviewed more than 9,300 survivors over eight years.[1] There have been seven state-specific surveys within five states, including surveys of victims in Arizona, California, Illinois, Michigan, Florida, and Texas, as well as two national studies, one conducted in 2016 and another in 2020.[2]

The results reveal a sharp contrast between the popular tropes of the vengeful victim and the actual criminal justice priorities that diverse victims express wanting. Instead of clamoring for maximum punishments, the research turns those myths on their head. The majority of crime victims report a preference for crime prevention, rehabilitation, and mental health treatment over the standard tough-on-crime policies of the mass incarceration era.[3] By large percentages, victims surveyed prefer shorter sentences with more prevention investments than a focus on securing the longest sentences possible.[4] For example, roughly 60 percent of all victims of violent crime think rehabilitation is more effective than punishment, and roughly 63 percent prefer shorter sentences and more spending on prevention than lengthy incarceration. The vast majority also believe investments in prevention should trump spending on incarceration.[5] Most also believe imprisonment has little to no impact on reducing future crimes and more often than not makes matters worse.[6]

The false narrative that victims want tough-on-crime policies has contributed to immense growth in the power and discretion of justice bureaucracies. But the very constituency that many politicians use to justify tough criminal justice policies is not actually clamoring for those policies. Instead, research reveals much more nuanced and varied opinions. And interviews with survivors living in the communities hardest hit by both crime and incarceration reveal a lot of agreement that the extreme sentencing policies of the

1990s came back like a boomerang to hurt the communities they allegedly sought to help.

After completing its inaugural research survey in 2013 in California, Crime Survivors for Safety and Justice issued the first of a series of *Crime Survivors Speak* reports to share the findings with public officials and reporters across the state. One reporter out of Monterey, California, was in such disbelief of the counterintuitive results that she stood on a busy downtown corner and asked passersby if any had experienced being a victim of violent crime, to get their take on the survey results. One person who told the reporter that she had been a victim glanced at the findings said, "Yes, that sounds right."

The myths about who victims are and what victims want influence nearly every aspect of the justice system and lead to unsafe criminal justice policies. The revelations revealed about survivor policy preferences found in the *Crime Survivors Speak* reports have garnered national surprise and attention. The studies have been cited more than 155 times in the media and academic sources in the seven years since the first report was released. These studies fundamentally undermine critical assumptions about victims' policy preferences—the very assumptions that have helped build the criminal justice system as we know it. Instead of holding on to myths, we can ask questions, offer acknowledgment, and listen to survivors to develop future public policy built on solid ground instead of on disastrously misguided assumptions.

Listening to the Data

What gets measured matters—a lot. Public safety leaders, justice system officials, and the larger public need an accurate, evidence-based understanding of who is vulnerable to victimization. Information on this is more important than crime rates, arrest rates, or conviction rates and can serve as the basis for public safety investments at the local, state, and national levels to prevent cycles of trauma. As of today, the justice system mostly measures itself. But measuring crimes reported to law enforcement and criminal justice responses to those reports, from arrest to prosecution and conviction, leaves enormous gaps in information, information about victimization and victim needs. Instead of measuring information the justice system has based on what is coming in, addressing victimization requires gathering new data.[7]

The deeply held and wildly inaccurate cultural notions of who is most vulnerable—specifically middle-class and elite white women—contribute to erasure of people who are actually more likely to be victimized and increase their vulnerability. Criminal justice priorities and expenditures flow from unfounded beliefs about who victims are, and when the justice system ignores the facts, the most vulnerable get repeatedly hurt or even criminalized.

Currently, the criminal justice system is failing to recognize many people who are vulnerable to victimization or who have been victims. The system's current perspective is focused on crime, not on victims, which is part of the reason public systems consistently interpret signs of vulnerability as signs of criminality. This happens on the person-to-person level and on the systems level.

Changes in data collection can alter harmful perceptions and transform public safety. One such shift, when the federal government commissioned the first-of-its-kind national victimization study in 1965, led to a big change in the justice system's understanding of crime. Prior to 1965, the prevalence of crime or violence was measured via crime reports gathered from law enforcement departments across the country. By contrast, the 1965 study interviewed households across the country to inquire about experiences of being *victims* of crime. The results were eye opening. The first major revelation was that most victims of crime do not report the crime to the criminal justice system. The second was that most victims do not receive help in the aftermath of experiencing harm. These two pieces of information significantly affected the public's understanding of both the prevalence of crime and violence and the need for victim services. This data helped shape the emergence of an entire field of victim compensation and victim assistance programs across the country.

While these breakthroughs in knowledge have been critical, significant limitations remain. The National Crime Victimization Study does not capture data about the three key vulnerabilities that lead to continued victimization: adverse childhood experiences; experiences of multiple victimizations; and experiences of co-victims, people who have suffered the loss of a family member to violence. In this sense, the criminal justice system is flying blind. Without an accurate picture of who is being repeatedly hurt or who is dealing with chronic trauma, how can we hope to effectively prevent repeat harm?

Beyond establishing an accurate understanding of who is most commonly lacking in safety, the people who work in public safety systems also need to become trauma literate. Knowledge of the impacts of trauma must become a core requirement for people interacting with survivors. Giving those working in the justice system the tools to recognize the signs and symptoms of someone who is likely being victimized or traumatized would change how public systems interact with survivors—and people entering courtrooms as defendants.

The field of public health offers an example of how collecting data about trauma can have a transformative effect. Adverse childhood experiences expert and the first California surgeon general Dr. Nadine Burke Harris launched ACEs Aware, a statewide initiative to train medical professionals in the health effects of toxic stress and trauma. The state offers financial support to health care providers who complete a certification training to screen patients—children and adults—for ACEs and to develop appropriate trauma treatment plans.[8] This level of awareness about the health effects of trauma has already led to innovation and collaboration with community-based programs to support healthy families and children.[9]

While these changes in public health are starting to take place, a major stressor, a major *health risk*, that many people living without safety face is their interaction with the criminal justice system. The long history of the hierarchy of harm and the present-day discrimination and violence that people experience along race and socioeconomic lines mean that for many Black and Brown people, interactions with police, courts, probation officers, or others can be stressful in the extreme, contributing to or worsening traumatic stress, rather than alleviating it.

The current trauma literacy level among criminal justice professionals is far too low given the frequency with which these bureaucracies interact with vulnerable people. New mandates should require that justice officials—police, court personnel, prison and jail staff, and probation and parole officers—become trauma aware: trained to recognize the signs and symptoms of unaddressed trauma and vulnerability to victimization, both among victims and among people who have committed crimes. With this awareness, justice officials can start to change standard protocols and criminal justice culture to become more consistently responsive to the needs of people living without safety.

Reorienting Around Public Safety

Crime Survivors for Safety and Justice has presented the findings from its state and national victim surveys to legislatures, governors, mayors, judges, police, victim service providers, community leaders, business leaders, and more. Reactions vary, but some responses reveal that deep-seated beliefs about what victims want can trump data, even when the data tell a very different story. Prosecutors in particular often do not believe the research. They say that most victims with whom they work to secure convictions want the harshest sentences possible. But prosecutors are typically evaluated based on their ability to achieve maximum penalties, which likely skews both victim behavior and prosecutor perception in the context of the courtroom. Although it is changing, the culture of prosecution is too often a culture of vengeance. The prosecutors considered the best are usually those who win the longest sentences; many victims encounter prosecutors who high-five one another when a conviction results in the maximum sentence possible. These same prosecutors call up victims out of the blue twenty years later to rally the victim to attend a parole hearing and to speak in opposition to release. The message to the victim is that the purpose of justice is to seek vengeance.

What if instead of being asked to focus on achieving the maximum sentence possible, justice officials discussed with victims the purpose of corrections and the various options to achieve that purpose? When the goal is public safety, the options for accountability look different. Victims can be active participants and leaders in discerning effective sentences that both hold the person accountable and reduce the likelihood of future crime involvement. Model programs in restorative justice provide a key example, and other rehabilitative sentencing options abound. When victims have agency in the accountability process, rehabilitative programs, not one-size-fits-all maximum sentences, receive a lot more support and even increase victim satisfaction. Victims might endorse a sentence of five years of focused rehabilitation instead of ten years of traumatic prison time, time that is unlikely to invoke positive behavioral change in the person who harmed them.

Over and over, victims report that the most important thing they want is for what happened to them never to happen again, to them or anyone else. If victims were offered options beyond incarceration, many would choose them. And since most people entering the justice system will return to communities at some point, preparing people for release requires a very different mandate than vengeance. Instead of setting victims up to feel wronged or slighted by the release of someone who may be elderly, ill, or no longer a threat to public safety, the justice system could inform victims on the front end of the public safety goals and what to expect.

System Humility

Public systems must be reoriented to demonstrate humility and to focus on listening to people experiencing a lack of safety rather than judging, shaming, or ignoring them. In 2011, when Jackson County prosecutor Jean Peters Baker began to grapple with the daunting fact that each year less than 20 percent of the nonfatal shootings in Kansas City, Missouri, a city with one of the highest rates of gun violence in the country, were reported or investigated, she knew she had to act.[10]

Many prosecutors accept the law enforcement tropes that if people don't come forward, nothing can be done and that the only response to low reporting is mass arrests. But Peters Baker saw it differently. As a prosecutor, she relied on victims' trust in her office and in the justice system, and to her, the 20 percent report rate was evidence enough of broken trust. When there is no trust in the justice system at the community level, people fear for their safety not just because of neighborhood violence but also because of the way the justice system responds to it. When residents see law enforcement use information shared by one resident in a way that later risks that resident's safety, people stop reporting and cooperating. When people see victims interrogated as if they were suspects and then denied compensatory support, they wonder why they should report at all. The chasm of trust is so great that the risk of reporting a crime starts to feel greater than the risk of *not* reporting. That's a chasm that is generations deep and not one that is going to be resolved through pressure to cooperate.

"The [statistics] made me start realizing, 'oh my God, we have to get out of this office,'" Peters Baker recalled. "We've got to figure out another way to reach victims; we're losing more legitimacy every week. Victims are just left to fend for themselves."[11]

Coming from a small farming community, she remembered the way neighbors supported one another when she was a kid: through casseroles. No need to ask what was going on, good or bad, just open the front door of your home and find a casserole from a neighbor. It was a way of showing support, ensuring that people felt others were looking out for them. She loved that tradition growing up. She gathered her victim advocate team together and asked them to start delivering food to shooting victims. No questions asked. No need to get into the case. Just send a message of concern. It was simple.[12]

At first, the idea seemed almost silly. How could food delivery possibly help? But after getting out of the office and knocking on people's doors, Peters Baker's victim advocates encountered survivors and their family members who were scared, isolated, and in physical and emotional pain—far more than they imagined. The fact that home visits were *not* part of the immediate response to victims as a matter of normal protocol suddenly seemed absurd. "Typically, the only time services are rendered is when the case is filed by the prosecutor. That's when most victims meet a victim advocate. But what if there is no case? Do we ignore those victims? That cannot be. And if you can't do it through a filed case, then you've got to do it through showing care and concern."[13]

The home deliveries of support grew, in both number and content. Along with groceries, her team started linking victims with other local resources, such as food banks and mental health support. They helped them apply for victim compensation. All the things that used to be provided only to the few victims who walked through the front door of a prosecutor's office. Then, Peters Baker's office started to offer relocation assistance and help filing unemployment claims—the things that are useful in getting people stabilized. Victim advocates started asking if people wanted in-home counseling services, or if they had broken windows, broken doors, or bullet holes in stucco, minor home repairs completed. "We also discovered that blood trails were often left at crime scenes without anyone coming to clean it up, so we added a cleanup system to the support."[14]

But not everyone thought providing basic help to victims in crisis was a good idea. Justice system officials often have a long list of technical reasons why keeping victims at arm's length is required by the job. What if the advocate learns something about the case while engaging with the victim? Or says something to the victim about what happened that affects their memory and diminishes the value of their potential testimony? Does that influence the investigation? It's all about the case. Even when there is very little chance of the case ever being filed. It's a familiar dynamic that's replayed in city after city. Be careful how much you get involved with crime victims. They may not be good witnesses for the prosecution. And if you influence them too much, you may jeopardize a good case by corrupting the evidence.

The blowback that Peters Baker received is emblematic of the bigger problem of making the justice system the primary vehicle by which survivors of crime access help. Shootings and other acts of violence in many communities are not effectively investigated. Yet attempts to offer additional help to victims are criticized as risking safety, even when safety is not there in the first place.

For Peters Baker, the moral obligation to help people in crisis was bigger than what happened in the courtrooms. Helping people when they are hurt is basic. She knew that the trust gap between the justice system and the residents was so great that the road to repair would be long—but that could not possibly mean system officials with knowledge of a harm should refrain from offering crisis assistance. By sending teams out to people's front doors with food and offers of basic help, with no questions asked, Peters Baker was aiming to see people's humanity and to build trust—something community members had not experienced from public systems much before.

The adversarial mindset of our current system means that many people in criminal courts cannot conceive of a scenario in which victims can be treated as more than a means to an end, and they cannot fathom that victims can be treated as witnesses and as people at the same time. It is an all-or-nothing approach. That case-first mindset among representatives of the justice system is well known among community members. "A lot of times, we are met with surprise when the victim advocates show up," Peters Baker noted. "We are not talking to residents about an investigation or asking about what happened. The message is 'I hope you recover, and I am concerned.'"[15]

The Power of Acknowledgment

Recognition for people who have been harmed is perhaps the most basic first step toward upending the hierarchy of harm and advancing true safety. The horror of generations of control without protection for far too many survivors must be acknowledged and addressed. The law-and-order brand of victims' rights buoyed mass incarceration while leaving millions of people invisible, vulnerable, and more likely to be criminalized than to be supported. It can be turned around. But achieving safety for all simply cannot happen without public recognition of the harms suffered.

Acknowledgment is a powerful agent for both healing and increasing safety.

What does it look like to recognize people who have been harmed? There is an urgent need for a broader awareness project at the level of culture, as well as a need for a more tangible awareness project at the level of decision-makers and government. A culture that recognizes harm is a culture that can build pathways to healing. Many survivor-led movements have already demonstrated the power of visibility in culture. The #MeToo movement transformed awareness of sexual assault and harassment, bringing visibility and dignity to millions of survivors. The topic is no longer as taboo to discuss or something people should feel shame about having experienced. A cultural sea change has taken place, with large-scale shifts in how people understand these issues and how they proactively address creating safe environments. The It Gets Better Project has brought visibility and belonging to millions of lesbian, gay, bisexual, and transgender young people experiencing isolation or bullying.

Tinisch Hollins of San Francisco joined Crime Survivors for Safety and Justice in 2018. In 2020, she created and launched We Are Survivors, a public education campaign in California to give survivors from low-income communities of color visibility and voice. "Most of the crime survivors I know have never even thought of themselves as a victim. The systems they interact with do not give them that dignity," Tinisch said. She traveled up and down the state, talking with community groups and the people they serve about what victims need and about what is missing from public safety strategies. Many people shared with her the lack of acknowledgment they experienced. "No one ever just said, 'I see you . . . and what happened was not right,'" one survivor told her. The We Are Survivors campaign has sought to offer that recognition. For Tinisch, acknowledgment is part of building a new approach to safety. When people are able to say "something happened to me, it's not my fault and I didn't cause this," it opens a new pathway to talk more about healing, about the fact that "people should have a right to heal."[16]

Beyond helping people heal, acknowledgment has also been linked to reducing vulnerability to re-victimization later in life. While the strongest predictor of future victimization is prior victimization, the cycle can be interrupted, starting with recognizing the humanity of people who have been harmed. Acknowledgment, rather than blame, can play a part in supporting recovery and protecting against repeat victimization. Surveys of women sexual assault survivors reveal important safety implications of acknowledgment. Women who have been sexually victimized earlier in life are at higher risk of being sexually victimized again later in life. Based on survey results, researchers have concluded that survivors of past trauma may be more vulnerable for a variety of reasons, including the long-term traumatic impacts of early victimization and a diminished ability to recognize danger cues.[17] Surveys also suggest that people whose prior victimization is acknowledged experience reduced rates of re-victimization. A 2009 study found an incidence rate of re-victimization to be half as prevalent among survivors whose past trauma was acknowledged compared to those for whom it was not.[18] While there is very limited research in this field, researchers speculate that acknowledgment of prior victimization increases a person's ability to assess danger cues and reduces the health impacts of unaddressed trauma, which can include substance use disorders or other risky behaviors.[19] These notions are consistent with the generally accepted concept that acknowledgment of past harms can support victims' healing.[20] In other words, acknowledging prior harms helps fortify survivors against future harms. Recognizing and acknowledging victims' harms on a large scale could help prevent repeat victimization and improve life outcomes for millions of people with unaddressed trauma.

After that first Day of Healing gathering in 2013 in Sacramento during Crime Victims' Rights Week, Adela Barajas suggested the event become annual and be turned into a conference in addition to a gathering at the capitol. The annual tradition of Survivors Speak was born. Each year since then, the number of participants and the size of the event have grown, from that first healing circle to a two-day conference, complete with trainings in policy, storytelling, and media; a healing room with on-site counseling support; speeches from governors and other elected officials; candlelight vigils; musical performances; poetry; and more. "These events are different," Adela said. "Legislators listen to us instead of us listening to them." Within a few years, the California event tripled in size and, with Aswad Thomas at the helm, Crime Survivors for Safety and Justice started organizing Survivors Speak events in state capitols across the country. In April 2019, Survivors Speak events took place in five different states and were attended by more than two thousand people. During the COVID-19 pandemic, the events went virtual, but the momentum for growth continued. In the eight years spanning 2013 to 2021, more than sixteen thousand people attended Survivors Speak events.

"I never knew I would find a community like this; my story matters here," one participant told Robert Rooks in 2015. "I listen to people who have been through what I have been through, and it gives me strength to keep going," another commented in 2017. Queen Brown, from Miami, Florida, was exhilarated to attend her first Survivors Speak convening in 2018. She spoke from the stage about the immense grief of losing her son to homicide, grief that was exacerbated by her inability to afford a headstone for his grave. "I would sit at the grave of my son all day long. It was just a plot of dirt. I didn't feel a sense of closure because that grave wasn't done." Nine months after his passing, she explained from the stage, another mother at the cemetery told her about victim compensation, which she had never heard of. She applied and received resources for a gravestone. As Queen left the Survivors Speak stage, three other mothers came up to her, emotional. They had all been in the same situation, unable to afford a headstone and unaware of victim compensation. And they all had previously thought they were alone. From the stage at Illinois Survivors Speak in 2019, Luz Doris Hernandez, from Chicago, told of meeting with elected officials there and why the events matter so much to her: "The most important thing that [the elected officials] did was they saw us as humans. Not as a number or statistics of the government and police. As humans."

In March 2019, Crime Survivors for Safety and Justice organized the first Survivors Speak in Ohio. Hundreds of survivors gathered in Columbus, the state capital, where they organized a healing circle inside the capitol building, met with legislators, and held a press conference. India Brown stood up and spoke at the press conference. She had never spoken at a press conference before. Among the people listening to her were legislators from different parts of the state. She talked about the loss of her life partner, Donald, who was murdered. She and their children had to flee the neighborhood to get to safety. They applied for victim compensation but the application was denied because Donald had a conviction for drugs. After talking about how important victim compensation can be in getting help for children of lost parents and in getting people to safety, she sat back down. House representative George Lang was standing there in tears. He represented the wealthiest district in Ohio. He walked over to her. He knelt, reached out for her hand, tears in his eyes, and said, "I'm so sorry for your loss, and I'm so sorry that you did not have help." Brown's bravery in sharing her story that day and talking about what was missing to keep her and her family safe led to change. Representative Lang has since been a major supporter of both victim services and justice reform. Ohio victim support policies are starting to change. Listening to victims will lead to policies enacted on behalf of victims' actual needs, not enacted just in their names.

12

A New Investment: Scaling Safety

On November 2, 2014, California voters passed Proposition 47, the Safe Neighborhoods and Schools Act—a ballot initiative to reclassify a range of low-level offenses from felony to misdemeanor and then reallocate the prison-cost savings into mental health, crime prevention, and trauma recovery centers. With 60 percent of voters endorsing the measure, the victory was decisive, albeit a surprise to some. It was the first time that voters anywhere in the country had elected to shorten numerous penal code sentences all at once for the purposes of reducing incarceration and redirecting prison money into community health. Just a few years prior, this kind of voter-enacted victory would have been considered politically impossible. After all, it was not that long ago that voters and politicians regularly did the opposite: enacting a wide range of tough-on-crime measures to drive incarceration and prison spending up, in the name of safety. A few days before the 2014 California election, Thad Kousser, a University of California, San Diego, political science professor, told the *Washington Post* that the passage of Proposition 47 "would officially end California's tough-on-crime era."[1]

While some political observers thought that ushering in large-scale criminal justice changes via voter-enacted reform was not possible, it turned out that not only was it possible, it was also popular. And the victory of Proposition 47 in 2014 spurred a sea change of additional reforms in subsequent years in California and beyond. Roughly forty years after California birthed the law-and-order brand of victims' rights and mass incarceration, the state that grew a prisons budget unparalleled in the nation became the state leading in a new direction, slashing incarceration, and passing dozens of legislative changes to expand community-based treatment, rehabilitation, violence prevention, and more.

Proposition 47 represented a political turning point for the United States because it demonstrated that the days of politicians selling tough-on-crime as public safety, and perpetually gaining political popularity as a result, were diminishing. The campaign offered voters a choice between different pathways to safety: spending billions to incarcerate people for petty offenses or redirecting prison money to help address neighborhood safety needs. As it turned out, voters were more interested in addressing crime through prevention than breaking the bank with bloated prisons.

Many precursors laid the foundation for voter receptivity to Proposition 47. Decades of litigation and grassroots organizing drove news media headlines, which meant the public was increasingly aware of extreme crowding in California prisons and the enormous price tag of incarceration, both financially and socially. Californians had been inundated with images of triple bunk beds filling prison gymnasiums and news about lawsuits for years. The California education system had fallen from being ranked one of the top in the nation to one of the bottom, while the prisons budget perpetually grew. Decades of social justice activism had also elevated the public's awareness of the racialized impact of mass incarceration.

But even with these precursors, the campaign to win the measure was difficult. Fearmongering opposition rolled out familiar messages. Most parts of the criminal justice bureaucracy vociferously opposed Proposition 47. Positioning themselves as the voice of public safety, opponents from the California Police Chiefs Association and the California District Attorneys Association raised alarm bells. "Prop. 47 will require the release of thousands of dangerous inmates," they argued.[2] Harriet Salarno, founder of the law-and-order victims' rights group Crime Victims United, warned that "[u]nfortunately, if Prop 47 passes, we will have a long, hard, retching future."[3]

However, this time around, fear-based messages did not persuade voters. Despite the familiar opposition, voters upended the historical priorities of the tough-on-crime state and decided that prevention was the future of public safety.

Perhaps the most unusual aspect of this early campaign for justice reform, and what ultimately propelled it to success, was the coalition of supporters that emerged to champion the measure. Californians for Safety and Justice steered the campaign and joined with forward-thinking law enforcement leader and then San Francisco district attorney George Gascón, who had been advocating to reduce incarceration for drug possession. DA Gascón was joined by San Diego police chief Bill Lansdowne and Santa Clara district attorney Jeff Rosen in breaking with their law enforcement peers to advance Proposition 47. Retired California parole director Tom Hoffman also joined the effort in strong support. Their numbers may have been small, but their leadership was transformative. Big-city law enforcement leaders favoring reduced incarceration gave many voters the reassurance they sought. Teachers, business titans, faith leaders, musical artists, celebrities, and senior figures in health care also endorsed the measure. The Los Angeles Chamber of Commerce. The California Teachers Association. The California Catholic Conference. John Legend. Jay Z. Newt Gingrich. The list of endorsers came from nearly every sector of society. And at the center of those endorsing Proposition 47 were the most unlikely supporters of all: a large and diverse coalition of victims of crime. Crime Survivors for Safety and Justice leaders were featured in television ads, radio spots, opinion editorials, testimony in public hearings, and voter outreach. Crime survivor leaders endorsed Proposition 47, with a voice and a message that few voters had encountered before.

Replacing, Not Just Reducing, Incarceration

The Proposition 47 victory was a national first and ushered in unprecedented change. But that change was not without controversy and challenges. The reforms enacted, while long overdue, were big, and as with most justice reforms both big and small, the implementation of them came with a lot of bureaucratic resistance.

It's frustrating that when a criminal justice policy is changed, it is precisely the opponents of that change, mostly criminal justice agencies, who are responsible for implementing it. They maintain leeway to interpret the change as they see fit, deciding to either make it work or make it fail without a lot of public transparency into how they do their jobs. Many of California's justice bureaucracies that had grown up in the era of mass incarceration had become very adept at operating their fiefdoms without much oversight. Bureaucratic self-preservation is probably what a lot of bureaucracies are best at, regardless of the effectiveness, or ineffectiveness, of what they are preserving.

The implementation of Proposition 47 faced immense backlash and was blamed for increases in crime within weeks of passage. Police officers expressed frustration that these low-level crimes were no longer chargeable as felonies. The paperwork was too much; they didn't want to take people to county jail for misdemeanors or sit in misdemeanor court to testify on the cases. Despite discretion in California's penal code to arrest and detain for both misdemeanors and felonies, many sheriffs of overcrowded jails were in the habit of releasing people after a few days, or immediately, if the charges were minor. So, some police decided responding to these crimes was not worth the hassle. In some cities, police even told residents they would no longer respond to theft incidents or, disturbingly, to some crimes unrelated to Proposition 47, like home burglary. An aggressive bureaucracy-driven media campaign piled on, telling the public nonstop that the measure was driving up crime.

While adjusting to law changes requires justice agencies to develop new approaches, and that can be difficult to do quickly, these agencies wield immense power. They have discretion to change their local practices to adapt to new state laws—like speeding up court dates so fewer people abscond between the date of citation and their court date or creating diversion, community service, or treatment programs that can hold people accountable without a jail cell. For bureaucracies that control large budgets and have discretionary authority, where there's a will, there's a way. Too often, when it comes to big changes like this, there is not a lot of will to adapt.

Beyond bureaucratic resistance to reform, Proposition 47 implementation also peeled back the curtain on the woeful lack of substance use disorder and mental health treatment available at the local level. Under the era of mass incarceration, detention became a one-size-fits-all solution to just about any kind of social problem. Gaps in needed substance use or mental health treatment remained—or in some places even worsened—while prisons grew. So, while reforms like Proposition 47 decreased incarceration and created new investments in community-based treatment and diversion, the need for these types of community programs remains vast.

From 2016 to 2022, under Proposition 47, more than half a billion dollars was reallocated from California's prisons budget to mental health and substance use treatment, reentry programs, diversion programs, youth programs, and trauma recovery centers.[4] The mental health, substance use, and housing support programs served more than forty thousand people in the first three years alone.[5] And data shows that people who have participated in Proposition 47–funded programs are less likely to recommit crimes and have experienced increased stability, with homelessness reduced by half and unemployment reduced by a third. All of this has been done at a fraction of the cost of incarceration: the average cost of participation in a Proposition 47–funded program is $3,000 annually while the cost of a state prison bed is more than $100,000 per year. These kinds of investments are just the start. They need to grow substantially to viably replace old approaches to public safety with new ones.

Identifying the Gaps

The gap between the availability of community-based crime prevention programs compared with the actual need for them has been enormous for many decades. What community leaders grappling with concentrated crime have advocated for, for many years, is a major scale-up of effective community-led crime prevention programs that work better to sustainably increase safety than does locking up millions of people.

For the most part, local, state, and federal officials have sporadically invested in boutique programs that often are capable of serving only a small number of people or a small geographic region. Most of these programs operate on a shoestring budget, without enough capacity to meet the need. If 200 people with mental health disorders enter a local criminal court each month, but the neighborhood has only 50 placements available in the local treatment program, the only option for the other 150 people is usually jail or nothing. And that becomes another excuse to limit justice reform. Instead of opposing reform because of an old tough-on-crime mentality that says every arrest should lead to tough punishments, some officials oppose reform because there is an inadequate supply of treatment programs that could serve as an alternative to jail. This vicious circle frequently prevents growth in the very community-based programs that could meet the need. A new approach to safety requires a much larger investment—an investment that can scale up prevention and treatment in the same way the criminal justice bureaucracies exploded during the mass incarceration era. After all, if we can grow prisons at a breakneck speed, it stands to reason we can grow networks of prevention programs at a similar pace and scale.

The Los Angeles Diversion, Outreach, and Opportunities for Recovery program (LA DOOR) is one example of a program—launched with Proposition 47 funds—that is demonstrating what new approaches to safety could look like. LA DOOR is a mobile crisis response team that conducts outreach to people who are homeless and have histories of addiction and mental illness, many of whom have outstanding arrest warrants, usually for failures to appear in court. The program enrolls people in mental health treatment, housing assistance, or substance use disorder treatment, depending on the need. Police can also refer arrested people to LA DOOR in lieu of sending them to jail or citing and releasing them with no intervention. In 2018, LA DOOR enrolled over 250 people in programs to address addiction, mental health, and homelessness. Only 13 percent of participants were rearrested after program participation, compared with 40 percent of a control group.[6] Proposition funds also grew programs like the San Diego Misdemeanants At Risk Track (SMART) program, which offers incentives to people with multiple misdemeanor arrests to enter treatment, with record expungement available to those who stabilize.[7]

These models work based on a few common principles. The main goal is to address the drivers of crime that lead people to cycle in and out of incarceration. Typically, those drivers are a combination of unaddressed trauma, addiction, mental health needs, and extreme poverty. To achieve that goal, accountability is built into the program, but it is accountability to addressing those drivers and staying out of the crime cycle. Instead of thinking of incarceration as accountability, in which unresolved issues often remain intact and people continue cycling in and out, the priority with these programs is to stop repeat crime through resolving core challenges people face that keep them in the cycle. Both inside and outside the justice system, pretty much everyone is more readily able to address the consequences of actions and change behavior when they have stability. Narrowly tailored, data-driven programs focused on resolving the underlying reasons people continue to cycle offer a key formula for addressing crime.

Unfortunately, these reasonable approaches to improving public safety, while growing, do not begin to address the amount of actual need. Rather than the run-of-the-mill courtroom calendars that blindly churn through case after case while people cycle in and out, the mainstream response to crime should be what is currently stuck in the pilot phase: the small but mighty programs changing lives.

Instead, prevention programs that can support people in crisis, offer pathways to address trauma, reduce conflicts, and increase well-being are not equipped to support everyone in need and most people entering justice systems languish in a system not truly designed to change outcomes while programs like LA DOOR can support only a fraction of the people that would benefit from these programs. In addition to the enormous number of people with underlying prior histories of trauma, almost 40 percent of the people entering prisons and jails across the country have experienced a mental health issue, and about 65 percent have a substance use disorder (many overlap and have both). For many, these challenges will not be addressed during incarceration, and these individuals face great risk of continuing to cycle in and out of jail and prison.

But what if voters and decision-makers understood, and agreed on, the prerequisites for public safety that every community deserves to have—and these prerequisites drove local, state, and federal policy making and financial investments? The prerequisites for public safety are knowable and scalable. Right now, however, many of these prerequisites to public safety are infrequently available in communities hardest hit by concentrated crime. Emergency law enforcement response, consisting mostly of intensified policing and incarceration, becomes the main option for addressing spikes in crime when the prerequisites to public safety are not met. When this kind of emergency response is the main response, the conditions remain largely unresolved. Cultivating safety must come from equipping communities with the essentials for prevention.

Scaling Up the Prerequisites for Safety

When talking about replacing mass incarceration with new approaches to safety, what begins as a criminal justice problem quickly becomes a math problem. For the most part, we know what kinds of new crime prevention and community-based safety programs are needed, but we know less about what it would take to fill the gaps. Exactly how much investment in prevention, treatment, and victim support is truly needed?

Although per capita need estimates have been developed in the other policy realms, such as education, health, and housing policy, a clear picture has not yet been developed for safety policy. Per capita assessments can be helpful to identify gaps in what is required to effectively meet a particular community need, compared with what exists, with a view toward driving change. Ratios can have a positive influence on government priorities. In the 1950s, student-to-teacher ratios emerged as a mechanism for estimating how well students would do in school. Since then, student-to-teacher ratios have been cut substantially, from twenty-seven students for every one teacher in 1955 to fifteen students to every one teacher in 2017. And this metric is continually used to assess school districts' resources and academic performance. There are other examples. The federal government considers any area in the United States with low physician-to-resident ratios to be "medically underserved areas," and that designation helps drive new investments in those areas. Housing ratios also point to areas for which housing development is sorely needed. The national estimate of 3,200 affordable housing units per 100,000 people is woefully lacking in many communities, and that assessment has motivated some cities to increase affordable housing construction.[8]

In 2022, after talking to experts in public health about approaches to violence prevention and mental health, reentry, and victim services, Alliance for Safety and Justice (the sponsor of Crime Survivors for Safety and Justice) developed rough per capita estimates for scaling new safety solutions. Looking at estimates about rates of victimization per one hundred thousand people, as well as rates for the prevalence of behavioral health needs and reentry populations, the group aimed to estimate what it might take to build up the kinds of programs that can equip communities with the prerequisites for safety. For every one hundred thousand residents, Alliance for Safety and Justice estimates that, minimally, a safe community would need one trauma recovery center, twenty domestic violence shelter beds, and one nonprofit that provides civil legal services to address the needs of violent crime victims. To have a robust violence prevention infrastructure, that same community of one hundred thousand people would need at least twenty-five violence prevention street outreach workers and a youth prevention program with capacity to serve about one hundred young people who need safe places to go and extra support. To ensure capacity to appropriately respond to mental health crises, that same community would need, minimally, a team of twenty-four mobile crisis response workers. And, to respond appropriately to the reentry needs of people exiting the justice system, that same community would need seven reentry navigators and at least sixty reentry housing placements.[9]

Alliance for Safety and Justice offered these estimates as a proposed floor, not a ceiling, for addressing long-standing safety gaps, especially in the areas of community-based crime prevention and crisis assistance. The estimates are based on interventions proven to improve safety but that are not yet available at scale.

Thinking about community public safety investments in ratios is not an exact science, but it paints a picture of just how imbalanced American public safety investments really are. Despite the immense popularity—and crucial importance—of crime prevention, mental health, reentry, and victim services, these foundational community safety programs have nowhere near the capacity needed to effectively stop cycles of trauma and crime.

Rethinking safety investments to prioritize prevention requires a big change in how a lot of public safety officials look at their jobs. Some officials are reluctant to see community-based programs as public safety. In 2017, Ohio corrections director Gary Mohr told the governor to cut—not grow—his budget by $50 million. Mohr requested that, instead, the governor give that money to the counties to build drug treatment programs, so people could enter those programs rather than be shipped off to the state prisons Mohr managed.[10] The governor embraced the idea. But the counties didn't. Even with free money on the table, they expressed concerns that the programs would not work and thought incarceration would be safer. It took legislative action to require the ten largest counties in the state to embrace the program. Eventually, other counties saw the impact and followed suit.

It's important to remember that closing these gaps helps victims as much as people who are arrested. The people helped by these programs may be individuals with an outstanding arrest warrant today, but they were likely to have been a victim yesterday, and tomorrow they are more likely to be victimized again. Instead of addressing that vulnerability, mass incarceration has grown bureaucracies that are effective at immediate incapacitation but do little to prevent most crime and violence. Reverse engineering that situation means starting with the actual safety gaps at the neighborhood level and filling them with the right kinds of prevention programs. To help victims, we must move from the surveillance and control method of public safety to drastically increasing investments in effective crime and violence prevention.

A Case Study: Newark, New Jersey

In 2011, Newark, New Jersey, was considered one of the "most dangerous" cities in the United States because of the extraordinary number of homicides that occurred there annually.[11] That year, more than thirty people per one hundred thousand were killed, and by 2013 the number had reached to over forty per one hundred thousand. Around the same time, the American Civil Liberties Union (ACLU) of New Jersey petitioned the Office of the U.S.

Attorney General to investigate unconstitutional policing practices in Newark, a petition that led to a federal investigation, a finding of widespread police misconduct, and a federal consent decree.

In 2014, Ras Baraka was elected Newark's mayor. He set out to address both the problem of rampant neighborhood violence and the deep distrust between a police department with a poor record and communities experiencing concentrated crime. Mayor Baraka contacted violence prevention expert Aqeela Sherrills for help. Aqeela helped the mayor build a new public safety approach for the struggling city. The outside-the-box effort contained a few critical elements: launching and scaling a community-based peace-making street outreach program; developing a program to protect children and teens before and after school; developing a hospital-based program; building a trauma recovery center; and—perhaps most important, and unusual—bringing the community into the city's public safety strategy as a full partner.[12]

Launched in 2016, the Newark Community Street Team is the hub of community-based public safety programs for Newark. At the center is a team of trusted Newark community members who had been previously involved in neighborhood violence, many of whom are formerly incarcerated, who conduct outreach in the South and East Wards of Newark, where the neighborhood violence has been most concentrated. Until this program launched, these neighborhood leaders were, like they are in so many cities, untapped assets. But they are key to public safety. They know, respect, and cherish the community; they have relationships with many residents; and they have the kind of mediation skills needed to build peace in the streets.[13]

Aqeela trained these neighborhood leaders in deescalating conflicts, providing mentorship, and preventing retaliatory violence. Aqeela had previously developed the neighborhood street outreach intervention model in Los Angeles, and he as well as many other violence prevention leaders have cultivated the model in numerous cities across the country, including Chicago and Boston.

While many cities have initiated this street outreach model, few have had the full backing of the city administration. Mayor Baraka brought this community-led approach into the center of the city's public safety strategy. He brought team members into meetings with police and required the police department and other city agencies to collaborate with the program and respect their independence and their role. Local police began regularly alerting trained outreach workers to reported homicides so that the interventionists can arrive on the scene, help the victims, and prevent retaliation.[14]

The Newark Community Street Team then branched out. With the mayor, they created a safe passages program to help children and teens get to and from school safely, after a neighborhood survey revealed higher violence problems just before and after school. Outreach workers talk to kids at bus stops, help people walk home, and stop arguments before violence breaks out. The mayor then invested in a hospital-based services program, in partnership with the Street Team, to support victims of shootings. And the Street Team added a full-time victims' advocate to help victims of gun violence with applications for compensation as well as secured state funding to open Newark's first trauma recovery center for longer-term comprehensive victim support services.[15]

Finally, the mayor and the Newark Community Street Team began hosting a public safety roundtable. At the bimonthly meetings, residents, police officers, health department officials, and many more talk together about emerging public safety issues. Instead of what Tom Hoffman experienced as a police officer in California, where there really was no "system" to the justice system and each agency was in a silo, not knowing much about what happened outside of its bailiwick, the Newark roundtable aims to make the local agencies collaborate with one another and to bring the community in as an equal.

As of 2022, over one hundred people regularly attend the meetings, and administrative reforms have emerged from the dialogues that occur there. For example, Newark Community Street Team members raised frustrations at a meeting about victim compensation denials. Police had been listing victims of shootings as suspects on police reports, which triggered automatic application denial for compensation. The police department changed its administrative practices and victims became eligible. "Before these meetings," Aqeela shared, "there was no point of entry for the community. But you cannot have public safety without the public."[16]

Mayor Baraka and Aqeela have developed one of the most comprehensive neighborhood-based public safety programs in the country, and the impact has been tremendous. The city's homicide rate in 2019 was the lowest it has been since 1961, and half of what it was just six years prior.[17] While violence rates across the United States spiked during the first two years of the COVID-19 pandemic, Newark's homicide rates remained essentially flat in 2020 and 2021, seeing far less fluctuation upward compared with other major cities across the country.[18]

From the outset, Newark Street Team leaders understood the failure of both traditional criminal justice *and* traditional victims' services to see many of the residents as victims of crime or as people vulnerable to being hurt. The effort has been about so much more than stopping conflicts; it has been about focusing on what victims need and on what communities want—and bringing the community into a full partnership with city officials as an essential part of the solution.

While the comprehensive city-community partnership approach in Newark stands out as nationally unique, evidence has piled up demonstrating the effectiveness of a wide range of alternatives to mass surveillance and mass incarceration. The "focused deterrence" model—which brings together law enforcement, credible community messengers, and service providers to set community norms against violence, offer support, and communicate a message of official responses to violence—has reduced neighborhood violence in dozens of cities between 30 and 60 percent, all without the typical over-policing responses that deepen mistrust and add to community trauma. California's Amity Foundation, a nationally renowned reentry organization providing housing, job training, peer support, and cognitive behavioral therapy, has demonstrated year after year that people exiting prison have much lower recidivism rates when they enter a meaningful program that helps with housing and employment. Amity's male community reentry program has resulted in a *92 percent decrease* in the average reconviction rate for people exiting prison one-year post-release.[19] CAHOOTS (Crisis Assistance Helping Out On The Streets), one of the longest-standing mental health crisis assistance programs in the United States, located in Portland, Oregon, has diverted thousands of 911 calls from police when the calls are related to a psychiatric crisis. The program, which stabilizes individuals experiencing mental health breakdowns before these individuals end up in jail or prison, has been so successful that it has been replicated in dozens of cities across the country.[20] The list of effective models that improve public safety through community partnership, victim-focused support, and public health goes on.

And voters strongly support these programs. Across the United States, Americans largely agree on what needs to be prioritized to improve public safety. However, the priorities of the current government policy do not match the public's expectations. In 2020, Alliance for Safety and Justice conducted a national survey of over four thousand Americans to ascertain their safety needs and public safety policy preferences. The survey interviewed crime victims, people who have experienced mental health or substance use disorders, and those living with past convictions and compared their needs with voters' preferences as they relate to public safety investments.[21]

The study found remarkable overlap—the very unmet safety needs identified by people vulnerable to the cycle of crime, such as mental health treatment, mirrored what voters thought were important priorities for safety investments. In other words, meeting the needs of people vulnerable to the cycle of crime is what most voters would want government spending to focus on.

The voter-endorsed safety programs that vulnerable populations identified as lacking included mental health crisis response and treatment, job training and placement programs for people released from prison, community-based violence prevention, an expanded 911 system to direct calls for mental health and substance use issues to trained mental health professionals instead of to police, an increase in hospital-based violence prevention workers, and expanded victims' services, including help for financial recovery and recovery from trauma. These policies have bipartisan support and support across gender, geography, race, and age.[22]

Importantly, voters support these solutions over incarceration. Voters support a wide range of strategies to reduce prison spending and increase prevention, including authorizing alternatives to incarceration for someone convicted of a crime who did not seriously injure someone else and authorizing the release of people who are a low risk to public safety, among many others.[23]

The gaps in safety are knowable and bridgeable. Strong majorities of the public support filling those gaps. And people who have faced a lack of safety place these solutions at the top of the list of safety priorities. So why is it so hard to scale these solutions? Why can't every neighborhood have a trauma recovery center, or street outreach workers, or mental health assistance programs, or reentry centers? Why do cities and states across the country still lack capacity to address even the most basic crime prevention and community safety needs for millions of people?

The law-and-order era that birthed mass incarceration emerged as a purported solution to a lack of public safety and a lack of support for victims of crime. That same justification for the emergence of mass incarceration remains the biggest obstacle to transforming our nation's approach to safety. The justice-related bureaucracies that ballooned over half a century have a built-in excuse for always dominating politics, media, and policy. The go-to stakeholders are the very bureaucracies that have benefited the most from wearing the public safety mask. Crime is up? We need more investments in criminal justice. Crime is down? That's because the criminal justice agencies are doing a good job. Too often, these are the first-resort, last-resort, and everything-in-between answers to anything related to public safety. As long as the opponents of reform can rest on an argument that any change will hurt public safety, the terms of the debate will be perpetually skewed against community-led prevention.

It is true that many hardworking people in the justice system raise genuine concerns about the impact of various reforms, and not every reform proposal is effective or easy to implement. The transition required, from a system of mass surveillance and incarceration as the primary approach to a partnership with communities that can prevent and alleviate trauma and cultivate well-being, is a seismic change. But it's one that most victims agree needs to happen.

Dionne Wilson was in her twenties when she met the man of her dreams at the gun store. When Dan walked in, she recalls it was love at first sight. They dated, got engaged, and got married. Dan was a police officer. They lived in a California suburb, spent weekends hunting, and grew their family.[24]

Dionne used to worry for Dan's safety when he worked. One night, her worst nightmare came true. She remembers getting a knock at the door, and three officers she knew broke the devastating news. Dan had had been shot and died instantly.[25]

The subsequent days were a blur. The police department staff, also devastated by the loss, looked after her. Calls to check in. Help to get her to court appearances. Flowers, cards, food. Having never experienced trauma like that, knowing she had support was a lifeline.[26]

When the day of sentencing came, the person who had killed her husband was sentenced to death. "It's finally over," she thought.

Then the next day came and went, and the next one after that. Her depression, anger, and sadness were still there.[27]

Robert Rooks met Dionne Wilson in 2013. She shared how, in searching for a way to process the continued grief she felt after sentencing, she started learning about the criminal justice system. She visited a prison and sat in a room with women who had committed homicide and other crimes. That first visit affected her. She met people with similar life struggles to hers. Facing hardships, dealing with pain of loss and the stress of life, making bad choices but not from a place of being permanently bad. "I thought that as long as our prisons were full, we were safe." But in these visits, she realized it was more complicated than that.[28]

Through Robert's invitation, she also met with crime survivors who were not police widows. Listening to the stories of everyday survivors, she understood that the aftermath of crime can be more complicated for victims, too. There was very little support for these survivors. For many, there was also no prosecution.

Months later, she stood in a room full of crime victims in Sacramento, California, at the first event organized by Crime Survivors for Safety and Justice. She looked around the room and said, "I received the gold standard of treatment. That help was so important to me. Now I know that help isn't always there. It's time to fix that."[29]

She championed trauma recovery centers and rehabilitation programs. She also joined the Proposition 47 campaign with Robert, David, Aqeela, Adela, and dozens of other survivors from around the state. And with their voices, the measure won.

The impact of Proposition 47 was immediate. Thousands of people sitting in jail facing felony sentences for crimes such as petty theft and drug possession were eligible for release the morning after the election. They had already been incarcerated longer than they would serve if convicted of a misdemeanor. Bewildered criminal court judges ordered their release; some prosecutors sat in disbelief.

Contra Costa County public defender Ellen McDonnell remembers the historic day the measure passed. She and other lawyers stayed up until the wee hours of the morning, reviewing hundreds of pending cases suddenly eligible for release. The next morning, defenders started filing petition after petition. While on a normal court day a handful of people would be released from jail, during that first day under the new law, jailors unlocked the doors for more than eighty people to exit the Contra Costa jail, one of the largest single-day releases ever.[30]

From her office window, McDonnell could see the sheriff's department across the street. People were streaming out. "I have never seen anything like it," she recalled years later. As attorneys told people that they would be released as soon as the judge arrived, many were stunned. Tears streamed down their faces. Some went from preparing to serve a three-year sentence to preparing for release that week.[31]

To manage the need for ongoing review of hundreds of cases, Contra Costa created a separate Proposition 47 court docket, held every Friday. People started referring to it as Freedom Fridays. "It was one of the most incredible experiences of my entire career as an attorney. . . . As public defenders, we rarely have good news to bring to clients. That felt like hope for the first time in a very long time," said McDonnell.[32]

Counties across California experienced the same revelatory outcomes in the days after the election. Jail populations dropped precipitously within months. At the time, roughly one-fourth of all felony cases moving through typical criminal courtrooms on any given day in California were for one of these low-level felony crimes that became misdemeanors. People in state prison started filing petitions for release as well, and thousands were released. Within a year, incarceration in California dropped by more than fifteen thousand people, and reductions continued in subsequent years. All the while, statewide crime rates remained at historic lows, until the COVID-19 pandemic, when crime rose across the nation.

One person released from state prison under Proposition 47 was Ingrid Archie, the former foster care youth who was incarcerated after stealing diapers and whose own children entered foster care after her imprisonment. Ingrid soon joined the effort to implement the measure and to help others seek release. "I was a survivor before I was ever convicted," she said. That old record prevented her from jobs and prevented her from being seen as a survivor. "The system doesn't ever see the other side."[33] A year after her release, she won custody of her children again and maintained two jobs to provide for her family: as an Uber driver and as a community organizer. And within a few years after that, she became a national organizer.

The fight to win Proposition 47 changed the lives of thousands of people. This campaign along with other reforms to expand rehabilitation and treatment made California a national leader in striving for a more balanced approach to safety. This is not about a lack of accountability. Rather, it is about building a better way to achieve it. Wasting taxpayer dollars on ineffective incarceration responses takes away the very resources needed to build up the prerequisites for safety in communities across the country and address the cause of so much crime.

And to be sustained, these victories must lead to a scale-up of government investments in what works better to stop cycles of crime and trauma. If you ask leaders from the Proposition 47 campaign what the secret is to scaling public safety, the things they say are not that complicated: We must respond to community needs for prevention and healing. We must build coalitions to upend public safety myths. And we must have faith that when voters are offered new safety solutions that will heal rather than hurt people, they will do the right thing.

13

A New Justice: Stopping the Cycle of Trauma and Poverty

Part V of this book has been devoted to solutions. These four chapters contain new and emerging strategies that could help transform our nation's approach and provide everyone a chance at safety. The chapters also contain stories from the leaders who are winning changes across the country and are helping to build a new safety movement, using their experiences, wisdom, and heart.

Chapter 10 calls for creating a new victim's right—a right to access trauma recovery. Accessing trauma recovery helps people overcome the crisis and hardship that being a victim of crime can bring and reduces the chance people will become victims again and again. Chapter 11 calls for a new lens—the more decision-makers listen to people chronically living without safety, the more the decisions they make will more effectively lead to increased safety and well-being. Listening leads to new insights and new solutions. Chapter 12 calls for an entirely new approach to investing in public safety. Prevention must come first, and it must be scaled to meet actual community need.

This chapter lays out a new way of advancing justice. The justice system should be the system of last resort—and it can be that if victims have a right to trauma recovery, if systems listen to survivors' needs, and if prevention programs are scaled up. But as a system of last resort in response to crime, what does justice look like? It looks like a system that first does no additional harm. That means preventing victims from falling into insurmountable debt or worsening trauma, and it also means preventing people convicted from being further traumatized or unable to reintegrate. And, beyond no additional harm, it looks like a justice system focused on stopping cycles.

The survivor leaders paving a pathway for this new future are not only leading at the community level. More and more, they're also becoming policy makers and government leaders who can make the goals of the new safety movement a reality. Jehan Gordon-Booth is that kind of policy maker.

Illinois state representative Jehan Gordon-Booth carries "the lens of a mother as well as the lens of a legislator" into every conversation she has in the Springfield State Capitol Building.[1] It is a lens that gives her personal insight into debates about public safety. In 2014, the Peoria-based policy maker was nine months pregnant when her twenty-year-old son, DJ, was shot and killed at a party during an argument with another partygoer. Ten days after his death, Gordon-Booth gave birth to her daughter. DJ had helped her decorate the baby room as her due date drew near, but he never got the chance to welcome his little sister home. Oscillating between unfathomable grief and immense joy was near impossible. The subsequent months brought the additional struggle of uncovering the failings of the justice system either to stop repeat crime or to help victims. Gordon-Booth's family had known the man who took her son's life. He had been in the justice system before, but his life trajectory was not redirected after earlier run-ins with the law. And even though it happened at a party, witnesses were traumatized and reluctant to get involved. "We ask victims and witnesses to help solve crimes but there is so little support or protection," Gordon-Booth explained.[2] Eventually, witnesses came forward and the prosecution resulted in a long prison sentence. But the trauma of the loss left her searching for answers.

Eighteen months later, she took a meeting in her small district office to discuss the Illinois justice system. Robert Rooks, Aqeela Sherrills, and others at Alliance for Safety and Justice had been working in Illinois for about a year, meeting with survivors and justice officials who lamented the dearth of victim support while prisons were perpetually overcrowded. When Gordon-Booth sat down, she was still grieving the loss of her son. Aqeela, in addition to his lifelong work to prevent violence, understood her pain intimately. His firstborn son, eighteen-year-old Terrell, while home from college for winter break, was shot and killed at a party, just as DJ had been. "Nothing prepares you for the loss of a child," he empathized.[3] From shared humanity, the conversation turned to solutions, and the ideas poured out.

They began envisioning legislative-reform concepts. Governor Bruce Rauner, a fiscal conservative, had recently launched a commission to make recommendations about how to reduce incarceration and prison costs. His openness to reform created an opportunity. But Illinois politics were also divisive; the Republican governor and Democratic-controlled legislature had been so deadlocked that the state had not passed a budget in three years, resulting in layoffs and school closures. Political observers characterized those years as some of the deepest partisan battles Illinois had seen. It was hard to imagine a breakthrough.

But Gordon-Booth was no average legislator. The youngest person and the first African American ever elected to represent Peoria, the state's eighth largest city and a town primarily organized around manufacturing and agriculture in central Illinois, she knew how to overcome unlikely odds.

The state legislator reached out to a bipartisan group of elected officials. Together, these officials traveled to San Francisco to visit Dr. B's Trauma Recovery Center. On that trip, conversations happened that are rarely possible in the day-to-day hustle of the statehouse, ranging from unaddressed trauma to the lack of rehabilitation for people who commit crimes. The Neighborhood Safety Act was born. The proposed reforms were not just about helping victims and not just about rehabilitating people who have committed crimes. The reforms were about both. The bill provided money for the creation of trauma recovery centers, eliminated mandatory incarceration terms for more than four hundred different penal code offenses, and expanded earned credit toward early release for incarcerated people participating in programs. More rehabilitation, less incarceration, more help for victims: a holistic approach to safety.

The bill was co-authored and championed by leading Democratic and Republican legislators, including then senator Kwame Raoul, who was later elected state attorney general. With strong bipartisan support, once the bill moved through the legislature, few opposed it. The governor, who saw it as an extension of his own commission's recommendations, signed it into law. It was the largest bipartisan justice reform bill ever passed. After enactment, the Illinois prison population dropped 20 percent. And the state established five trauma recovery centers. One of them is in Gordon-Booth's hometown of Peoria, a place for victims of all kinds to receive financial and therapeutic support.

Her leadership to advance a revamped approach to safety in Illinois did not stop there. She later expanded record-clearing opportunities to hundreds of thousands of Illinoisans with old records, to help people become eligible for jobs and housing. Seeing the cycle of the man who took DJ's life, Gordon-Booth knew all too well that after people have served time, getting their lives on track is key to public safety. And, as prison costs declined, she also secured significant increases in violence prevention funding and launched a multimillion-dollar workforce initiative to bring jobs to communities hardest hit by crime and incarceration. In just five years, Gordon-Booth championed a set of solutions that have the potential to refocus the state's public safety priorities. "It was not easy to work through differences and advance a bill that became the first major piece of justice reform in decades, but we were able to achieve this and other reforms by focusing on the facts about what improves safety and acknowledge what has not served us. This is about safety first."[4]

Reform proposals akin to the various new approaches Gordon-Booth has championed have emerged in many states across the country. But advancing these changes is usually an uphill battle when the justice system remains rooted in harmful myths that determine the machinery of everyday operations. How would the justice system itself need to be reoriented?

Stop Driving Victims into Debt and Instability

Tinisch Hollins describes the need to find emergency help when crisis erupts as a matter of life and death: "Victims of violent crime are like refugees," she reflected. "Unable to stay but with nowhere else to go."[5] Helping people recover from harm is foundational to what the justice system should be doing. Fortifying victims is arguably the most direct route to less repeat victimization, less vulnerability, and less crime. In addition to offering acknowledgment, the We Are Survivors campaign Tinisch launched in 2021 also provided flexible grants to community-based victim services providers to ensure the victims they support can get basic crisis needs met. The effort provided roughly 200 victims with money for car seats, emergency hotel stays, headstones, and more. "These were resources for emergency safety needs and some type of closure," she said.[6] And this is the kind of help and dignity survivors rarely get from government compensation programs.

Victim compensation in the United States needs a complete overhaul. There is no rational public safety reason to prevent people experiencing hardship arising from victimization from attaining stability. First, most of the common eligibility restrictions must be eliminated. Regardless of the circumstances in which most people become victims, the crisis that erupts in the aftermath has lasting ripple effects for families and communities, from worsened poverty, to unaddressed trauma, to physical ailments, to shorter life spans. When assistance is unreachable, this toll is borne by victims whose health and economic burdens mount, by public health systems whose emergency rooms are overrun, by taxpayers who end up subsidizing the cycle of trauma, and by communities that suffer when victims are repeatedly hurt.

Second, flexible up-front emergency assistance should be provided to alleviate immediate crises. Many survivors face sudden afflictions. Wading through a lengthy, difficult application process only to qualify for reimbursement when capacity to pay is limited or nonexistent worsens the crisis. Flexible, up-front financial and logistical assistance ought to be a basic response.

It is not impossible to imagine providing this scale of flexible relief to people traumatized by violence. The changes in procedural protocols that emerged in the aftermath of the Oklahoma City bombing and the 9/11 attacks demonstrate what is possible. Flexible, up-front help, increased financial contributions, and logistical support to participate in proceedings and access services were made available. And the federal government encouraged private contributions and facilitated the distribution of private dollars to help pay for the wide range of support sought. This kind of regulations change is both needed—and possible.

Slowly but surely, compensation program limitations are changing. Fourteen-year-old Cleveland, Ohio, resident LaTaevia Williams was shot and killed while standing outside at a birthday party when a fight broke out across the street. LaTaevia's inconsolable mother, Latanya, needed assistance to pay for funeral costs, and she reached out to Shakyra Diaz for help. Looking at the compensation application, they noticed a question about whether the deceased or the applicant had a criminal record. To Shakyra, reading that felt like a gut punch. After joining Alliance for Safety and Justice to expand the Crime Survivors for Safety and Justice program in Ohio, in 2018 Shakyra proposed changing this compensation prohibition to Republican state senator Nathan Manning. He authored a bill to eliminate compensation eligibility prohibitions for people with prior records and for people under the influence at the time of victimization and to expand burial expense coverage.

The Ohio bill was one of dozens of compensation reform proposals that Crime Survivors for Safety and Justice has championed across the country. From 2016 to 2022, the group has secured the passage of twelve bills in five states that have revamped compensation practices to reach more people and to provide new eligibility to more than five hundred thousand victims across the country. The Ohio victim compensation reform bill failed twice but finally succeeded in 2021. When Ohio governor Mike DeWine signed the bill, Shakyra Diaz teared up. "This one is in LaTaevia's honor," she said.[7]

Stop Traumatizing and Incarcerating Victims

Justice system officials must stop practices that re-traumatize, blame, or criminalize victims. Put simply, case is not above all else. Yes, holding people that harm others accountable matters a great deal, but what happens in court is not the true measure of justice. Stopping the cycle of trauma is. By and large, most people working in the justice system are not trained in the physiological impacts of trauma, how to engage with people in crisis, or how to propose case resolutions that reduce future harm. Hostile courtroom tactics, suspicion-laden interrogations of people reporting crime, jailing reluctant victims, and prosecuting victims—these are practices that worsen the cycle of trauma, reduce system legitimacy, and make communities less safe. These harmful practices diminish when justice agencies feel accountable to the communities they serve. Across the country, grassroots leaders are holding justice agencies accountable to end discriminatory, traumatizing practices and are demanding fairness.

Launched in 2007, Court Watch NOLA did not start off as an organization concerned about the treatment of crime victims. The New Orleans justice system was in deep disarray in the aftermath of Hurricane Katrina in 2005. The flood and the devastating loss of life and land shocked the world. The disaster also wreaked havoc on local justice agencies. People were left incarcerated as the waters rose in the local Orleans Parish Prison; police were documented shooting at people stranded in the city after the storm; and the flood ruined computer databases and paper files, with thousands of records lost.[8] As the city rebuilt, the justice system did not easily bounce back. Resident complaints mounted: judges not showing up, police not responding to emergency calls, cases not being investigated, and incidences of crime rising. Business leaders, community members, and city leaders joined with a local city council member to create Court Watch NOLA to monitor court proceedings. Carrying bright yellow clipboards, volunteers documented whether judges showed up and how cases were resolved. The group started issuing reports about their observations. This kind of public accountability for the functioning of local criminal justice was rare, and it got attention.[9]

When Simone Levine signed on as the organization's new executive director, she expanded Court Watch NOLA's monitoring role. She had previously served in the Office of the Independent Police Monitor, a police oversight agency that was also formed in the aftermath of Katrina. She anticipated receiving complaints of misconduct from people being arrested but found that "most of the complaints the Police Monitor took were actually from crime survivors."[10] Being degraded by officers, left in the dark about their case status, threatened with arrest, and more. Through Court Watch NOLA, Levine began documenting victims' experiences in court.

That is when the practice of jailing victims like Renata Singleton came to light. Court monitors discovered that, not only was it humiliating and traumatic, but their practice of jailing victims was also illegal. The material witness statute, the law under which this practice is authorized, is only legally approved by a judge—no other authority can mandate the arrest of a crime victim. Yet the subpoenas from the New Orleans District Attorney's Office were signed by assistant prosecutors, not judges. In other words, they were fake. The shocked Court Watch NOLA volunteers drafted a report for public release. Levine brought the data to Leon Cannizzaro, the elected district attorney, as a courtesy, months prior to public release. He was unfazed. "The prosecutors in my office did nothing wrong," he later told inquiring reporters.[11]

While DA Cannizzaro may have felt his agency was above reproach, everyone else who learned about the jailing of victims reacted quite differently. The release of the Court Watch NOLA report generated local news stories and investigations. National papers picked it up. Top-notch civil rights lawyers from Civil Rights Corps and the ACLU filed lawsuits on behalf of the victims. The New Orleans City Council passed two resolutions against the practice. And DA Cannizzaro decided against running for a third term after criticism of the fake subpoenas reached a fever pitch.[12]

After four years of intensive litigation, in October 2021, the new district attorney of New Orleans agreed to settle the lawsuits. The settlement included payments to the victims, a ban on fake subpoenas, restrictions on the use of the material witness statute, and third-party monitoring to oversee the office's interactions with victims and witnesses.[13] By design, it was a settlement to change policies and practices, far more than monetary compensation. "We invested the entire community of New Orleans in the settlement," Civil Rights Corps attorney Tara Mikkilineni reflected.[14]

The day the lawsuit finally settled was an emotional day for lead plaintiff Renata Singleton. She was stunned at the battle she and her fellow plaintiffs had to endure to achieve justice in the face of deep bureaucratic reluctance. "It was like pulling teeth" to secure an agreement to treat victims with more dignity. But for her, pursuing justice was not optional. "I would never want another single mother to go through what I felt. I would never want another child to have to answer the other line of a telephone call from jail" like her children did when she was a victim.[15] The Court Watch NOLA activism and the hard-won legal settlement ushered in a new era. The exposure of harmful bureaucratic practices by clipboard-wielding volunteers stopped the jailing of victims and drew national attention to the issue of how victims are treated.

Grassroots leaders have also advanced reform to stop the criminalization of victims for acts committed in response to being a victim of life-threatening violence. Reformers have won the enactment of new laws to protect and support survivors of domestic violence and human trafficking who have been arrested, prosecuted, and jailed for crimes they were forced to commit while being trafficked or abused and for crimes they committed to escape the violence.

Leaders in states like New York and California have enacted groundbreaking laws to authorize courts to consider prior trauma a mitigating factor, allowing victims of domestic violence and trafficking to receive lesser sentences for crimes committed in response to abuse. The 2019 Domestic Violence Survivors Justice Act in New York provides survivors of domestic abuse the opportunity to receive less than the minimum sentence when the offense they committed arose from the abuse they experienced. The idea for the law came from women in prison, who had suffered domestic violence. The Coalition for Women Prisoners and other advocates advanced the legislation, which was supported by more than 130 organizations. It took ten years for the law to finally pass the legislature and become law.[16]

In California, a coalition of grassroots organizations like the Young Women's Freedom Center and Survived and Punished championed a similar bill, AB 124, that was signed into law in October 2021. The idea for AB 124 gained momentum after Maggy Krell, renowned human trafficking prosecutor, met Keiana Aldrich. Keiana, like many thousands of young women, mostly low-income girls of color, was forced into sex trafficking as a child and then convicted of crimes stemming from the robbery of a man who was trying to exploit her when she was seventeen. Krell secured Keiana's release. After the ordeal, they decided the law needed to change. This trailblazing legislation, which garnered support of more than seventy organizations, requires California courts to consider the impact of prior trauma on people facing conviction or have been previously sentenced, allowing for lesser sentences or resentencing and release. The bill also expands the affirmative defense of coercion for human trafficking victims and expands criminal conviction expungement relief to victims of intimate partner violence and sexual violence.[17]

Alleviating Trauma Is Safer Than Vengeance

In addition to providing relief to incarcerated survivors, what's remarkable about the reforms to stop criminalizing victims is the door they open to an entirely new way of looking at most crime incidents. The belief, fortified under mass incarceration, that people who commit crimes are inherently bad is dangerous. It lets public systems off the hook, because if people are just bad, there's no way the justice system can be held accountable for preventing crime. But when you take this belief out of the public safety equation, justice officials would need to look at what caused a crime to happen, and the lack of safety that preceded many crime incidents— in cases of domestic abuse, trafficking, and beyond—would have to be acknowledged. Looking at contexts and circumstances, not just blind adherence to mandatory penal code sections, opens new opportunities to consider what it takes to stop future harm by specifically addressing the trauma that drove so much of the past harm.

President Reagan famously said, "We must reject the idea that every time a law's broken, society is guilty rather than the law-breaker." This way of thinking underlies much of the law-and-order political agenda: we cannot coddle people who commit crimes by blaming society for the choices they made. The way it's framed—that you either hold people accountable or make excuses for them—assumes that the only reason to consider environmental circumstances is to absolve harmful behavior. But the reason to understand the why is not to make excuses—it is to stop future harm. The options are not between blaming society and letting crime run rampant or blaming individuals and getting tough. That's a false—and dangerous—dichotomy. The reason to understand contexts and circumstances is to stop the cycle and prevent similar devastating outcomes in the future. Understanding the why can prevent future harm committed by the person and can prevent others from facing the same dire circumstances. As with solving a health ailment, understanding the cause leads to solutions and, importantly, prevents more illness.

It is extremely *unsafe* to develop policy based on the simplified worldview that bad people just do bad things. There are sophisticated organized crime operations engaged in exploitation and violence for monetary or political gain, but these are not the typical kinds of crimes that fill most criminal courts across the country. Instead, the most common incidents that drive the everyday machinations of our justice system are often driven by interpersonal conflict or desperation. Instead of the one-size-fits-all bad people stance, the safer stance would be to embrace the truth that—more often than not—hurt people hurt people and to build an approach to safety focused on healing. What most people understand intuitively, and what neuroscience confirms, is that compassion and empathy are the *safest* way to respond when people commit crimes. That response is not in contrast to accountability; it is a *more effective* approach to accountability.

Extraordinary examples of effective accountability programs, rooted in empathy and compassion, abound. Restorative justice programs are a key example. Restorative justice seeks to repair the harm caused by crime through engagement with all the impacted parties—those who commit harm and those who are victimized by it. This approach is the opposite of an adversarial process, where opposing parties—the state and the defendant—are in a contest to prove innocence or guilt, with a predetermined sentence that usually involves the harmful practices of supervision or incarceration, without support or rehabilitation. Bringing the stakeholders together through the restorative justice process takes many forms. Powerful restorative justice programs across the country are achieving accountability without increasing trauma. Restorative justice programs are among the most powerful models of alternative approaches to justice that work better than the adversarial system, with new evidence supporting their efficacy emerging all the time.[18]

Rehabilitation programs such as workforce development, educational programs, life skills training, and cognitive behavioral therapy also provide opportunities for people both to accept responsibility for harm caused and to foster new connections and new capacities that allow for stable lives after sentences are completed. All programs that successfully reduce recidivism share an approach that sees the humanity of the people who have committed harm. Such an approach makes it possible for people to face the impact of the crimes they have committed and to come to terms with the harm they have caused. Humanity, compassion, and empathy *increase* opportunities for accountability. Together, they provide a pathway to alleviating trauma and to reducing the physiological responses that keep people in the cycle of trauma.

We have been using the wrong metrics to assess our criminal justice system. Instead of counting crimes committed and how many people we lock up and for how long, we must start to measure how much trauma the system causes and how much it alleviates. Unaddressed trauma often brought on by systematic indifference toward chronically unsafe conditions is what fuels most crime and undermines a lot of public safety. Putting safety first would not only change sentencing considerations and expand solutions like restorative justice and community-based rehabilitation but also change how we look at American incarceration practices. Locking people up in conditions that are extraordinarily toxic makes us all less safe. Punishment that intentionally exposes people to more violence as part of the presumed punishment is all but certain to perpetuate cycles of trauma and to lead to further crime.

We cannot credibly claim to be pursuing public safety while we are intentionally traumatizing millions of individuals entering the justice system each year.

End Post-conviction Poverty

Preventing victims from falling into insurmountable debt, changing practices that traumatize victims, and responding to crime incidents and people who commit crimes with a view toward alleviating trauma would transform most aspects of criminal justice. And then it's critical that we make rehabilitation meaningful in the lives of people who have paid their debts to society. Permanent exclusion—preventing people from jobs, housing, loans, licenses, and more because of an old conviction—drives people deeper into poverty and contributes to the cycle of trauma.

Shortly after the passage of California's Proposition 47, the measure's proponents sat down to figure out how to spread the word to people who might benefit from it. While most of the attention focused on the fact that the measure reduced incarceration, it was also the first ballot initiative in the nation to authorize large-scale record change. Anyone with an old record for one of the crimes reclassified from felony to misdemeanor, no matter how old, could petition to remove the felony from their record. More than 1.5 million Californians became eligible, most with records that were decades old. Californians for Safety and Justice joined with others to host free record change and resource fairs—big community events to help people review their records and to complete the record change petitions. For the first fair, the organization recruited over one hundred volunteer attorneys and three hundred event volunteers.[19]

At six in the morning on September 27, 2015, volunteers arrived at the Los Angeles EXPO Center to set up tents and attorney meet-and-greet stations for the event that was scheduled to begin at eleven. When the volunteers arrived, they were surprised to find people already waiting to get in. Some were sitting in lawn chairs, and others were on blankets. The first person had arrived at four in the morning—he did not want to miss a chance to remove an old felony record.

By the time the event started, thousands of people were standing in line, many of whom had already waited for hours. Staff were overwhelmed—they had not predicted this many people would attend. Temperatures rose to over 100 degrees. Organizers made trips to the store for water to keep people hydrated while they waited to meet with a lawyer. Volunteers handed out granola bars. Despite computer problems, chaos, confusion, and the hot sun, people stayed in line, no matter how long it took. Removing an old record to gain a bit more stability was well worth the wait.

Adela Barajas brought her nephew, Joey, to the event. He had a few old convictions preventing him from stable work. Joey told her he didn't want to go, that he probably would not qualify. Adela did what she always did, she took a stand for him and got him in the car. The lawyer reviewed Joey's rap sheet, and he qualified. Within a few months, he no longer had those felony convictions on his record, and he could become a licensed mechanic.[20] The trauma that emerged in response to his mother's death had led Joey down a path of crime. At that fair, a different path emerged. This is part of stopping the cycle of trauma. This is turning hurt into healing and changing lives.

Released from prison in 2012, Jay Jordan moved from Stockton to Los Angeles to become a community organizer. There he met Robert Rooks and learned about the massive record change fair. After a few meetings with Robert, Jay joined the team, along with leaders like Aswad Thomas, Shakyra Diaz, and so many others who Robert recruited to join Alliance for Safety and Justice and its various programs. Jay organized two more record change fairs, one of which was in his hometown of Stockton. After the fairs, he and the team surveyed more than nine thousand people with records in California, documenting the immense barriers that records have posed to recovery. They wanted to go even further in giving people with records meaningful redemption, economic mobility, and a chance to become full citizens again. From there, TimeDone was born, a national effort Jay spearheaded to sunset convictions, provide people with records with economic empowerment, and let people live past their past. And part of that was about showing people what the real lifetime impacts of convictions are. Jay constructed a "wall of consequences," to physically demonstrate the number of post-conviction legal restrictions placed on people with old records—a wall that stands thirty feet high and seventy feet long, with more than forty thousand laws printed on it. Whenever the wall is displayed, public officials are aghast. It's hard to confront a wall of barriers and conclude our system is fair. Alliance for Safety and Justice's TimeDone efforts have had enormous impact. Since 2018, the group has changed laws to provide more than 5 million people with eligibility to clear an old record.[21]

In American culture, justice has been understood to mean vengeance, getting the maximum punishment or making people pay for their crimes. But, at its foundation, a full understanding of the cycle of trauma should lead us to very different conclusions about what we mean by justice. There can be no justice in the continuation of the cycle of harm. And the popular understanding of justice as vengeance or permanent exclusion is also a continuation of the cycle of harm. A different kind of justice, a safer justice, would seek to break the cycle. Reducing trauma, alleviating trauma, preventing financial ruin, supporting stability, and addressing the drivers of crime—these become ways to advance a safer justice. This is justice for victims and justice for community. Justice is stopping the cycle.

Conclusion: A Shared Safety

In 2009, during the days Aswad spent on his mother's couch recuperating from a life-altering gun violence injury, there was one person he felt he could talk to, who understood what he was going through, and who offered him a lifeline in the wake of a planned-for future that had so quickly disappeared. Aswad's eldest brother, Negus, called him every day, three times a day, without fail. Negus was calling from prison. He used all his allotted phone time to lift Aswad's spirits, to listen, and to help him process the grief that was swirling around in his head nonstop. It was through those conversations that Aswad found meaning in life again. Negus helped him make the decision to earn a master of social work degree and to dedicate his life to helping other survivors. Aswad has said Negus is a big part of the reason he does the work he does today. But for Negus's presence and support, Aswad may not have been able to emotionally recover from being shot.

Negus had to process his own grief to become fully present in Aswad's time of crisis. When he first learned of the shooting, Negus was extremely distraught. In their first phone call, Aswad revealed that the injury had destroyed his chance to play professional basketball, commenting that he felt his "life was over." Negus cried after they hung up, sitting with the pain of what his youngest brother was experiencing. Negus made it a personal mission to show Aswad that life was not over. It would be different, but it could still be a meaningful life.

He sought to help Aswad through the trauma because his own

life had been derailed by gun violence. Saving his brother from
a downward spiral meant saving Aswad from the life outcomes
that Negus had experienced. Sixteen years before Aswad was shot,
Negus witnessed the murder of his best friend, Carl, a few yards
away from Negus and Aswad's family home in Highland Park,
Michigan. Negus was sixteen at the time, a basketball player who
aspired to play professionally, just as Aswad later would. Negus and
Carl were tossing a football back and forth outside when a man
approached them, pointing a gun. The two teens thought it was a
robbery, and they panicked and ran. Negus dove under a minivan
to hide; as he did so, he heard a shot ring out. The bullet hit Carl
in the back of the head, killing him instantly. Seeing his friend on
the ground "locked into [his] mind, heart, and soul" and changed
the course of Negus's life.

Negus was petrified that the assailant would return. He did not
sleep for a month, staying up all night in case something happened,
so that he could protect Aswad, his other siblings, and his mother.
The eldest of five children, Negus could not stomach the thought
of something happening to them, something like what happened
to ten-year-old Aswad's best friend, Reubin, killed in a drive-by
shooting just months earlier. He was scared to go outside. Unable
to concentrate on school. Developing paranoia and anxiety. Yet
no person in the school system, justice system, or any other public system seemed to recognize what was happening. No mention
of victim assistance, no referral to counseling or peer support, no
change in routine or extra help. Literally nothing happened in
response, despite the shocking horror his young mind and body
were processing.

A few years later, after the family relocated to Hartford, Negus
was in college but still grappling with the effects of his experiences
in Highland Park. One afternoon, two men robbed him outside
his home, and one put a gun to his temple. Terrorized, Negus's
mind went to Carl, and he went into a trance. As the assailants
left, Negus chased after them, fired a shot, and one of the men who

had robbed him died. Negus was in shock at what just transpired. The cycle of trauma had continued. Negus was sentenced to life in prison. As a result, when Aswad was shot sixteen years later, the main person supporting his recovery was locked away.

Under Aswad's leadership, Crime Survivors for Safety and Justice has grown to more than 100,000 members. People from all walks of life who have been harmed by crime are organizing for a new approach to safety, a shared safety that can belong to everyone. Across the country, he trains survivors in leadership, advocates for policy reform, and helps survivors connect with recovery resources. As Aswad travels city to city meeting with other survivors and talking to public officials, he often talks about his personal experiences and the cycle of trauma. "I don't tell my story because it is unique," he said. "I tell my story because it is *not*. There are so many people like me, but we have to be acknowledged to change how our public safety systems operate."

What would it look like if stopping the cycle of trauma became the central goal of our public safety investments? What if Aswad's family had received help to relocate to safety or grief counseling or crisis assistance? Or, what if violence prevention street outreach workers were available and reached teenage Negus after he witnessed his friend's homicide—and long before his own trauma and lack of protection led him down the all-too-familiar dangerous path of illegal guns?

If stopping the cycle of trauma were central to public safety, it would mean that children and youth exposed to violence would have support in school and would have safe, supportive places to be after school. Families in dire straits would have access to supportive crisis assistance to help reduce extreme stress. Trauma recovery centers would be ubiquitous. As would be community-based programs for mental health and financial assistance, and so much more. Those lifesaving interventions would have been possible and could have positively changed the fates of millions of people, if stopping the cycle of harm and healing trauma rose to the top of our safety priorities. It would have been possible only if the humanity, vulnerability, and worth of so many survivors had been more readily recognized—and responded to—by the public systems around them.

And then, there's me.

In contrast to Aswad and Negus, and millions like them, as a white woman occupying an altogether different spot on the hierarchy of harm, I have had many experiences throughout my life where I was treated as a victim-in-the-making. Even when I've been the one breaking the law.

I grew up a military brat, moving around with my air force father and homemaker mother until my father retired in California as I entered my teens. By the time I was in high school, rebellion was the main way I liked to express myself. From skipping school to shaving my head, I was determined to rebuff expectations to fit in. That landed me in occasional trouble, but a lot of the people who interacted with me as a wayward teen saw me as someone in need of help. My family had resources for therapy and helped me apply for jobs. Teachers gave me passing grades despite my not having actually passed. And store owners and police let me go home instead of hauling me off to juvenile hall when I was caught shoplifting or with drugs. These kinds of responses are not unusual. Many middle-class white Americans report similar experiences of forgiveness and concern, rather than condemnation, when they have gotten in trouble.

At the same time that I was given second and third chances on my way to adulthood, California was in the midst of a prison-building boom. The state was getting tough on crime and on juvenile "superpredators," often by cracking down on nearly everyone living in urban communities of color, especially young people, for anything, including minor infractions. That drastic change in public safety policy did not affect everyone. Middle-class white kids were still mostly perceived of as more victim than perpetrator. So I was offered help and concern instead of handcuffs or expulsion.

Years later, when I began advocating for families of incarcerated youth as a new attorney, I met many youths whose initial contacts with the justice system were for choices that were not that different from decisions I had made. It was not uncommon for those first contacts with the justice system to be followed by many more. Some ended up in the adult prison system for most of their lives. Instead of finding safety *for* them in response to those early signals of distress, officials interacting with them too often focused more on giving everyone else a false sense of safety *from* them.

While it may seem difficult to imagine a public safety orientation focused on stopping cycles, where helping people being hurt—or getting into trouble—is a central strategy, it should not be. It is already the common orientation public systems have toward many people recognized as innocent and worthy, primarily along race and socioeconomic lines, and at times even regardless of whether they are the ones in trouble, or the ones hurt by crime.

The future of public safety begins with confronting what has been extremely unsafe about the country's approach thus far. The severe unfairness of who experiences imprisonment and who does not, of who is surveilled for minor transgressions and who is not, is a key feature of mass incarceration. And—the other side of the same coin—who is recognized as having a right to safety and who is not is also a key feature. The marriage between victims' rights and criminal justice lobbies that spawned mass incarceration ultimately meant that millions of people ended up being excluded from that right to safety.

Shared safety starts with equipping all communities with meaningful access to well-being and prevention, and building those prerequisites to safety in genuine partnership with communities. The basic, and knowable, elements of safe environments—youth programs, health clinics, crisis assistance, mental health support, economic mobility, and more—must be available to as many people as possible. Looking at violence, and much of crime, as a public health issue is a long overdue pathway to build this kind of prevention. Instead of disregarding safety and letting crisis devolve into crime over and over again, most crime and violence can be prevented through building strong communities.

As paramount as an authentic investment into prevention is for the future of public safety, so is the recognition of what is happening right now when people are hurt. Victim assistance is a central, yet somehow all too elusive, public safety strategy. The choice is simple: Are we helping victims recover—and therefore reducing their immediate situational vulnerability to becoming a victim again—or are we adding to their trauma and vulnerability? We are either supporting healing or increasing the chance of more victimization. Instead of making it hard for survivors to recover, public safety demands that we make it easy. Acknowledging the harm, helping people. These are basic elements of safety.

And the future of public safety means the justice system must do less—less damage to people and communities hurt by crime and violence and less damage to people convicted of hurting others. This is not to reject accountability when people commit crime. Rather, the myriad changes proposed in this book would make accountability more possible and more effective. Strong prevention and victim assistance will reduce crime and instances of repeat victimization. And a smaller justice system focused primarily on smart, data-driven approaches to address sophisticated and serious crime, while also responding to that crime in ways that are likely to reduce future harm, would bring about more accountability than the current emphasis on blunt incapacitation and vengeance toward those convicted. Instead of wreaking havoc, justice systems should focus on restoration. Offering empathy, connection and recovery fosters deep change and safety. Vengeance does not.

Organizing to build political power is key to achieving a future for public safety that looks like this. Government leaders are more restrained, responsive, and effective when communities are organized, politically active, and running their own institutions. Community power can outlast the comings and goings of elected officials or agency leaders. Reform-minded elected officials can be critical to enacting change, but are rarely sufficient to sustain it. In large bureaucracies, no matter who sits at the top of the agency, the autopilot approaches among rank-and-file staff do not change very quickly. And those staff who aim to resist reform can just wait it out until the next elected official or agency head comes around. But when communities most affected by unaccountable justice systems and concentrated violence have visible, lasting influence and organized political power, local and state government priorities shift a lot faster. Investing in organizing gives communities a seat at the table in a different way: they become stakeholders equal to, or even more powerful than, the bureaucracies responsible for improving safety.

In the 2020s, the United States began experiencing a resurgence of the tough-on-crime rhetoric of the 1980s and 1990s. Criminal justice reform again became a boogeyman, at times being blamed for a resurgence of violent crime in cities across the country. Political pundits are sounding off about the need for more money for criminal justice, tougher penalties, and less leniency. And some of the same rhetoric about protecting victims through these law-and-order tactics is rearing its head. The nation is at risk of returning to the old ways of doing business. This is a risk that cannot be tolerated.

Political leaders of all stripes can stand up against mass incarceration and for public safety at the same time. In fact, the only way to really stand up for the future of public safety is to soundly reject mass incarceration as unsafe. And all sides of the political spectrum must take ownership of the new vision for safety. Just as we cannot attain safety through mass incarceration, we also cannot end mass incarceration by reducing incarceration alone. While justice reform efforts often focus on reduced incarceration as the top metric, that is severely inadequate. Ending the legacy of mass incarceration cannot happen without actually providing everyone a meaningful and attainable right to safety.

Since the 1990s, which was the high-water mark of the law-and-order victims' rights political agenda, a lot has changed among victim advocates across the country. Nationally renowned victim advocate Anne Seymour retells the days of applauding prison construction in the name of victims as a mea culpa, to acknowledge errors in the victims' rights political agenda of the past. For her, everything changed when she learned about restorative justice. Witnessing the transformation that takes place, for both survivors and the people who harmed them, through a process of addressing and repairing harm was a breakthrough in her viewpoints about how to achieve public safety. "This is what we should be doing," she said. She, along with many other victims' rights leaders, have since championed expanded access to victim/survivor services and trauma recovery for diverse survivors, along with more rehabilitation, restorative justice programming, and reasoned criminal justice policy.

Key victims' rights leaders like Seymour openly discuss the wrongs of earlier iterations of victims' rights and join with justice reformers to advance change. For some, the changed outlook emerged from deepening partnerships with leaders from communities overrun by both violence and mass incarceration and from recognizing the ways in which calling for a more powerful justice system hurt these communities—and ultimately everyone. These new alliances have the potential to foster an entirely new approach to safety.

And the safety solutions that can replace mass incarceration already exist. Thousands of leaders across the country are demonstrating success through community-based violence prevention, victim services, mental health assistance, financial recovery programs, reentry programs, and so much more.

The main barrier to investing in these solutions at the scale needed is fundamentally a political barrier. As crime rates shift, politicians too often look for simple headline-driving solutions. Those usually revolve around increased investments into the same criminal justice bureaucracies that grew exponentially over the last forty years. But those kinds of solutions will bring forth the same dynamics we have already seen.

It's more important than ever to do something different. After all, it's no secret who is vulnerable to the cycle of harm or what victims need to heal. We already know what to do.

But as violence is once again on the rise in the aftermath of the COVID-19 pandemic, the law-and-order mantras shouted across the morning headlines risk regurgitating the disastrous mythologies that have already failed the nation once. We are at a crossroads: Do we reify the hierarchy of harm once more? Do we once again grow the power and reach of the justice system and act as if that will bring about safety for all? Or do we truly set out to see all victims and build something safer in *their* names?

For every leader who appeared in this book, the answer is clear— and after spending 275 pages with their stories, I hope your answer is too.

Author's Note

I wrote this book after spending a decade advocating for changes to public safety policy in numerous states across the country. It began in 2012, when I left my leadership position in the San Francisco District Attorney's Office to launch a new philanthropy-backed effort to advance criminal justice reform in California, Californians for Safety and Justice, focused on policy advocacy and grassroots mobilization. Crime Survivors for Safety and Justice was the first program we built, to reach underrepresented victims and bring their voices to bear in policy debates. California's Proposition 47 was our first major campaign. In 2016, Robert Rooks and I co-founded Alliance for Safety and Justice, a national offshoot of our California work, advancing reform in the nation's largest states. That organization grew to become the umbrella that now houses Californians for Safety and Justice, Crime Survivors for Safety and Justice, and other advocacy efforts mentioned herein.

Together, and in collaboration with other groups, the reforms we achieved in ten years, from 2012 to 2022, have resulted in more than half a billion dollars reallocated from prison budgets to prevention; expanded victim compensation eligibility for hundreds of thousands of people; reduced incarceration for hundreds of thousands of people; opportunities to clear old records for millions of people; and forty new trauma recovery centers built to support victims of violence, among other reforms.

More than 50,000 everyday people from all walks of life mobilized to win these changes. Portions of this book discuss the ideas and solutions that have emerged through these efforts—work that has certainly not been mine alone. My discussion of it reflects lessons learned through a decade of partnerships. I share credit for all the positive outcomes with the leaders in this book, and many more. Any errors in retelling or representation are mine alone.

Acknowledgments

Words cannot adequately convey the depth of my gratitude for my family. To Mom and Dad, thank you for your unrelenting support and for teaching me about passion and hard work. I am blessed beyond measure to have you as my parents. To my fantastic siblings, Sean, Michelle, and Adrienne, and my beloved children, Kioni, Nyame, Tehya, and Jael, you have been constant sources of encouragement, laughter, and love. You have made it possible for me to learn and grow, make mistakes, and try again, and accomplish many things. Thank you. A few of you have been especially supportive during the book writing process. My precious daughter Kioni, you went from an infant to nearly a teenager in the decade I spent building the work of Alliance for Safety and Justice. And, more recently, you have endured many a boring night watching me write. Thank you for your patience, and for telling me when it was time to put the computer away and play. Your bright eyes make every day better and I love you more than you could ever know. My sister Michelle Anderson, you were my earliest and most influential mentor. Thank you for teaching me about purpose and justice, and continually cheering me on. My brother Sean, your fierce loyalty and quiet support has been a gift, especially these last few years. And Mom, it would be impossible to imagine how I could have managed anything without your help over the last ten years. There are many other wonderful people in our extended family; you have been so kind and loving throughout the years and I appreciate all of you.

Thank you so much to the people featured in this book, who both shared so much of themselves in the process and provided invaluable feedback to help me bring this book into being. To Robert Rooks, whenever I said I didn't have time to write, you pushed and motivated me to keep at it. Thank you for believing in me, and for the past decade of working together. It has been transformative—from marathon meetings to nonstop travel, remarkable wins, devastating losses, and the constant unfolding of unexpected challenges and opportunities. Together we built an organization and body of work I am so proud of. I am deeply grateful for your unwavering commitment. To Aswad Thomas, Annie Nichol, Jess Nichol, Renata Singleton, Pete Baroni, Suzy Loftus, Ray Winans, Tinisch Hollins, Shakyra Diaz, Rachel Dissell, Tom Hoffman, Jean Peters Baker, Aqeela Sherrills, David Guizar, Jay Jordan, Gary Mohr, Alicia Boccellari, Mark Leno, Adela Barajas, Jehan Gordan-Booth, Simone Levine, Negus Thomas, and many others, thank you so much for your inspiration, support, input, and wisdom. To all the additional people who I interviewed or who I talked with about the topics of this book, as well as those who provided invaluable research help, feedback, or other support along the way, thank you immensely, including: Caroline Reilly, Sophia Magnolia Hunt, Allen Hopper, Sasha Abramsky, Cyrus O'Brien, Andi Gentile, Cheryl Green, Matt Carle, Nell Bernstein, Colby Bruno, Mai Fernandez, Jennifer Johnson, David Kennedy, Maggy Krell, Tara Mikkilineni, Anne Seymour, Sejal Singh, Patrick Sharkey, Tom Synan, Anjuli Verma, and Kamilah Willingham, among many others. Extra special thanks to Lauren Hamlin and Aaron Shulman, the two best writing coaches ever, and Diane Wachtell, Emily Albarillo, Rachel Vega-DeCesario, and the entire brilliant (and patient) team at The New Press. It has been an honor to bring this book to life with your help.

Thank you to everyone who has worked on staff and given blood, sweat, and tears to build Alliance for Safety and Justice and Californians for Safety and Justice with Robert and me, most especially

Andrea Broxton, Shakyra Diaz, Tinisch Hollins, Shaena Fazal, Jay Jordan, Aswad Thomas, Seema Sadanandan, Anna Cho, and John Cutler. I think you all have capes hidden somewhere. Thank you also to all of the past and current staff, including many people who have been pivotal in building the work in our early years and big transitions, including Ingrid Archie, Marisa Arrona, John Bauters, Milena Blake, Hillary Blout, Sara Blumenfrucht, Rima Chaudry, Juan Pablo Chavez, Roger Cox, Kimberly Deterline, Brittanie Dial, Anthony DiMartino, Vickey Flores, Tricia Forbes, Kenny Foster, Andi Gentile, David Guizar, Latiah Hill, Jessica Hong, Seung Hong, Gilbert Johnson, Mandela Jones, Subhash Kateel, Karalyn Lacey, Tesha Laurante, Jonathan Lewis, Kung Li, John Maki, Julien Martinez, Will Matthews, Tashante McCoy, Devon McGriff, Danny Montes, Suman Murthy, Stephanie Ong, Caroline Perez, Kyla Perry, Nathan Pirtle, Jessica Reid, Terry Rillera, Liz Sanchez, Elizabeth Siggins, Mike Smith, Terrance Stewart, Jenny Montoya Tansey, Selena Teji, Terra Tucker, Annie Whalen, Keevy Wilkerson, Jason Ziedenberg, and many more. The list of instrumental people who have advanced our operations, communications, advocacy, and organizing work goes on. Thank you to all of you, deeply.

Thank you to the dynamic leaders who have built and grown Crime Survivors for Safety and Justice across the country. From the Founders Circle, including sujatha baliga, Adela Barajas, David Guizar, Vickey Lindsey, Deldep Medina, sonya shah, Aqeela Sherrills, Heather Warnken, Dionne Wilson, and Kathy Young-Hood; to the more than forty chapter coordinators building membership, including leaders such as India Brown, Dolores Castenada, Kimesha Coleman, Kevin Dolphin, LaNaisha Edwards, Agnes Fury, Luz Doris Hernandez, Megan Hobson, Pam Hubbard, Bertha Purnell, Elizabeth Reubman, Shari Ware, and so many others; to the many more people who have participated in Survivors Speak, held healing vigils, offered mutual support, and continually advocated for a new approach to safety. You have had immeasurable impact.

Thank you to everyone who made Californians for Safety and Justice and Alliance for Safety and Justice possible and who helped us grow through immense support, guidance, partnerships, and advice, especially the incomparable Tim Silard, without whom we would have never begun, and many other wonderful advisors, partners, supporters, or investors including Doug Bond, Anne Marie Burgoyne, Susan Burton, Seiji Carpenter, Pat Clark, Chloe Cockburn, Tanya Coke, Quinn Delaney, Jonah Edelman, Julio Escobar, Betsy Fairbanks, Mark Faucette, Neill Franklin, Seema Gajwani, James Harrison, J. Hilton, Latanya Hilton, Wayne Hughes Jr., Will Ing, William Johnston, David Kordus, Karren Lane, Bill Lansdowne, Monica Larenas, Kirsten Levingston, Michael Madnick, Mary McClymont, Desmond Meade, Dan Newman, Lenny Noisette, Karen Pank, Sasha Post, Susan Pritzker, Patty Quillin, David Rattray, Barbara Raymond, Nina Revoyr, Laura Rodriguez, david rogers, Jilian Roland, Mike Romano, Jeff Rosen, Bob Ross, Mattie Scott, Dan Seeman, Lateefah Simon, Liz Simons, Lowell Simpson, Ace Smith, Mark Soloman, Darrell Steinberg, Anthony Thigpenn, Jeremy Travis, Michael Troncoso, Butch Trusty, Jehan Velji, Darren Walker, Billy Watterson, David Weil, Dana Williamson, Lori Wortz, Bill Wortz, Ana Zamora, Ken Zimmerman, and many, many more. Some of these remarkable people, and other pivotal backers, come from supporting philanthropic foundations such as Rosenberg Foundation, Arnold Ventures, Art for Justice, The Ballmer Group, Blue Meridian Partners (JAM Fund), The California Endowment, The California Wellness Foundation, Chan Zuckerberg Initiative/The Just Trust, Ford Foundation, Fund for Nonviolence, Galaxy Gives, Lakeshore Foundation, MacArthur Foundation, Meadow Fund, Open Philanthropy, Open Society Foundation, Public Welfare Foundation, Schusterman Family Philanthropies, and many more.

Finally, I am deeply grateful for the inspirational mentors and friends who have supported me and taught me so much over the years. To my first boss in social justice, Van Jones, you were a life-changing mentor; thank you so much for teaching me about campaigning, tenacity, and especially leadership. I am lucky to have learned so much from many extraordinary leaders for whom I worked over the years, including Gavin Newsom, Ron Dellums, Kamala Harris, George Gascón, and more. And, there have also been so many other supportive colleagues, friends, and cherished people who have influenced me along the way, including Jakada Imani, Xochitl Bervera, Sheri Costa, Lourdes Duarte, Charity Harbo, Patricia Houts, Nadine Burke Harris, Kari Hong, Kathleen Kelly Janus, Shahidah Lacey, Debbie Mesloh, Zach Norris, David Onek, Will Roy, Marlene Sanchez, Lateefah Simon, Anjana Samant, and so many more—too many to adequately name.

To everyone mentioned here and many more who have impacted me, thank you. There is truly no way I would be standing strong without you.

Notes

Chapter 1: A Traumatized Nation

1. Alliance for Safety and Justice, *Crime Survivors Speak: The First-Ever National Survey of Victims' Views on Safety and Justice*, 2017, allianceforsafety andjustice.org/crimesurvivorsspeak. A generation ago, the last time the federal government estimated how many people would be victimized by crime, the estimate was nearly everyone would at some point. U.S. Department of Justice, *Lifetime Likelihood of Victimization*, technical report by the Bureau of Justice Statistics, March 1987, www.ojp.gov/pdffiles1/bjs/104274.pdf.

2. Rachel E. Morgan and Jennifer Truman, *Criminal Victimization, 2019* (NCJ 255113), U.S. Department of Justice, Bureau of Justice Statistics, September 2020, bjs.ojp.gov/content/pub/pdf/cv19.pdf.

3. Alexandra Thompson, Rachel E. Morgan, Heather Warnken, and Barbara A. Oudekerk, *Services for Crime Victims, 2019* (NCJ 300741), U.S. Department of Justice, Bureau of Justice Statistics, October 6, 2021, www.ojp.gov /news/news-release/services-crime-victims-2019; see also Heather Warnken, "A Vision for Equity in Victim Services: What Do the Data Tell Us About the Work Ahead?" Video presentation, U.S. Department of Justice, Office for Victims of Crime, June 8, 2021, ovc.ojp.gov/media/video/12971#transcript—0; Erika Harrell, *Crimes Against Persons with Disabilities, 2009–2019 Statistical Tables* (CSJ 301-367), U.S. Department of Justice, Bureau of Justice Statistics, November 2021; Illinois Criminal Justice Information Authority (2019), *Victimization and Help-Seeking Experiences of LGBTQ+ Individuals*; S. E. James, J. L. Herman, S. Rankin, M. Keisling, L. Mottet, & M. Anafi (2016), *The Report of the 2015 U.S. Transgender Survey*, Washington, DC: National Center for Transgender Equality, transequality.org/sites/default/files/docs/usts/USTS -Full-Report-Dec17.pdf; Alliance for Safety and Justice, *Crime Survivors Speak: The First-Ever National Survey of Victims' Views on Safety and Justice*, 2017, allianceforsafetyandjustice.org/crimesurvivorsspeak.

4. Ibid.

5. Aswad Thomas, *The Stars Represent You and Me* (Cleveland, OH: King and Queen Publishing, 2021).

6. Sarah Brown Hammond, "Enforcing and Evaluating Victims' Rights

Laws," *National Conference of State Legislatures LEGISBRIEF* 13, no. 13 (March 2005): 1; Anne Seymour and Pat Nolan, "Reagan Had It Right: We Must Not Forget America's Crime Victims," May 7, 2015, Fox News, www.foxnews.com /opinion/reagan-had-it-right-we-must-not-forget-americas-crime-victims.

7. See "Highest to Lowest—Prison Population Rate" data tables, www .prisonstudies.org/highest-to-lowest/prison_population_rate?field_region _taxonomy_tid=All; see also *The Crime Victims Fund: Federal Support for Victims of Crime*, Congressional Research Service, updated April 2, 2020, crsreports.congress.gov/product/pdf/R/R42672.

8. Aswad Thomas, interviewed by the author, August 12, 2020.

9. Ibid.

10. *Criminal Victimization* 2019; Alliance for Safety and Justice, *Crime Survivors Speak: The First-Ever National Survey of Victims' Views on Safety and Justice*, 2017, allianceforsafetyandjustice.org/crimesurvivorsspeak.

11. Ibid.

12. In 2020, only 40 percent of violent crimes were reported. In 2019, only 46 percent of reported crimes resulted in an arrest, with even fewer resulting in prosecution. Rachel E. Morgan and Alexandra Thompson, *Criminal Victimization, 2020*, Bureau of Justice Statistics, October 18, 2021, table 4, bjs.ojp.gov/library/publications/criminal-victimization-2020; and *Crime in the United States, 2019*, Federal Bureau of Investigation, table 25, ucr.fbi.gov /crime-in-the-u.s/2019/crime-in-the-u.s.-2019/topic-pages/tables/table-25.

13. Robert J. Smith and Justin D. Levinson, "The Impact of Implicit Racial Bias on the Exercise of Prosecutorial Discretion," *Seattle University Law Review* 35 (2011): 795–826; Lucy Adams, "Death by Discretion: Who Decides Who Lives and Dies in the United States of America," *American Journal of Criminal Justice* 32 (2004): 389–90; Michael L. Radelet and Glenn L. Pierce, "Race and Prosecutorial Discretion in Homicide Cases," *Law & Society Review* 19 (1985): 587–622; Rory K. Little, "What Federal Prosecutors Really Think: The Puzzle of Statistical Race Disparity Versus Specific Guilt, and the Specter of Timothy McVeigh," *DePaul Law Review* 53 (2003): 1590–1600.

14. For a discussion of more grassroots victims' rights solutions, see Marie Gottschalk, *The Prison and the Gallows* (New York: Cambridge University Press, 2006), esp. 128–38.

15. Based on an analysis of data from the Census Bureau's 2020 Annual Survey of Public Employment & Payroll combined with employment figures published by the U.S. Department of Justice and U.S. Courts. The number of agricultural works, including fishing, hunting, and forestry, was reported by the Bureau of Labor Statistics. See U.S. Census Bureau. 2020 Annual Survey of Public Employment & Payroll, Individual Unit Files, www.census.gov /data/datasets/2020/econ/apes/annual-apes.html; U.S. Department of Justice, FY2020 Budget Request at a Glance, www.justice.gov/jmd/page/file/1398931 /download; U.S. Courts, 2021 Annual Report, www.uscourts.gov/statistics -reports/annual-report-2021; U.S. Bureau of Labor Statistics, Employment

Projections Program, Employment by Major Industry Sector, September 8, 2021, www.bls.gov/emp/tables/employment-by-major-industry-sector.htm.

16. Emily D. Buehler, *Justice Expenditures and Employment in the United States, 2017*, Bureau of Justice Statistics, June 17, 2021, bjs.ojp.gov/library /publications/justice-expenditures-and-employment-united-states-2017; and National Association of State Budget Officers, *State Expenditure Report*, 2021, www.nasbo.org/reports-data/state-expenditure-report.

17. Calculated from Prison Policy Initiative, state prisons, local jails, and federal prisons, incarceration rates and counts, 1925–2020, n.d., www .prisonpolicy.org/data. Jail population for 1972 was not available, so the relevant figure from 1970 was used.

18. Emily Wirda and Tiana Herring, *States of Incarceration: The Global Context 2021*, Prison Policy Initiative, September 2021, www.prisonpolicy.org /global/2021.html.

19. For prominent court cases that diminished protections against search and seizure, see Supreme Court of the United States, *Terry v. Ohio* (1968); Supreme Court of the United States, *Michigan v. Long* (1983); Supreme Court of the United States, *Hiibel v. Sixth Judicial District Court of Nevada* (2004); and Supreme Court of the United States, *Heien v. North Carolina* (2014).

20. Jeffrey Bellin, "Reassessing Prosecutorial Power Through the Lens of Mass Incarceration," *Michigan Law Review* 116.6 (2018): 835–57; Jeffery T. Ulmer, Megan C. Kurlychek, and John H. Kramer, "Prosecutorial Discretion and the Imposition of Mandatory Minimum Sentences," *Journal of Research in Crime and Delinquency* 44.4 (2007): 427–58.

21. Thomas P. Bonczar, *Prevalence of Imprisonment in the U.S. Population, 1974–2001* (Czechia: Good Press, 2003).

22. Racial disparities are so embedded in U.S. justice systems that entire fields and academic journals are dedicated to studying their causes and impacts. For overviews of these fields, see journals such as the *Michigan Journal of Race and Law*; *Race and Justice, Gender, Race and Justice*; *Race and Social Justice Law Review*; *St. Mary's Law Review on Race and Social Justice*, to list only a few. For an early account, see Joan Petersilia, *Racial Disparities in the Criminal Justice System* (Santa Monica, CA: Rand Corporation, 1983). For an accessible summary, see National Research Council, *The Growth of Incarceration in the United States: Exploring Causes and Consequences* (Washington, DC: The National Academies Press, 2014), 56–67, doi.org/10.17226/18613.

23. Californians for Safety and Justice, *Repairing the Road to Redemption in California*, 2018, safeandjust.org/wp-content/uploads/CSJ_SecondChances -ONLINE-May14.pdf.

24. "Crime Survivors Speak: The First-Ever National Survey of Victims' Views on Safety and Justice," Alliance for Safety and Justice, 2017; "Crime Survivors Speak: Florida Victims' Views on Safety and Justice," Alliance for Safety and Justice, 2018; "California Crime Survivors Speak: A Statewide Survey of California Victims' Views on Safety and Justice," 2018; "Crime

Survivors Speak: Texas Victims Experiences with Recovery and Views on
Criminal Justice," Alliance for Safety and Justice, 2019; "Illinois Crime Victims' Voices: The First-Ever Survey of Illinois Victims' Views on Safety and
Justice," Alliance for Safety and Justice, 2017; "Crime Survivors Speak: Michigan Victims' Views on Safety and Justice," Alliance for Safety and Justice,
2018. All available at allianceforsafetyandjustice.org.

Chapter 2: How the Call for Victims' Rights Led to Mass Incarceration

1. Annie and Jess Nichol, interview by the author, January 15, 2021.

2. Michelle Locke, Associated Press, "The Polly Klaas Story Unfolded
Through a Veil of Many Tears," *Southcoast Today*, August 11, 1996, www
.southcoasttoday.com/story/news/1996/08/11/the-polly-klaas-story-unfolded
/50637248007.

3. Associated Press, "Actress Offers Reward to Find Kidnaped Girl," *Los
Angeles Times*, October 10, 1993, www.latimes.com/archives/la-xpm-1993-10
-10-mn-44456-story.html; Lori A. Carter, "Tearful Petaluma Remembers
Polly Klaas," *Press Democrat*, October 5, 2013, www.petaluma360.com/article
/news/tearful-petaluma-remembers-polly-klaas.

4. Annie and Jess Nichol, interview by the author, January 15, 2021.

5. Ibid.

6. Daniel W. Stiller, Note, "Initiative 593: Washington's Voters Go Down
Swinging," *Gonzaga Law Review* 30 (1994): 433.

7. Victor S. Sze, "A Tale of Three Strikes Slogan Triumphs over Substance as
Our Bumper-Sticker Mentality Comes Home to Roost," *Loyola of Los Angeles
Law Review* 28, no. 3 (1995): 1047, 1053–57 & n. 54.

8. Philip Heymann, remarks during C-Span broadcast, C-Span, March 1,
1994, www.c-span.org/video/?54956-1/crime-legislation, at 1:15.

9. William J. Eaton, "House Approves Crime Bill, 285-141: Congress:
$28-Billion Measure Would Add More Police, Build More Prisons, Expand
Death Penalty. The Vote Sends the Legislation to Be Reconciled with Senate
Version," *Los Angeles Times*, April 22, 1994, www.latimes.com/archives/la-xpm
-1994-04-22-mn-49015-story.html.

10. DeNeen L. Brown, "For Clinton, Questions from the Heart," *Washington Post*, March 20, 1994; "President Clinton Answering Children's Questions," ABC News, March 19, 1994, www.youtube.com/watch?v=Tbjnk
_jYn90&t=1s.

11. Jennifer K. Wood, "In Whose Name? Victims' Rights Policy and the
Punishing Power of Protection," *2005 NWSA Journal* 17, no. 3 (Autumn
2005): 12.

12. "California Proposition 184, Three Strikes Sentencing Initia-

tive (1994)," Ballotpedia, ballotpedia.org/California_Proposition_184, _Three_Strikes_Sentencing_Initiative_(1994).

13. Prison Policy Initiative, "Three Strikes Laws: Five Years Later," 1998 https://static.prisonpolicy.org/scans/sp/3strikes.pdf.

14. Annie and Jess Nichol, interview by the author, January 15, 2021.

15. "The Three Strikes and You're Out Law," California Legislative Analyst's Office, February 22, 1995, lao.ca.gov/analysis_1995/3strikes.html.

16. E. Ann Carson and Joseph Mulako-Wangota. Count of total jurisdiction population, generated using the Corrections Statistical Analysis Tool (CSAT)—Prisoners at Bureau of Justice Statistics, January 10, 2022, www.bjs .gov.

17. Findings of Fact and Conclusions of Law re Appointment of Receiver, *Plata v. Schwarzenegger*, No. C01-1351 TEH CLASS ACTION (N.D. Cal. Oct. 3, 2005), pp. 1–2, casetext.com/case/plata-v-schwarzenegger-29.

18. Annie and Jess Nichol, interview by the author, January 15, 2021.

19. Ibid.

20. Barry W. Hancock and Paul Sharp, *Criminal Justice in America: Theory, Practice and Policy*, 3rd ed. (Hoboken, NJ: Prentice Hall, 2003), 16–35; see also *The History of the Crime Victims Movement in the United States*, Office for Victims of Crime Oral History Project, December 2004, www.ncjrs.gov /ovc_archives/ncvrw/2005/pg4c.html.

21. Frank G. Carrington and Wayne W. Schmidt, "The Man Who Swam Upstream," *Journal of Criminal Law and Criminology* 68, no. 2 (Summer 1977), scholarlycommons.law.northwestern.edu/cgi/viewcontent .cgi?article=6017&context=jclc.

22. Judith Greene, "Getting Tough On Crime: The History and Political Context of Sentencing Reform Developments Leading to the Passage of the 1994 Crime Act," in C. Tata and N. Hutton (eds.), *Sentencing and Society: International Perspectives*, p. 10 (England: Ashgate Publishing Limited, 2002).

23. Elizabeth Hinton, *From the War on Poverty to the War on Crime* (Harvard: Harvard University Press, 2016), 139–41; National Research Council, *The Growth of Incarceration in the United States: Exploring Causes and Consequences* (Washington, DC: The National Academies Press, 2014), 78–85, doi.org/10 .17226/18613; Julilly Kohler-Hausmann, "'The Attila the Hun Law': New York's Rockefeller Drug Laws and the Making of a Punitive State," *Journal of Social History* (2010): 71–95.

24. L.A. Addington and C.M. Rennison, "U.S. National Crime Victimization Survey," in *Encyclopedia of Criminology and Criminal Justice*, ed. G. Bruinsma and D. Weisburd (New York: Springer, 2014), doi.org/10.1007/978 -1-4614-5690-2_448.

25. See Gillian Greensite, "History of the Rape Crisis Movement and Sexual

Violence Prevention," PreventConnect, 2003, wiki.preventconnect.org/history
-of-the-rape-crisis-movement-and-sexual-violence-prevention.

26. For an analysis of these campaigns, see Donna Coker, "Crime Control
and Feminist Law Reform in Domestic Violence Law: A Critical Review," *Buf-
falo Criminal Law Review* 4, no. 2 (2001): 801–60.

27. Marie Gottschalk, *Caught: The Prison State and the Lockdown of American
Politics* (Princeton, NJ: Princeton University Press, 2014), 274–76.

28. Los Angeles Times Staff, "'Good Samaritan' Bill Signed by Governor,"
Los Angeles Times, July 22, 1965, p. 3.

29. Kathleen A. Cairns, *The Case of Rose Bird; Gender, Politics and the California Courts* (Lincoln, Nebraska, and London: University of Nebraska Press,
2016) 1–3, 150–95.

30. Patrick K. Brown, "The Rise and Fall of Rose Bird: A Career Killed by
the Death Penalty" (master's thesis, California State University, Fullerton,
2007), www.cschs.org/wp-content/uploads/2014/03/CSCHS_2007-Brown
.pdf.

31. See Michael C. Campbell, "The Emergence of Penal Extremism in California: A Dynamic View of Institutional Structures and Political Processes,"
Law & Society Review 48, no. 2 (2014): 377–409, http://www.jstor.org/stable
/43670397.

32. Candace McCoy, *Politics and Plea Bargaining: Victims' Rights in California* (Philadelphia: University of Pennsylvania Press, 1993), 21–39.

33. California Proposition 8, Victims' Bill of Rights (June 1982), ballotpedia
.org/California_Proposition_8,_Victims%27_Bill_of_Rights_(June_1982).

34. Ibid.

35. Michael C. Campbell, "The Emergence of Penal Extremism in California: A Dynamic View of Institutional Structures and Political Processes," *Law
& Society Review* 48, no. 2 (2014): 377–409.

36. McCoy, *Politics and Plea Bargaining*, 28–32.

37. Ibid.

38. Ronald Reagan, "Remarks on Signing Executive Order 12360, Establishing the President's Task Force on Victims of Crime," Ronald Reagan Presidential Library & Museum, April 23, 1982, www.reaganlibrary.gov/archives
/speech/remarks-signing-executive-order-12360-establishing-presidents-task
-force-victims.

39. Louis Haight Herrington et. al., *Final Report of the President's Task
Force on Victims of Crime* (December 1982), pp. 16–18, ovc.ojp.gov/library
/publications/final-report-presidents-task-force-victims-crime.

40. John Hurst, "The Big House That Don Novey Built: Working the PR,
Spreading Big Bucks, a Canny Union Boss Demands More Prisons and Top
Pay for His Guards," *Los Angeles Times*, February 6, 1994.

41. See Heather Ann Thompson, "Downsizing the Carceral State: The

Policy Implications of Prison Guard Unions," *Criminology and Public Policy* 10 (2011): 771–80.

42. Dan Boyd, *Compensation Analysis: California Correctional Peace Officers Bargaining Unit 6,* Govern for California, January 6, 2022, governforcalifornia.org/research/2022/1/6/compensation-analysis-california-correctional -peace-officers-bargaining-unit-6.

43. "CCPOA Information Sheet," Center on Juvenile and Criminal Justice (August 2011), p. 2, www.cjcj.org/uploads/cjcj/documents /CCPOA_Information_Sheet.pdf.

44. Penne Usher, "A Precious Life Was Taken Too Young," Gold Country Media, November 3, 2006, goldcountrymedia.com/news/105835/a-precious -life-was-taken-too-young.

45. Bill Ainsworth, "A Marriage of Convenience," *Sacramento Bee*, December 11, 1994, sacbee.newspapers.com/image/626713526.

46. Ibid.

47. Ibid.

48. See CCPOA website, "California Correctional Peace Officers Association Representing the Men and Women Who Walk the Toughest Beat in the State," www.ccpoa.org.

49. Ibid.

50. Ibid.

51. "CCPOA Information Sheet," Center on Juvenile and Criminal Justice (August 2011), p. 2, www.cjcj.org/uploads/cjcj/documents/CCPOA _Information_Sheet.pdf.

52. David Cox, "You Will Do More Time for a Gun Crime Gov. Bush Signed the Get-Tough Measure That Sets Tougher Minimum Sentences for Criminal Gunmen," *Orlando Sentinel*, April 1, 1999, www.proquest.com /docview/279281845.

53. Ibid.

54. Transcript of Hearing on SB 1462 before the California Senate Committee on Public Safety, Senator Loni Hancock, Chair, 2011–12 Regular Session, April 17, 2012.

55. Ibid.

56. Robert Rooks, interviewed by the author, August 14, 2020.

57. Robert Rooks, "Lack of Humanity Makes Justice System More Dangerous for Blacks Long Before Cops Interact: Victims of Crimes Too Often Made to Feel like Suspects. Spend Less Money on Police, Prisons and More on Treatment, Communities," *USA Today*, June 9, 2020.

58. The account here and on the following two pages is from Robert Rooks, interviewed by the author, August 14, 2020.

59. Annie and Jess Nichol, interviewed by the author, January 15, 2021.

60. Annie Nichol and Jess Nichol, "Op-Ed: Polly Klaas Was Our Sister. We Don't Want Unjust Laws to Be Her Legacy," *Los Angeles Times*, October 18, 2020.

61. Madison Feller, "Their Sister's Murder Was Used to Justify Tough on Crime Laws. Now They Want to Build Her a Different Legacy," *Elle*, February 25, 2022.

Chapter 3: Victims Seen and Unseen

1. *Singleton v. Cannizzaro*, United States District Court for the Eastern District of Louisiana, United States, 2017 DKT No. 2:17-cv-10721, www.aclu .org/legal-document/singleton-v-cannizzaro-complaint.

2. Interview of Renata Singleton appears in "New Orleans DA Jailed Crime Victims," ACLU of Louisiana, n.d., www.aclu.org/video/new-orleans-da-jailed -crime-victims.

3. Ibid.

4. Interview of Renata Singleton appears in "New Orleans DA Jailed Crime Victims," ACLU of Louisiana, n.d., www.aclu.org/video/new-orleans-da-jailed -crime-victims.

5. Sarah Stillman, "Why Are Prosecutors Putting Innocent Witnesses in Jail?" *New Yorker*, October 17, 2017.

6. American Civil Liberties Union of Louisiana, Civil Rights Corp and ACLU Sue District Attorney Leon Cannizzaro to End the Coercion and Jailing of Crime Victims and Witnesses Based on Fake, Illegal Subpoenas and False Information Provided to the Courts (October 17, 2017), www.laaclu .org/en/press-releases/civil-rights-corps-and-aclu-sue-district-attorney-leon -cannizzaro.

7. Ibid.

8. Rebecca Woolington, "Prosecutor: Alleged Victim Jailed in Prison Sex Misconduct Case Is 'Complicit,'" *Oregonian/OregonLive*, September 16, 2016, updated January 9, 2019, www.oregonlive.com/hillsboro/2016/09 /prosecutor_alleged_victim_comp.html.

9. *Trafficking in Persons Report, 20th Edition*, U.S. Department of State, June 2020, www.state.gov/wp-content/uploads/2020/06/2020-TIP-Report -Complete-062420-FINAL.pdf.

10. William Goodall, *The American Slave Code in Theory and Practice: Its Distinctive Features* (New York: American and Foreign Anti-slavery Society, 1853).

11. Lawrence M. Friedman, *A History of American Law*, 4th ed. (New York: Oxford University Press, 2019), 11.

12. Ibid., 18–21.

13. Thomas D. Morris, *Southern Slavery and the Law, 1619–1860* (Chapel Hill: University of North Carolina Press, 1996), 37–58.

14. Peter Kolchin, *American Slavery: 1619–1877* (New York: Hill and Wang, 1993); Brenda E. Stevenson, *What Is Slavery?* (Malden, MA: Polity Press, 2015).

15. Edward Baptist, *The Half Has Never Been Told* (New York: Basic Books, 2014); Ariela Gross, *Double Character* (Princeton, NJ: Princeton University Press, 2000); Edward L. Ayers, *Vengeance and Justice: Crime and Punishment in the 19th Century American South* (Oxford: Oxford University Press, 1984).

16. Morris, *Southern Slavery and the Law,* 161–71.

17. Private prosecution gave way to public justice gradually and unevenly in different jurisdictions. According to some scholars, victims maintained some prosecutorial powers throughout much of the nineteenth century. See ibid., 276–77; Juan Cardenas, "The Crime Victim in the Prosecutorial Process," *Harvard Journal of Law & Public Policy* 9, no. 2 (Spring 1986): 357–98; and Douglas E. Beloof and Paul G. Cassell, "The Crime Victim's Right to Attend the Trial: The Reascendant National Consensus," *Lewis & Clark Law Review* 9, no. 3 (Fall 2005): 481–546.

18. Friedman, *A History of American Law,* 276–77; Daniel J. Flanigan, "Criminal Procedure in Slave Trials in the Antebellum South," *Journal of Southern History* 40, no. 4 (1974): 537–64.

19. A vast body of scholarship highlights the violence enslaved people experienced, their resistance to oppression, and remarkable demonstrations of human resilience. For a few examples, see Edward Baptist, *The Half Has Never Been Told: Slavery and the Making of American Capitalism* (New York: Basic Books, 2014); Daina Ramey Berry, *The Price for Their Pound of Flesh: The Value of the Enslaved, from Womb to Grave, in the Building of a Nation* (Boston: Beacon, 2017); Stephanie M.H. Camp, *Closer to Freedom: Enslaved Women and Everyday Resistance in the Plantation South* (Chapel Hill: University of North Carolina Press, 2005); Walter Johnson, *Soul by Soul: Life Inside the Antebellum Slave Market* (Cambridge, MA: Harvard University Press, 1999); and Eugene D. Genovese, *Roll, Jordan, Roll: The World the Slaves Made* (New York: Pantheon Books, 1974).

20. Gross, *Double Character,* 114–16.

21. Euguene Genovese, *From Rebellion to Revolution* (Baton Rouge: Louisiana State University Press, 1979).

22. Melton McLaurin, *Celia, a Slave: A True Story* (Athens: University of Georgia Press, 1991); see also Ta-Nehisi Coates, "The Black Family in the Age of Mass Incarceration," *Atlantic,* October 2015.

23. Ibid.

24. Kate Masur, *Until Justice Be Done: America's First Civil Rights Movement, from the Revolution to Reconstruction* (New York: W.W. Norton, 2021).

25. Alfred Avins, "Anti-miscegenation Law and the Fourteenth Amendment: The Original Intent," *Virginia Law Review* 52, no. 7 (November 1966): 1224–55.

26. The historian Ariela Gross calls this legal contradiction *double character*:

enslaved people were at once property *and* people in the eyes of courts. See Gross, *Double Character*.

27. Daniel J. Flanigan, "Criminal Procedure in Slave Trials in the Antebellum South," *Journal of Southern History* 40, no. 4 (1974): 537–64, doi.org/10.2307/2206354.

28. Alfred Avins, "The Right to Be a Witness and the Fourteenth Amendment," *Missouri Law Review* 31, no. 4 (Fall 1966): 471–504, scholarship.law.missouri.edu/mlr/vol31/iss4/1.

29. See Gross, *Double Character*, 66–71.

30. Estelle B. Freedman, *Redefining Rape* (Cambridge, MA: Harvard University Press, 2013).

31. Aaron O'Neill, *Black and Slave Population in the United States from 1790 to 1880*, Statista, March 19, 2021, www.statista.com/statistics/1010169/black-and-slave-population-us-1790-1880.

32. Gross, *Double Character*, 112.

33. Joan R. Gundersen and Gwen Victor Gampel, "Married Women's Legal Status in Eighteenth-Century New York and Virginia," The Family in Early American History and Culture, *William and Mary Quarterly* 39, no. 1 (January 1982): 114–34, www.jstor.org/stable/1923419.

34. Gross, *Double Character*, 112.

35. Linda Gordon, *Heroes of Their Own Lives: The Politics and History of Family Violence* (Urbana: University of Illinois Press, 2002).

36. *State v. A. B. Rhodes*, Supreme Court of North Carolina, Raleigh. 61 N.C. 453 January 1868, la.utexas.edu/users/jmciver/357L/61NC453.html.

37. For an account of progressive era efforts to establish more protections, see Michael Willrich, *City of Courts: Socializing Justice in Progressive Era Chicago* (Cambridge: Cambridge University Press, 2003).

38. Gordon, *Heroes of Their Own Lives*, 217–18.

39. Frederick W. Benteen to Theodore Goldin, 14 February and 17 February 1896, quoted in Sherry L. Smith, "Beyond Princess and Squaw: Army Officers' Perceptions of Indian Women," in *The Women's West*, ed. Susan Armitage and Elizabeth Jameson (Norman: University of Oklahoma Press, 1987), 70.

40. For instance, a California law barred testimony "against any white man by African Americans, mulattoes, and Indians." In 1862, the California Supreme Court ruled in *Ling Sing v. Washburn* that, based upon that statute, a Chinese witness could not testify against a white man accused of murder. After George Hall was convicted of the murder of Ling Sing, based on the testimony of three Chinese witnesses, Hall's lawyer argued that the California statute barring testimony by "African Americans, mulattoes, and Indians" applied to *all* nonwhites. The court concurred, stating, "We are of the opinion that the words 'white,' 'Negro,' 'mulatto,' 'Indian,' and 'black person,' wherever they occur in our Constitution and laws, must be taken in their generic sense, and that, even

admitting the Indian of this continent is not of the Mongolian type, that the words 'black person,' in the 14th section, must be taken as contradistinguished from white, and necessary excludes all races other than the Caucasian." For an overview of Native American legal rights, see Bethany R. Berger, "Red: Racism and the American Indian," *UCLA Law Review* 56 (2008): 591. For details of treaty rights negotiated in different colonies and in different nations, see Alden T. Vaughan, *Early American Indian Documents: Treaties and Laws, 1607–1789* (Washington, DC: University Publications of America, 1979).

41. Eric Foner, *Reconstruction: America's Unfinished Revolution, 1863–1877* (New York: Harper and Row, 1988).

42. Leon Litwack, *Trouble in Mind: Black Southerners in the Age of Jim Crow* (New York: Knopf, 1998), 253.

43. Ibid, 254.

44. Alfred Avins, "Right to Be a Witness," 471–504.

45. Jeffrey S. Adler, "Less Crime, More Punishment: Violence, Race, and Criminal Justice in Early Twentieth-Century America," *Journal of American History* 102, no. 1 (June 2015), doi.org/10.1093/jahist/jav173.

46. Freedman, *Redefining Rape*, 41–43, 50–51, 154.

47. Danielle McGuire, *At the Dark End of the Street: Black Women, Rape, and Resistance—A New History of the Civil Rights Movement from Rosa Parks to the Rise of Black Power* (New York: Knopf, 2010).

48. Ibid.

49. Litwack, *Trouble in Mind*, 269.

50. Equal Justice Institute, *Lynching in America: Confronting the Legacy of Racial Terror*, 3rd ed., 2015, lynchinginamerica.eji.org/report.

51. Manfred Berg, *Popular Justice: A History of Lynching in America* (New York: Rowman & Littlefield, 2015, 2011), 153.

52. Litwack, *Trouble in Mind*, 278.

Chapter 4: A Tale of Two Cities

1. Lauren Eagan, "Biden to Visit Tulsa to Commemorate 100th Anniversary of Tulsa Race Massacre: The Attack, One of the Worst Incidents of Racial Violence in American History, Has for Years Been Ignored on the National Level," NBCNews.com, May 25, 2021.

2. See *Tulsa Race Riot: A Report by the Oklahoma Commission to Study the Tulsa Race Riot of 1921*, Final Report of the of Findings and Recommendations of the 1921 Tulsa Race Riot Commission, February 28, 2001, iv–v, 56–89, www.okhistory.org/research/forms/freport.pdf; see also "1921 Tulsa Race Massacre," Oklahoma Historical Society and Museum, and documents collected there, www.tulsahistory.org/exhibit/1921-tulsa-race-massacre.

3. Tulsa Race Riot Commission, *Tulsa Race Riot*, viii, 64–70.

4. Farrell Evans, "What Role Did Airplanes Play in the Tulsa Race Massacre?" History.com, May 13, 2021www.history.com/news/1921-tulsa-race-massacre-planes-aerial-attack; Tulsa Race Riot Commission, *Tulsa Race Riot*: 103–8.

5. Tulsa Race Riot Commission, *Tulsa Race Riot*, 11–12 ("People, some of them agents of government, also deliberately burned or otherwise destroyed homes credibly estimated to have numbered 1,256, along with virtually every other structure—including churches, schools, businesses, even a hospital and library—in the Greenwood district").

6. Walter White, "The Eruption of Tulsa," *Nation* 112 (June 29, 1921): 909–10, reprinted at historymatters.gmu.edu/d/5119.

7. Alexis Clark, "How the Tulsa Race Massacre Was Covered Up: A Search for Mass Graves of the Victims of the 1921 Tulsa Race Massacre Highlights an Event That Some Had Tried to Erase from History," History.com, January 27, 2021, www.history.com/news/tulsa-race-massacre-cover-up.

8. Tulsa Race Riot Commission, *Tulsa Race Riot*; Oklahoma Historical Society, "1921 Tulsa Race Massacre."

9. Tulsa Race Riot Commission, *Tulsa Race Riot*, 13.

10. Randy Krehbiel, "Tulsa Race Massacre: In Aftermath, No One Prosecuted for Killings, and Insurance Claims Were Rejected but Greenwood Persevered," *Tulsa World*, May 31, 2020, updated July 6, 2021, tulsaworld.com/news/local/racemassacre/tulsa-race-massacre-in-aftermath-no-one-prosecuted-for-killings-and-insurance-claims-were-rejected/article_3ba23c3c-886d-5821-9970-02153261960a.html.

11. "Convict Tulsa Police Chief, Jury Blames Him for Terrible Death Toll: Class Him as Modern Nero; He Laughed While Tulsa Burned," *Chicago Whip*, July 30, 1921, front page.

12. Randy Krehbiel, "Tulsa Race Massacre: In Aftermath, No One Prosecuted for Killings, and Insurance Claims Were Rejected but Greenwood Persevered," *Tulsa World*, May 31, 2020, updated July 6, 2021, tulsaworld.com/news/local/racemassacre/tulsa-race-massacre-in-aftermath-no-one-prosecuted-for-killings-and-insurance-claims-were-rejected/article_3ba23c3c-886d-5821-9970-02153261960a.html.

13. Tulsa Race Riot Commission, *Tulsa Race Riot*, 144–45 and note 4.

14. Krehbiel, "Tulsa Race Massacre," *Tulsa World*.

15. See "The Case for Reparations in Tulsa, Oklahoma: A Human Rights Argument," Human Rights Watch, May 29, 2020, www.hrw.org/news/2020/05/29/case-reparations-tulsa-oklahoma#.

16. See "Oklahoma City Bombing," U.S. Department of Justice, Federal Bureau of Investigation, www.fbi.gov/history/famous-cases/oklahoma-city-bombing; see also "An Investigation of the Belated Production of Documents in the Oklahoma City Bombing Case," U.S. Department of Justice, Office

of the Inspector General, March 19, 2002, oig.justice.gov/sites/default/files
/archive/special/0203/chapter1.htm.

17. Sarah Pruitt, "How Ruby Ridge and Waco Led to the Oklahoma City
Bombing," History.com, May 22, 2018, updated April 2, 2020, www.history
.com/news/how-ruby-ridge-and-waco-led-to-the-oklahoma-city-bombing.

18. "Oklahoma City Bombing," U.S. Department of Justice, Federal Bureau
of Investigation.

19. Ibid.

20. Ibid.

21. Jody L. Madeira, "When It's So Hard to Relate: Can the Legal System
Mitigate the Trauma of Victim-Offender Relationships?" 46 *Houston L. Rev.*
401 (2009–2010): 434.

22. Victim Rights Clarification Act of 1997, Pub. L. No. 105-6, 111 Stat. 12
(codified as amended at 18 U.S.C. § 3510 (2006)). See also Jody L. Madeira,
"When It's So Hard to Relate: Can the Legal System Mitigate the Trauma of
Victim-Offender Relationships?": 434 and note 152, citing David E. Aaronson,
"New Rights and Remedies: The Federal Crime Victim Rights Act of 2004,"
28 Pace L. Rev. 623 (2008): 629 (explaining the origins of the Victim Rights
Clarification Act of 1997).

23. Jill Lepore, "The Rise of the Victims'-Rights Movement: How a Conservative Agenda and a Feminist Cause Came Together to Transform Criminal
Justice," *New Yorker*, May 21, 2018, www.newyorker.com/magazine/2018/05
/21/the-rise-of-the-victims-rights-movement.

24. Kaila Hale-Stern, "This Live Stream of Gymnasts Describing Their Sexual Assault in Court Is Hard to Watch but Incredibly Important," *The Mary Sue*,
January 22, 2018, www.themarysue.com/victim-impact-statements-nassar.
Victim impact statements can be important for victims to receive recognition
within the criminal justice system, but these statements also suffer from the
same hierarchy of harm dynamics found in every aspect of American justice:
racial, gender, and class bias that filters which impact statements are deemed
compelling and which are not. They have also been critiqued as inappropriate
for influencing sentencing, even if they have value in giving voice to victim
experiences. For criticisms of victim impact statements, see Rebecca Makkai,
"The Power and Limitations of Victim-Impact Statements," *New Yorker*,
June 8, 2016, www.newyorker.com/culture/culture-desk/the-power-and
-limitations-of-victim-impact-statements; Susan Bandes, "What Are Victim-
Impact Statements For?," *The Atlantic*, July 23, 2016, www.theatlantic.com
/politics/archive/2016/07/what-are-victim-impact-statements-for/492443;
Erin Shelley, "Reverberations of the Victim's 'Voice': Victim Impact Statements and the Cultural Project of Punishment," *Indiana Law Journal* 87, no. 3
(2012); Riannon Davies and Lorana Bartels, "The Use of Victim Impact Statements in Sexual Offence Sentencing: A Critique of Judicial Practice," *Criminal
Law Journal* 45 (2021): 168–84.

25. U.S. Department of Justice Office of Justice Programs Office for Victims

of Crime, *Responding to Terrorism Victims: Oklahoma City and Beyond*, October 2000, ovc.ojp.gov/sites/g/files/xyckuh226/files/media/document/ncj183949 .pdf.

26. Penny Owen, "Bombing Victims, Family Members Find Haven in Denver Organizers Try to Ease Trial's Stress," *The Oklahoman*, March 26, 1997, oklahoman.com/story/news/1997/03/26/bombing-victims-family-members -find-haven-in-denver-organizers-try-to-ease-trials-stress/62319814007; "Ordinary People Doing Extraordinary Things: A Report to the Community," Oklahoma City Disaster Relief Fund, September, 1996, www.occf.org /publications/okcdisasterrelief.pdf; Keara Pringle, "Coping with the Oklahoma City Bombing: Emphasizing Ideas of Rescue and Recovery in the Face of Tragedy for Children," *Prologue: A First-Year Writing Journal* 2, article 10: 38 (2010), digitalcommons.denison.edu/cgi/viewcontent.cgi?article=1037&co ntext=prologue; Associated Press, "A Nation Challenged: The Victims; Oklahomans Questioning Sept. 11 Aid," *New York Times*, December 23, 2001.

27. U.S. Department of Justice Office of Justice Programs Office for Victims of Crime, *Responding to Terrorism Victims: Oklahoma City and Beyond*, October 2000, ovc.ojp.gov/sites/g/files/xyckuh226/files/media/document/ncj183949 .pdf.

28. U.S. Department of Justice Office of Justice Programs Office for Victims of Crime, *Responding to Terrorism Victims*.

29. Office of Victims of Crime Fact Sheet, Crime Victims Fund, www.ncjrs .gov/ovc_archives/factsheets/cvf2010/intro.html#go2.

30. "9/11 Victim Compensation Fund Pay over 2.6 Billion to Date," U.S. Department of Justice Press Release, April 1, 2004, www.justice.gov/archive /opa/pr/2004/April/04_civ_207.htm.

31. Keynote address of Janet Reno, U.S. Attorney General, at the Adams Mark Hotel, Tulsa, Oklahoma (August 15, 1996): 6, 28, www.justice.gov /archive/ag/speeches/1996/08-15-1996.pdf.

Chapter 5: Good Victims, Bad Victims

1. Pete Baroni, interviewed by the author, July 13, 2021.

2. Ibid.

3. Suzy Loftus, interview by the author, June 22, 2021; Lauren Smiley, "Trial by Fire," *SF Weekly*, May 27, 2009, www.sfweekly.com/news/trial-by -fire.

4. Suzy Loftus, interview by the author, June 22, 2021.

5. The Florida Supreme Court's Gender Bias Study Implementation Commission of 1994–96, *Gender Bias—Then and Now*, footnote 7, page 5, citing Stacey Kabat, remarks from presentation at Harvard School of Public Health, Center for Health Communication, June 1991, www.flcourts.org/content /download/218236/file/1996RPT.pdf.

6. Allison Bass, "Women Far Less Likely to Kill Than Men; No One Sure Why," *Boston Globe*, February 24, 1992, p. 27, as cited in Caroline Gillis, "Domestic Violence and Self-Defense: Respecting Women's Autonomy by Creating a Woman-Centered Law of Self-Defense," Digital Commons @ American University Washington College of Law, 2020, page 1.

7. Bryan Robinson, "Mystery Over 'Other' Missing Girl," ABC News, June 21, 2002.

8. Mark Johnson and Annysa Johnson, "2 Missing Girls' Cases Show Media Disparity: Alexis Gets Little Notice; Utah Girl Widely Covered," *Milwaukee Journal Sentinel*, June 15, 2002, archive.jsonline.com/news/milwaukee/2-missing-girls-cases-show-media-disparity-385118501.html.

9. Scripps Howard News Service, "News Coverage Ignoring Missing Minority Children," *Gainesville Sun*, December 2, 2005, www.gainesville.com/news/20051202/news-coverage-ignoring-missing-minority-children [https://perma.cc/WLA3-VL8N]; Seong-Jae Min and John C. Feaster, "Missing Children in National News Coverage: Racial and Gender Representations of Missing Children Cases," *Communication Research Reports* 27, no. 3 (2010): 207–16; C. Simmons and J. Woods, "The Overrepresentation of White Missing Children in National Television News," *Communication Research Reports* 32, no. 3 (2015): 239–42.

10. Studies collected in Jada L. Moss, "The Forgotten Victims of Missing White Woman Syndrome: An Examination of Legal Measures That Contribute to the Lack of Search and Recovery of Missing Black Girls and Women," *William and Mary Journal of Women and the Law* 25, no. 3 (2018–2019), scholarship.law.wm.edu/wmjowl/vol25/iss3/9; see also Arnout van de Rijt, Hyang-Gi Song, Eran Shor, and Rebekah Burroway, "Racial and Gender Differences in Missing Children's Recovery Chances," *PLOS ONE*, December 31, 2018, doi.org/10.1371/journal.pone.0207742.

11. Tracy Everbach, "Women's (mis) Representation in News Media," in *Media Disparity: A Gender Battleground*, ed. Cory L. Armstrong (Lanham, MD: Lexington, 2013): 15, 21.

12. See *2018 NCIC Missing Person and Unidentified Person Statistics*, National Crime Information Center, www.fbi.gov/file-repository/2018-ncic-missing-person-and-unidentified-person-statistics.pdf/view.

13. Simmons and Woods, "Overrepresentation of White Missing Children," 239–45.

14. Harmeet Kaur, "Black Kids Go Missing at a Higher Rate Than White Kids. Here's Why We Don't Hear About Them," CNN, November 3, 2019, cnn.com/2019/11/03/us/missing-children-of-color-trnd/index.html.

15. Cheryl L. Neely, *You're Dead—So What?: Media, Police, and the Invisibility of Black Women as Victims of Homicide* (East Lansing: Michigan State University Press, 2015).

16. K. White, F. Stuart, and S.L. Morrissey, "Whose Lives Matter? Race,

Space, and the Devaluation of Homicide Victims in Minority Communities," *Sociology of Race and Ethnicity* 7, no. 3 (2021): 333–49, doi:10.1177/2332649220948184.

17. C.T. Harris and J. Gruenewald, *News Media Trends in the Framing of Immigration and Crime, 1990–2013* (2019).

18. G.C. Ousey and C.E. Kubrin, "Immigration and Crime: Assessing a Contentious Issue," *Annual Review of Criminology* 1 (2018): 63–84; P. Orrenius and M. Zavodny, "Do Immigrants Threaten US Public Safety" (2019); M.T. Light and T. Miller, "Does Undocumented Immigration Increase Violent Crime?" *Criminology* 56, no. 2 (2018): 370–401; A. Nowrasteh, "Immigration and Crime—What the Research Says" (Cato Institute, 2015); A. Flagg, "Is There a Connection Between Undocumented Immigrants and Crime?" (The Marshall Project, 2019).

19. F. Wood, A. Carrillo, and E. Monk-Turner, "Visibly Unknown: Media Depiction of Murdered Transgender Women of Color," *Race and Justice* 1-19 (2019), www.researchgate.net/publication/337770819_Visibly_Unknown_Media_Depiction_of_Murdered_Transgender_Women_of_Color.

20. D. Perry, "On Media Coverage of the Murder of People with Disabilities by Their Caregivers," 2019, rudermanfoundation.org/wp-content/uploads/2017/08/Murders-by-Caregivers-WP_final_final.pdf.

21. Julie Carr Smyth, "Black Victims Underrepresented in Named Violent Crime Laws," Associated Press, December 3, 2019, apnews.com/article/us-news-ap-top-news-laws-cleveland-crime-30d5a2a0b8464aec9593f4918cfa51d4.

22. William Glaberson, "Stranger on the Block—A Special Report: At Center of 'Megan's Law' Case, a Man No One Could Reach," *New York Times*, May 28, 1996.

23. Rich Shapiro, "Parents of Little Girl Who Inspired Megan's Law Recall Brutal Rape, Murder of Their Daughter 20 Years Later," *New York Daily News*, July 27, 2014.

24. Lakeidra Chavis and Daniel Nass, "Illinois Has a Program to Compensate Victims of Violent Crimes. Few Applicants Receive Funds. Less Than 40 Percent of Applicants Are Compensated, but Many More Never Apply in the First Place," *Trace*, July 9, 2021, www.thetrace.org/2021/07/illinois-violent-crime-victim-compensation-application-data.

25. Californians for Safety and Justice, *Los Angeles County Crime Victim Survey*, February 2021.

26. Ray Winans, interviewed by the author, July 18, 2021.

27. Amnesty International, *Scars of Survival, Gun Violence and Barriers to Reparation in the USA*, 2019, 29–32.

28. Ray Winans, interviewed by the author, July 18, 2021.

29. Ibid.

30. Ibid.

31. Ibid.

32. Alysia Santo, "The Victims Who Don't Count: Seven States Won't Give Victim Aid to People with Criminal Histories. The Policies Fall Hardest on Black Families," The Marshall Project, September 13, 2018, www .themarshallproject.org/2018/09/13/the-victims-who-don-t-count.

33. Alisia Santo, "States Have Money to Help Victims of Crime but Seven Ban Aid for People with Criminal Records. A Close Look at Two Reveals It Hurts Black Families the Most," The Marshall Project, September 13, 2018, www.themarshallproject.org/2018/09/13/the-victims-who-don-t-count. The law has changed in two states since the publication of this article.

34. Public records request, Alliance for Safety and Justice, January 2021.

35. Alameda County Grand Jury, "Final Report: Racial Inequities in Police Responses to Victims' Needs," 2021, grandjury.acgov.org/grandjury-assets /docs/2020-2021/Racial%20Disparities.pdf.

36. S. Andrews et al., *Post-Assault Healthcare and Crime Victim Compensation for Immigrant Victims of Violence—Medical Coverage and Services for Immigrants* (National Immigrant Women's Advocacy Project, American University, Washington College of Law, 2017).

37. N. Smith and C. Hope, *Helping Those Who Help Others: Key Findings from a Comprehensive Needs Assessment of the Crime Victims Field* (The National Resource Center for Reaching Victims, 2020).

38. National Coalition of Anti-Violence Programs, "Lesbian, Gay, Bisexual, Transgender, Queer, and HIV-Affected Intimate Partner Violence in 2015," 2016, avp.org/wp-content/uploads/2017/04/2015_ncavp_lgbtqipvreport.pdf.

39. S.E. James, J.L. Herman, S. Rankin et al., *The Report of the 2015 U.S. Transgender Survey* (Washington, DC: National Center for Transgender Equality, 2016), transequality.org/sites/default/files/docs/usts/USTS-Full -Report-Dec17.pdf.

40. N. Smith and C. Hope, *Culture, Language, and Access: Key Consideration for Serving Deaf Survivors of Domestic and Sexual Violence* (Vera Institute, Center on Victimization and Safety, 2015).

41. Illinois Criminal Justice Information Authority, *2016 Victim Needs Assessment*, 2017, www.icjia.state.il.us/assets/articles/2016_ICJIA_Victim _Needs_Assessment_Summary_Report.pdf.

42. Committee on the Revision of the Penal Code, *First Supplement to Memorandum 2022-02 Crime Victims' Rights and Services Panelist Materials*, www.clrc.ca.gov/CRPC/Pub/Memos/CRPC22-02s1.pdf.

43. Analysis of US Department of Justice, *Office for Victims of Crime, FY 2019 Annual Performance Measures Reports—Victim Compensation Formula Grant Program*, fifty state and District of Columbia reports, ovc.ojp.gov/states.

44. Office for Victims of Crime, *Victims of Crime Act Compensation Grant Program: Fiscal Year 2019 Data Analysis Report*, ovc.ojp.gov/sites/g/files

/xyckuh226/files/media/document/fy-2019-voca-compensation-performance
-report.pdf.

45. Office for Victims of Crime, *Victims of Crime Act Victim Assistance
Formula Grant Program: Fiscal Year 2019 Data Analysis Report*, ovc.ojp.gov
/sites/g/files/xyckuh226/files/media/document/fy-2019-voca-assistance
-performance-report.pdf; see also Heather Warnken, "A Vision for Equity in
Victim Services: What Do the Data Tell Us About the Work Ahead?" video
presentation, U.S. Department of Justice, Office for Victims of Crime, June 8,
2021, ovc.ojp.gov/media/video/12971#transcript—0.

46. Ray Winans, interviewed by the author, July 18, 2021.

Chapter 6: Up Is Down and Down Is Up

1. Shakyra Diaz, interviewed by the author, August 13, 2020.

2. Ibid.

3. Ibid.

4. "Reinvestigating Rape: Old Evidence, New Answers," *Plain Dealer*,
Cleveland.com, www.cleveland.com/rape-kits; Rachel Dissell, "Cleveland
Sex Crime Unit's Persistent Problems Illuminated by Latest Investigation into
Unsubmitted Rape Kits," *Plain Dealer*, November 4, 2018, updated March 8,
2019, www.cleveland.com/metro/2018/11/cleveland-sex-crime-units-persistent
-problems-illuminated-by-latest-investigation-into-unsubmitted-rape-kits
.html.

5. Shakyra Diaz, interviewed by the author, August 13, 2020.

6. For an overview of the history of grand jury reports and racial disparity
in charging crack pipe cases in Cleveland, see Dan Harkins, "Disparate Times
Even Judges See the Disparities in Drug Prosecutions in Cuyahoga County,"
Cleveland Scene, June 30, 2008, www.clevescene.com/cleveland/disparate
-times/Content?oid=1520517.

7. Mona Lynch, "Crack Pipes and Policing: A Case Study of Institutional Racism and Remedial Action in Cleveland," *Law and Policy* 33 (2011):
179–214, doi.org/10.1111/j.1467-9930.2010.00334.x; see also "If You're Arrested for Drugs, You're More Likely to Get a Second Chance If You're White,"
Plain Dealer, Cleveland.com, October 19, 2008, updated January 13, 2019,
www.cleveland.com/metro/2008/10/race_and_drug_use.html.

8. "If You're Arrested for Drugs, You're More Likely to Get a Second Chance
If You're White," *Plain Dealer*, Cleveland.com, October 19, 2008, updated
January 13, 2019, www.cleveland.com/metro/2008/10/race_and_drug_use
.html; Mark Puente, "Cleveland Eases Charges for Some Crack-Pipe Cases,"
Plain Dealer, Cleveland.com, November 10, 2008, updated March 28, 2019,
www.cleveland.com/metro/2008/11/cleveland_adjusts_policy_for_c.html;
see also Mona Lynch, "Crack Pipes and Policing: A Case Study of Institu-

tional Racism and Remedial Action in Cleveland," *Law and Policy* 33 (2011): 179–214, doi.org/10.1111/j.1467-9930.2010.00334.x.

9. Shakyra Diaz, interviewed by the author, August 13, 2020.

10. Joel Rubin, "LAPD Clears Decades-Old Backlog of Untested DNA Evidence," *Los Angeles Times*, February 2, 2011; Joel Rubin, "LAPD Closes Backlog of Untested Rape Kits," *Los Angeles Times*, April 28, 2011.

11. Lee Romney and Kevin Johnson, "O.C. Making Drugs for Officers to Sell: Santa Ana Police Arrest 350 Small Buyers in 'Reverse Stings' After Taking the Crack Cocaine to Streets," *Los Angeles Times*, October 20, 1994.

12. Ibid.

13. National, statewide, and local homicide and clearance rates for 1990 to 2010 are available via the Federal Bureau of Investigation Crime Data Explorer interactive comparative statistical tool, crime-data-explorer.fr.cloud.gov/pages /explorer/crime/crime-trend.

14. Sarah Favot, "What Cities Are Doing to Solve More Homicides," *Los Angeles Daily News*, December 26, 2015, updated August 28, 2017, www .dailynews.com/2015/12/26/what-cities-are-doing-to-solve-more-homicides; Dexter Filkins and Geoff Boucher, "Half of O.C. Killings Are Going Unsolved," *Los Angeles Times*, December 16, 1996.

15. *State v. Williams*, 623 So. 2d 462, Florida Supreme Court 1993, affirming *Kelly v. State*, 593 So. 2d 1060, Florida Dist. Court of Appeals, 4th Dist. 1992.

16. Fort Lauderdale is the county seat and largest city of Broward County. According to the Vera Institute of Justice, Broward County clearance rates for homicide and rape for 1990 through 1993 were: 1990–homicide 75%, rape 64.42%; 1991–homicide 83.53%, rape 66.96%; 1992–homicide 80%, rape 62.3%; 1993–homicide 75%, rape 50.38%. See arresttrends.vera.org /clearance-rates.

17. Eric Young and Alicia Di Rado, "Homicides in Santa Ana Tie Yearly Record: Crime: With Three Months Left to Go, Murders Already Equal the 59 Committed in 1991. Police Don't Know Why the Rate Is So High, But More Than Half the Cases Are Gang-Related," *Los Angeles Times*, September 16, 1993.

18. Max Felker-Kantor, *Policing Los Angeles: Race, Resistance, and the Rise of the LAPD* (Chapel Hill: University of North Carolina Press, 2018).

19. Ibid.

20. Simon Balto, *Occupied Territory: Policing Black Chicago from Red Summer to Black Power* (Chapel Hill: University of North Carolina Press, 2019), 159–60.

21. Ibid., 60.

22. Lieutenant Jean Delafuente, quoted in Emily Badger, "The Most Damning Passages in the New York Stop and Frisk Ruling," *Bloomberg CityLab*

(August 13, 2013), www.bloomberg.com/news/articles/2013-08-13/the-most
-damning-passages-in-the-new-york-stop-and-frisk-ruling.

23. Elizabeth Hinton, *From the War on Poverty to the War on Crime* (Harvard: Harvard University Press, 2016), 10–26.

24. Ibid., 2.

25. Ibid., 3.

26. Ibid., 4.

27. Ibid., 123, 220–48; 279–81.

28. Lauren-Brooke Eisen, "The Federal Funding That Fuels Mass Incarceration: Decades of Financial Incentives by the Federal Government Have Encouraged States and Cities to Put More People Behind Bars for Longer, with Devastating Results," Brennan Center for Justice at New York University School of Law, 2017, www.brennancenter.org/our-work/analysis-opinion /federal-funding-fuels-mass-incarceration.

29. Joel Brinkley, "Anti-Drug Law: Words, Deeds, Political Expediency," *New York Times*, October 27, 1986.

30. Ronald Reagan, "Remarks on Signing Anti-Drug Abuse Act of 1986," The American Presidency Project, www.presidency.ucsb.edu/documents /remarks-signing-the-anti-drug-abuse-act-1986.

31. Hinton, *From the War on Poverty*, 283.

32. City of Cleveland Department of Finance Single Audit reports showing federal grant monies received and expended, available on the city government website at www.clevelandohio.gov/CityofCleveland/Home/Government /CityAgencies/Finance/formsandpublication?field_category_forms_pubs _tid=All&title=audit&cck_multiple_field_remove_fields.

33. J. Dionne Jr., "Clinton Charges Bush with Inaction on Crime," *Washington Post*, April 22, 1992, www.washingtonpost.com/archive/politics/1992/04 /22/clinton-charges-bush-with-inaction-on-crime/8376b1c8-9582-4adb-b181 -99c561f31bfd.

34. For the program priorities of Department of Justice grants, see Bureau of Justice Assistance, Local Law Enforcement Blog Grants Program, May 24, 1996, www.ojp.gov/sites/g/files/xyckuh241/files/media/document/llebgfs.pdf; see also R. Cox and J.P. Cunningham, "Financing the War on Drugs: The Impact of Law Enforcement Grants on Racial Disparities in Drug Arrests," *Journal of Policy Analysis and Management* 40, no. 1 (2021): 191–224.

35. Ingrid Archie, interviewed by author, December 15, 2021; see also "Ingrid Archie's Story," My Prop 47, myprop47.org/share-my-story/ingrid -archies-story-light-switch-came.

36. Markus D. Dubber, *Victims in the War on Crime: The Use and Abuse of Victims' Rights* (New York: New York University Press, 2002), 32–92.

37. Dubber, *Victims in the War on Crime*, 14.

38. Arrests and Clearance Rates, OpenJustice, California Department of Justice, openjustice.doj.ca.gov/arrests/overview.html.

39. Mona Lynch, "Crack Pipes and Policing: A Case Study of Institutional Racism and Remedial Action in Cleveland," *Law and Policy* 33 (2011): 179–214, doi.org/10.1111/j.1467-9930.2010.00334.x.

40. See Nicole Fortier and Inimai Chettiar, *Success-Oriented Funding: Reforming Federal Criminal Justice Grants*, Brennan Center for Justice at New York University School of Law, 2014, www.brennancenter .org/sites/default/files/publications/Success-OrientedFunding-Reforming FederalCriminalJusticeGrants.pdf; see also *Drug Policy Alliance, Federal Byrne Grants: Drug War Funds Available for Drug Treatment*, Drug Policy Alliance, September 2010, drugpolicy.org/sites/default/files/FactSheet_ByrneJAG_Sept .%202010.pdf.

41. Amy E. Lerman and Vesla M. Weaver, *Arresting Citizenship: The Democratic Consequences of American Crime Control* (Chicago: University of Chicago Press, 2014), 51.

42. *Report of the Independent Commission on the Los Angeles Police Department*, Independent Commission on the Los Angeles Police Department, 1991, www.ojp.gov/ncjrs/virtual-library/abstracts/report-independent-commission -los-angeles-police-department-0.

43. Dubber, *Victims in the War on Crime*, 15–16.

44. See Carroll Bogert and Lynnell Hancock, "Superpredator: The Media Myth That Demonized a Generation of Black Youth," Marshall Project, www .themarshallproject.org/2020/11/20/superpredator-the-media-myth-that -demonized-a-generation-of-black-youth.

45. Howard N. Snyder and Melissa Sickmund, *Juvenile Offenders and Victims: 2006 National Report*, Washington, DC: U.S. Department of Justice, Office of Justice Programs, Office of Juvenile Justice and Delinquency Prevention, 2006, pp. 199 and 235.

46. John DiIulio, "The Coming of the Super-Predators," *Weekly Standard*, November 27, 1995, www.washingtonexaminer.com/weekly-standard/the -coming-of-the-super-predators.

47. See Bogert and Hancock, "Superpredator."

48. Hillary Clinton speech at Keene State College in Keene, NH, in 1996, C-SPAN, available at www.themarshallproject.org/2020/11/20/superpredator -the-media-myth-that-demonized-a-generation-of-black-youth.

49. Associated Press, "Dole Seeks to Get Tough on Young Criminals," *Los Angeles Times*, July 7, 1996, www.latimes.com/archives/la-xpm-1996-07-07 -mn-22017-story.html.

50. Crime Victims United, Measure 11, www.crimevictimsunited.org /measure11/index.htm.

51. The official arguments in support of Proposition 21 were signed by Maggie Elvey, assistant director, Crime Victims United; Grover Trask, president,

California District Attorneys Association; and Chief Richard Tefank, president, California Police Chiefs Association and are available at ballotpedia .org/California_Proposition_21,Treatment_of_Juvenile_Offenders_Init iative_(March_2000).

52. K.G. Muhammad, *The Condemnation of Blackness: Race, Crime, and the Making of Modern Urban America, with a New Preface* (Cambridge, MA: Harvard University Press, 2019).

53. Ibid., 146–61.

54. Ibid., 194.

55. Ibid., 198–204, 211–24.

56. Karen Farkas, "Anthony Sowell, Accused of Killing 11 Women, to Go on Trial Sept. 7," *Cleveland Plain Dealer*, May 6, 2010, updated January 12, 2019, www.cleveland.com/metro/2010/05/anthony_sowell_accused_of_kill.html; see also "Anthony Sowell on Trial: Index of Plain Dealer Coverage," *Cleveland Plain Dealer*, June 7, 2011, updated January 12, 2019, www.cleveland.com /anthony-sowell/2011/06/the_trial_of_anthony_sowell.html.

57. Leila Atassi, "Pleasant Conversations with Anthony Sowell Turned Violent Without Warning, 3 Women Testify," *Cleveland Plain Dealer*, July 1, 2011, updated January 12, 2019, www.cleveland.com/anthony-sowell /2011/06/pleasant_conversations_with_anthony_sowell_turned_violent _without_warning_three_women_testify.html.

58. Ibid.

59. See also Kathy Wray Coleman, "Five Families of Imperial Avenue Murder Victims Sue City of Cleveland, Others Relative to Sowell Capital Murder Case," Kathy Wray Coleman Online, December 9, 2010, www .kathywraycolemanonlinenewsblog.com/2010/12/five-families-of-imperial -avenue-murder.html.

60. Rachel Dissell, interviewed by the author, August 5, 2021.

Chapter 7: The Public Safety Myth

1. Tom Hoffman, interviewed by the author, January 19, 2021.

2. Ibid.

3. Ibid.

4. Ibid.

5. Robert Farley, "Bill Clinton and the 1994 Crime Bill," FactCheck.org, April 12, 2016, www.factcheck.org/2016/04/bill-clinton-and-the-1994-crime -bill.

6. A federal judge in Wisconsin wrote in 1974, "I am persuaded that the institution of prison probably must end. In many respects it is as intolerable within the United States as was the institution of slavery, equally brutalizing to all involved, equally toxic to the social system, equally subversive of

the brotherhood of man, even more costly by some standards, and probably less rational." Judge James Doyle, Western District of Wisconsin, *Morales v. Schmidt* 340 Federal Supplement (W.D. Wis. 1972), pp. 544, 548–49. See also President's Commission on Law Enforcement and Administration of Justice, *Task Force Report—Corrections: A Report to the President's Commission on Law Enforcement and Administration of Justice* (Washington, 1967), 11; American Friends Service Committee, *A Struggle for Justice: A Report on Crime and Justice in America* (Farrar, Straus and Giroux, 1971); Michelle Alexander, *The New Jim Crow: Mass Incarceration in the Age of Colorblindness* (New York: New Press, 2010).

7. See Ames Grawert, Matthew Friedman, and James Cullen, *Crime Trends: 1990–2016*, Brennan Center for Justice at New York University School of Law, April 18, 2017, www.brennancenter.org/our-work/research-reports/crime -trends-1990-2016; Federal Bureau of Investigation, Crime in the United States – 2019, https://ucr.fbi.gov/crime-in-the-u.s.

8. See National Research Council, *The Growth of Incarceration in the United States: Exploring Causes and Consequences*, Committee on Causes and Consequences of High Rates of Incarceration, J. Travis, B. Western, and S. Redburn, editors, Committee on Law and Justice, Division of Behavioral and Social Sciences and Education (Washington, DC: The National Academies Press, 2014), 5, 155.

9. Christopher S. Koper et al., "The Long-Term and System-Level Impacts of Institutionalizing Hot Spot Policing in a Small City," *Policing: A Journal of Policy and Practice* 15, no. 2 (June 2021); Anthony Allan Braga and David Weisburd, *Policing Problem Places: Crime Hot Spots and Effective Prevention* (Oxford: Oxford University Press, 2010); A. Braga, A. Papachristos, and D. Hureau, "Hot Spots Policing Effects on Crime," *Campbell Systematic Reviews* 8, no. 1 (2012): 1–96.

10. Patrick Sharkey, *Uneasy Peace: The Great Crime Decline, the Renewal of City Life, and the Next War on Violence* (New York: W.W. Norton, 2018), 157–58.

11. See, for example, Tuttle, James, Patricia McCall, and Kenneth Land, "The Crime Decline in Cross-National Context: A Panel Analysis of Homicide Rates Within Latent Trajectory Groups," *Global Crime* 22, no. 3 (2021): 240–64; Paul Knepper, "An International Crime Decline: Lessons for Social Welfare Crime Policy?" *Social Policy & Administration* 46, no. 4. (2012): 359–76.

12. Rachel E. Morgan and Jennifer L. Truman, *Criminal Victimization, 2019*, U.S. Department of Justice, Office of Justice Programs, Bureau of Justice Statistics, September 2020, bjs.ojp.gov/content/pub/pdf/cv19.pdf.

13. See Lynn Langton, Marcus Berzofsky, Christopher Krebs, and Hope Smiley-McDonald, *Victimizations Not Reported to the Police, 2006–2010*, U.S. Department of Justice, Office of Justice Programs, Bureau of Justice Statistics, August 2012, bjs.ojp.gov/content/pub/pdf/vnrp0610.pdf.

14. Alliance for Safety and Justice, *Crime Survivors Speak: The First-Ever National Survey of Victims' Views on Safety and Justice* (2016), allianceforsafety andjustice.org/crimesurvivorsspeak.

15. Jean Peters Baker, interviewed by the author.

16. Federal Bureau of Investigation, *Crime in the United States, 2019*, Table 27: Percent of Offenses Cleared by Arrest or Exceptional Means, ucr.fbi .gov/crime-in-the-u.s/2019/crime-in-the-u.s.-2019/topic-pages/tables/table-27.

17. See Memorandum from Oakland Police Captain Trevelon Jones to Chief of Police LeRonne Armstrong re: Gunshot Location Detection System (ShotSpotter)—2020 Annual Report, June 7, 2021, cao-94612.s3.amazonaws .com/documents/Special-Meeting-Packet.pdf.

18. For a review of demographic explanation of crime, see Vanessa Barker, "Explaining the Great American Crime Decline: A Review of Blumstein and Wallman, Goldberger and Rosenfeld, and Zimring," *Law & Social Inquiry* 35, no. 2 (2010): 489–516; and Maria Tcherni-Buzzeo, "The 'Great American Crime Decline': Possible Explanations," in *Handbook on Crime and Deviance* (Springer, Cham, 2019), 309–35.

19. M.E. Slater and H.R. Alpert, *Surveillance Report #117 Apparent Per Capita Alcohol Consumption: National, State, and Regional Trends, 1977–2019*, 2021, pubs.niaaa.nih.gov/publications/surveillance110/CONS16.htm.

20. S.M. Boles and K. Miotto, "Substance Abuse and Violence: A Review of the Literature," *Aggression and Violent Behavior* 8, no. 2 (2003): 155–74.

21. For a more nuanced discussion of the relationship between the U.S. economic system and crime, see Steven F. Messner and Richard Rosenfeld, *Crime and the American Dream* (Boston, MA: Cengage Learning, 2012).

22. Kevin M. Drakulich and Robert D. Crutchfield, "The Role of Perceptions of the Police in Informal Social Control: Implications for the Racial Stratification of Crime and Control," *Social Problems* 60, no. 3 (August 2013): 383–407, academic.oup.com/socpro/article-abstract/60/3/383 /1691335.

23. Rick Nevin, "Understanding International Crime Trends: The Legacy of Preschool Lead Exposure," *Environmental Research* 104, no. 3 (2007): 315–36; and Mark Patrick Taylor et al., "The Relationship Between Atmospheric Lead Emissions and Aggressive Crime: An Ecological Study," *Environmental Health* 15, no. 1 (2016): 1–10.

24. Jay P. Kennedy, Melissa Rorie, and Michael L. Benson. "COVID-19 Frauds: An Exploratory Study of Victimization During a Global Crisis," *Criminology and Public Policy* 20, no. 3 (2021): 493–543.

25. Hefei Wen, Jason M. Hockenberry, and Janet R. Cummings, "The Effect of Medicaid Expansion on Crime Reduction: Evidence from HIFA-Waiver Expansions," *Journal of Public Economics* 154 (2017): 67–94; Jacob Vogler, "Access to Healthcare and Criminal Behavior: Evidence from the ACA Medicaid Expansions," *Journal of Policy Analysis and Management* 39, no. 4 (2020):

1166–1213; Erkmen Giray Aslim et al., "The Effect of Public Health Insurance on Criminal Recidivism," *George Mason Law and Economics Research Paper* 19-19 (2020).

26. Charles C. Branas et al., "Citywide Cluster Randomized Trial to Restore Blighted Vacant Land and Its Effects on Violence, Crime, and Fear," *Proceedings of the National Academy of Sciences* 115, no. 12 (2018): 2946–51; Eugenia C. Garvin, Carolyn C. Cannuscio, and Charles C. Branas, "Greening Vacant Lots to Reduce Violent Crime: A Randomised Controlled Trial," *Injury Prevention* 19, no. 3 (2013): 198–203; John Macdonald et al., "Reducing Crime by Remediating Vacant Lots: The Moderating Effect of Nearby Land Uses," *Journal of Experimental Criminology* (2021): 1–26.

27. Rahini Mahendran et al., "Interpersonal Violence Associated with Hot Weather," *Lancet Planetary Health* 5, no. 9 (2021): e571–e572.

28. Jonathan Easley, "The Day the Drug War Really Started" [Interview with Eric Sterling], *Salon* (June 19, 2011), www.salon.com/2011/06/19/len_bias_cocaine_tragedy_still_affecting_us_drug_law.

29. Wide-Ranging Online Data for Epidemiologic Research (WONDER) (Atlanta, GA: CDC, National Center for Health Statistics, 2020), wonder.cdc .gov.

30. Centers for Disease Control and Prevention, *Drug Overdose Deaths in the U.S. Top 100,000 Annually* (November 17, 2021), www.cdc.gov/nchs/pressroom/nchs_press_releases/2021/20211117.htm.

31. Charlie Lloyd, "Risk Factors for Problem Drug Use: Identifying Vulnerable Groups," *Drugs: Education, Prevention and Policy* 5, no. 3 (1998): 217–32.

32. Nora D. Volkow, "Addiction Should Be Treated, Not Penalized," *Neuropsychopharmacology* 46, no. 12 (2021): 2048–50; see also Carl Mazza, "A Pound of Flesh: The Psychological, Familial and Social Consequences of Mandatory Long-Term Sentencing Laws for Drug Offenses," *Journal of Social Work Practice in the Addictions* 4, no. 3 (2004): 65–81.

33. Molly M. Gill, "Correcting Course: Lessons from the 1970 Repeal of Mandatory Minimums," *Federal Sentencing Reporter* 21, no. 1 (2008): 55–67.

34. United States Sentencing Commission, *Special Report to the Congress: Mandatory Minimum Penalties in the Federal Criminal Justice System* (August 1991), www.ussc.gov/research/congressional-reports/1991-report-congress -mandatory-minimum-penalties-federal-criminal-justice-system.

35. Robert Reinhold, "Gang Violence Shocks Los Angeles," *New York Times*, February 8, 1988, A10.

36. Reinhold, "Gang Violence"; John M. Glionna, "A Murder That Woke Up L.A.," *Los Angeles Times*, January 30, 1998; Margaret Carlson, "The Price of Life in Los Angeles," *Time*, February 22, 1988.

37. Reinhold, "Gang Violence."

38. Jerry Gillam and Daniel M. Weintraub, "Governor Signs Curbs on Gangs, Drugs," *Los Angeles Times*, September 25, 1988.

39. The Intersector Project, *Intersector Case Study: Reducing Gang Violence and Providing Youth Development in Los Angeles*, n.d., intersector.com/case/advancementproject_california.

40. Center for Juvenile Law and Policy, LMU Loyola Law School, *50 Years of Deputy Gangs: Identifying Root Causes and Effects to Advocate for Meaningful Reform* (2021), www.lls.edu/academics/centers/centerforjuvenilelawpolicy/cjlpdeputygangreport, 3.

41. Benjamin Lessing, "Counterproductive Punishment: How Prison Gangs Undermine State Authority," *Rationality and Society* 29, no. 3 (2017): 257–97.

42. Patrick McGreevy, "Newsom Signs Bills Restricting Sentencing Enhancements for Many Crimes," *Los Angeles Times*, October 8, 2021.

43. ACLU, Northern California, "Union City Students Reach Groundbreaking Settlement with Union City and School District," news release, May 18, 2005, www.aclunc.org/news/union-city-students-reach-groundbreaking-settlement-union-city-and-school-district.

44. Victor M. Rios, *Punished: Policing the Lives of Black and Latino Boys* (New York: New York University Press, 2011), 52, 76–95.

45. Illinois Channel TV, Hearing on Changing Gun Sentencing Guidelines, YouTube, May 26, 2017, www.youtube.com/watch?v=D5ML2IJmgIQ [https://perma.cc/96GA-SG4Q], as quoted in Wally Hilke, "The Truth Limps After: Sentence Enhancements and the Punishment Paradigm," *University of Pennsylvania Journal of Law and Social Change* 23, no. 2 (2020): 115, fn. 254.

46. City of Chicago, Shootings, *Chicago Data Portal* (updated March 2022), data.cityofchicago.org/Public-Safety/Shootings/vqmv-zqjm.

47. Reis Thebault, and Danielle Rindler, "Shootings Never Stopped During the Pandemic: 2020 Was the Deadliest Gun Violence Year in Decades," *Washington Post*, March 23, 2021.

48. Illinois Sentencing Policy Advisory Council, *Unlawful Use of a Weapon Trends Analysis* (2014), spac.icjiaapi.cloud/uploads/SPAC_Trends_Analysis_Report_09_2014-20191127T15204111.pdf.

49. See Hilke, "The Truth Limps After," 74.

50. National Research Council, *Firearms and Violence: A Critical Review* (Washington, DC: The National Academies Press, 2005).

51. See for example David S. Abrams, "Estimating the Deterrent Effect of Incarceration Using Sentencing Enhancements," *American Economic Journal: Applied Economics* 4, no. 4 (2012): 32–56; and David McDowall, Colin Loftin, and Brian Wiersema, "A Comparative Study of the Preventive Effects of Mandatory Sentencing Laws for Gun Crimes," *Quantitative Methods in Criminology* (London: Routledge, 2017), 521–37.

52. Jeffrey A. Butts et al., "Cure Violence: A Public Health Model to Reduce Gun Violence," *Annual Review of Public Health* 36 (2015): 39–53.

53. Alice Goffman, *On the Run: Fugitive Life in an American City* (Chicago: University of Chicago Press, 2014).

54. Nancy Loo and Erik Runge, "Police: Boy Brought Gun to School Because He Was Being Bullied," WGN9News.com, September 16, 2014, wgntv.com/news/12-year-old-took-gun-to-his-grade-school.

55. "9-Year-Old Manassas Boy Arrested, Charged with Taking Gun to School," NBCWashington.com, April 25, 2014, updated April 26, 2014.

56. Jennifer Mascia, "Why Would a Nine-Year-Old Bring a Gun to School? Since the Start of the School Year, More Than Two Dozen Kids Have Been Caught Bringing Firearms to Class. A Sociologist Helps to Understand the Phenomenon," *Trace*, September 21, 2015, www.thetrace.org/2015/09/gun-to -school-child-firearm.

57. "9-Year-Old Manassas Boy Arrested," NBCWashington.com.

58. Jake Allen, "Fourth Grader at North Naples Elementary School Arrested, Accused of Taking Unloaded Gun to School," *Naples Daily News*, March 2, 2021, www.naplesnews.com/story/news/crime/2021/03/02/north-naples -elementary-school-student-arrested/6888179002.

59. Tammy B. Pham, Lana E. Schapiro, Majnu John, and Andrew Adesman, "Weapon Carrying Among Victims of Bullying," *Pediatrics* 140, no. 6 (November 2017): e20170353, pediatrics.aappublications.org/content/early /2017/11/22/peds.2017-0353.

60. See Human Rights Watch, *No Easy Answers: Sex Offender Laws in the U.S.*, September 11, 2077, www.hrw.org/report/2007/09/11/no-easy-answers /sex-offender-laws-us.

61. ACLU, "ACLU Challenges Miami-Dade County's 2,500-Foot Sex Offender Residency Restriction," press release, July 9, 2009, www.aclu.org /press-releases/aclu-challenges-miami-dade-countys-2500-foot-sex-offender -residency-restriction.

62. Dara Lind, "Why the Sex Offender Registry Isn't the Right Way to Punish Rapists," *Vox*, July 5, 2016, www.vox.com/2016/7/5/11883784/sex -offender-registry.

63. Allegra M. McLeod, "Regulating Sexual Harm: Strangers, Intimates, and Social Institutional Reform," *California Law Review* 102, no. 6 (2014): 1553–1621 (at p. 1559 and n. 29), www.jstor.org/stable/24758177.

64. "Patty Wetterling Questions Sex Offender Laws," Citizens for Criminal Justice Reform–New Hampshire, August 1, 2014, www.ccjrnh.org /sex_offender_laws_treatment/patty_wetterling_questions_sex_offender _laws.

65. Amy M. Zelcer, "Battling Domestic Violence: Replacing Mandatory Arrest Laws with a Trifecta of Preferential Arrest, Officer Education, and Batterer Treatment Programs," *American Criminal Law Review* 51 (2014): 541; Scott W. Phillips and James J. Sobol, "Twenty Years of Mandatory Arrest: Police Decision Making in the Face of Legal Requirements," *Criminal Justice Policy Review* 21, no. 1 (2010): 98–118.

66. Peter S. Hovmand et al., "Victims Arrested for Domestic Violence:

Unintended Consequences of Arrest Policies," *System Dynamics Review: The Journal of the System Dynamics Society* 25, no. 3 (2009): 161–81.

67. Jennifer L. Doleac, "Study After Study Shows Ex-prisoners Would Be Better Off Without Intense Supervision," Brookings Institution Blog (July 2, 2018), www.brookings.edu/blog/up-front/2018/07/02/study-after-study-shows-ex-prisoners-would-be-better-off-without-intense-supervision; see also Jennifer L. Doleac, "Strategies to Productively Reincorporate the Formerly-Incarcerated into Communities: A Review of the Literature," available at SSRN 3198112 (2018).

Chapter 8: The Cycle of Trauma

1. Aswad Thomas, interviewed by the author, August 12, 2020.

2. Ibid.

3. Ibid.

4. Ibid.

5. See Rafael Javier, Elizabeth Owen, and Jemour Maddux, *Assessing Trauma in Forensic Contexts* (Cham: Springer, 2020): 42, 86 and articles cited therein.

6. Nancy Wolff and Jing Shi, "Childhood and Adult Trauma Experiences of Incarcerated Persons and Their Relationship to Adult Behavioral Health Problems and Treatment," *International Journal of Environmental Research and Public Health* 9, no. 5 (May 2012): 1908–26.

7. Nancy Wolff, Jessica Huening, Jing Shi, and B. Christopher Frueh, "Trauma Exposure and Posttraumatic Stress Disorder Among Incarcerated Men," *Journal of Urban Health* 91, no. 4 (August 2014): 707–19 (at pp. 715–16).

8. Ibid.

9. Javier, Owen, and Maddux, *Assessing Trauma*, 9 and articles cited therein.

10. B.L. Green, J. Miranda, A. Daroowalla, and J. Siddique, "Trauma Exposure, Mental Health Functioning, and Program Needs of Women in Jail," *Crime and Delinquency* 51, no. 1 (2005): 133–51.

11. Javier, Owen, and Maddux, *Assessing Trauma*, 445 and articles cited therein.

12. Lauren Aaron and Danielle H. Dallaire, "Parental Incarceration and Multiple Risk Experiences: Effects on Family Dynamics and Children's Delinquency," *Journal of Youth and Adolescence* 39, no. 12 (2010): 1471–84.

13. Kaiser study can be found at www.ajpmonline.org/article/S0749-3797(98)00017-8/fulltext.

14. V.J. Felitti, R.F. Anda, D. Nordenberg, D.F. Williamson, A.M. Spitz, V. Edwards, and J.S. Marks, "Relationship of Childhood Abuse and Household Dysfunction to Many of the Leading Causes of Death in Adults: The Adverse

Childhood Experiences (ACE) Study," *American Journal of Preventive Medicine* 14, no. 4 (1998): 245–58.

15. Craig Haney, "Criminality in Context: The Psychological Foundations of Criminal Justice Reform," *American Psychological Association* (2020), doi.org /10.1037/0000172-000, 108.

16. James A. Reavis, Jan Looman, Kristina A. Franco, and Briana Rojas, "Adverse Childhood Experiences and Adult Criminality: How Long Must We Live Before We Possess Our Own Lives?" *Permanente Journal* 17, no. 2 (Spring 2013): 44–48.

17. Ibid.

18. Ibid.

19. Michael Baglivio, Nathan Epps, K. Swartz, Mona Sayedul Huq, A. Sheer, and N.S. Hardt, "The Prevalence of Adverse Childhood Experiences (ACE) in the Lives of Juvenile Offenders," *Journal of Juvenile Justice* 3 (2014): 1–23.

20. Ibid.

21. C.B. Dierkhising, S.J. Ko, B. Woods-Jaeger, E.C. Briggs, R. Lee, and R.S. Pynoos, "Trauma Histories Among Justice-Involved Youth: Findings from the National Child Traumatic Stress Network," *European Journal of Psychotraumatology* 4 (2013).

22. Ibid.

23. E.N. Taylor, C. Timko, A. Nash, M.D. Owens, A.H. Harris, and A.K. Finlay, "Posttraumatic Stress Disorder and Justice Involvement Among Military Veterans: A Systematic Review and Meta-Analysis," *Journal of Traumatic Stress* 33 (2020): 804–12, doi.org/10.1002/jts.22526.

24. J. Bronson, A. Carson, M. Noonan, and M. Berzofsky, *Veterans in Prison and Jail 2011–12* (Washington, DC: U.S. Department of Justice, Office of Justice Programs, Bureau of Justice Statistics, 2015).

25. Eli Hager, "Fit to Be Killed? The Impending Execution of a Decorated Soldier Shows the Limits of the PTSD Defense," Marshall Project, January 13, 2015, www.themarshallproject.org/2015/01/13/fit-to-be-killed.

26. L. Keyser-Marcus, A. Alvanzo, T. Rieckmann, L. Thacker, A. Sepulveda, A. Forcehimes, and D.S. Svikis, "Trauma, Gender, and Mental Health Symptoms in Individuals with Substance Use Disorders," *Journal of Interpersonal Violence* 30, no. 1 (2015): 3–24.

27. Trevor Bennett, Katy Holloway, and David Farrington, "The Statistical Association Between Drug Misuse and Crime: A Meta-Analysis," *Aggression and Violent Behavior* 13, no. 2 (2008): 107–18; Lana Harrison and Joseph Gfroerer, "The Intersection of Drug Use and Criminal Behavior: Results from the National Household Survey on Drug Abuse," *Crime and Delinquency* 38, no. 4 (1992): 422–43.

28. Nadine Burke Harris, *The Deepest Well: Healing the Long-Term Effects of Childhood Adversity* (Boston: Houghton Mifflin Harcourt, 2018), 39.

29. Haney, *Criminality in Context*, 110.

30. Haney, *Criminality in Context*, 49–80.

31. Rex Huppke, "McDonald's CEO Tries Victim-Blaming Parents of Slain Chicago Kids. Bad Idea," *Chicago Tribune*, November 3, 2021.

32. Aqeela Sherrills, interviewed by the author, February 10, 2021.

33. Ibid.

34. Ibid.

35. Ibid.

36. Janet L. Lauritsen and John H. Laub, "Understanding the Link Between Victimization and Offending: New Reflections on an Old Idea," *Crime Prevention Studies* 22 (2007): 55–75, reprinted in J.M. Hough and Michael J. Maxfield, *Surveying Crime in the 21st Century* (New York: Criminal Justice Press, 2007).

37. Ibid., 56.

38. Ibid., abstract, 55.

39. K.M. Thompson and R. Braaten-Antrim, "Youth Maltreatment and Gang Involvement," *Journal of Interpersonal Violence* 13 (1998): 328–45.

40. E. Bocanegra and B. Stolbach, "Trauma Histories and Recruitment of Gang Involved Youth in Chicago" (paper presentation, 28th Meeting of the International Society for Traumatic Stress Studies, Los Angeles, CA, November 1, 2012).

41. Ibid.

42. David Guizar, interviewed by the author, February 10, 2021.

43. Ibid.

44. Ibid.

45. Ibid.

46. Aqeela Sherrills, interviewed by the author, February 10, 2021.

47. Ibid.

48. See Burke Harris, *Deepest Well*, 145–46.

49. Ibid.

50. Ibid.

51. Aqeela Sherrills, interviewed by the author, February 10, 2021.

52. Ibid.

53. Ibid.

54. L.M. Najavits, *Seeking Safety: A Treatment Manual for PTSD and Substance Abuse* (New York: Guilford Press, 2002).

55. Ibid.

56. Precious Skinner-Osei, Laura Mangan, Mara Liggett, Michelle Kerrigan, and Jill S. Levenson, "Justice-Involved Youth and Trauma-Informed Interventions," *Justice Policy Journal* 6, no. 2 (Fall 2019): 13.

57. Ibid.

58. Burke Harris, *Deepest Well*, 112–15.

59. Aqeela Sherrills, interviewed by the author, February 10, 2021.

60. Studies exploring the impact of ACEs on adult diseases have found higher odds ratios than studies examining family history. See Karen Hughes et al., "The Effect of Multiple Adverse Childhood Experiences on Health: A Systematic Review and Meta-analysis," *Lancet Public Health* 2, no. 8 (2017): e356–e366, especially as compared to Karin Leander et al., "Family History of Coronary Heart Disease, a Strong Risk Factor for Myocardial Infarction Interacting with Other Cardiovascular Risk Factors: Results from the Stockholm Heart Epidemiology Program (SHEEP)," *Epidemiology* (2001): 215–21.

61. David Guizar, interview by the author, February 10, 2021.

62. Aswad Thomas, interview by the author, August 12, 2020.

63. Ibid.

64. Ibid.

65. Ibid.

Chapter 9: The Trauma of the Justice System

1. Witness and Books Not Bars, *System Failure: Violence Abuse and Neglect in the California Youth Authority*, August 2004, YouTube, www.youtube.com /watch?v=ptC0mJD3l4Y.

2. Ibid.

3. Ibid.

4. Ibid.

5. Nisha Ajmani and Erica Webster, "Failure After Farrell: Violence and Inadequate Mental Health Care in California's Division of Juvenile Justice," Center on Juvenile and Criminal Justice, August 2016, www.cjcj.org/uploads /cjcj/documents/failure_after_farrell_djj.pdf.

6. Witness and Books Not Bars, *System Failure*.

7. Witness and Books Not Bars, *System Failure*.

8. Barry Krisberg, Linh Vuong, Christopher Hartney, and Susan Marchionna, "A New Era in California Juvenile Justice: Downsizing the State Youth Corrections System," Berkeley Center for Criminal Justice, October 2010, www.law.berkeley.edu/files/bccj/New_Era.pdf.

9. Mark Gladstone and James Rainey, "Abuse Reports Cloud Youth Authority," *Los Angeles Times*, December 24, 1999.

10. Mika'il Deveaux, "The Trauma of the Incarceration Experience," *Harvard Civil Rights–Civil Liberties Law Review* 48 (2013): 257–77.

11. Ibid.

12. Ibid.

13. Ibid.

14. Emily Widra, "No Escape: The Trauma of Witnessing Violence in Prison," Prison Policy Initiative, December 2, 2020, www.prisonpolicy.org/blog/2020/12/02/witnessing-prison-violence.

15. Meghan A. Novisky and Robert L. Peralta, "Gladiator School: Returning Citizens' Experiences with Secondary Violence Exposure in Prison," *Victims and Offenders* 15, no. 5 (2020): 594–618.

16. Ibid.

17. Ibid.

18. Josh Sweigart, "Oregon District Shooting Survivors, Family Denied State Aid for Crime Victims," *Dayton Daily News*, April 14, 2020, www.daytondailynews.com/news/oregon-district-shooting-survivors-family-denied-state-aid-for-crime-victims/3Z4ZWDCMDZABNJCNNKOALE5KN4.

19. See Widra, "No Escape."

20. Novisky and Peralta, "Gladiator School."

21. Ibid.

22. Correctional Association of New York, "Lockdown New York: Disciplinary Confinement in New York State Prisons," October 2003, p. 7, www.prisonpolicy.org/scans/lockdown-new-york-1.pdf (citing declaration of Dr. Stuart Grassian submitted in *Eng v. Coughlin*, 865 F.2d 521 [2d Cir. 1989]).

23. Donald Clemmer, "Observations on Imprisonment as a Source of Criminality," *Journal of Criminal Law and Criminology* 43, no. 3 (1950): article 6, scholarlycommons.law.northwestern.edu/cgi/viewcontent.cgi?article=3795&context=jclc.

24. National Research Council, *The Growth of Incarceration in the United States: Exploring Causes and Consequences* (Washington, DC: National Academies Press, 2014), 174–79.

25. Craig Haney, "From Prison to Home: The Effect of Incarceration and Reentry on Children, Families, and Communities; The Psychological Impact of Incarceration: Implications for Post-Prison Adjustment," U.S. Department of Health and Human Services, ASPE, November 30, 2001, aspe.hhs.gov/reports/psychological-impact-incarceration-implications-post-prison-adjustment-0.

26. N.A. Miller and L.M. Najavits, "Creating Trauma-Informed Correctional Care: A Balance of Goals and Environment," *European Journal of Psychotraumatology* 3 (2012), doi.org/10.3402/ejpt.v3i0.17246.

27. Ibid.

28. Dasha Lisitsina, "Prison Guards Can Never Be Weak: The Hidden PTSD Crisis in America's Jails," *Guardian*, May 20, 2015.

29. Caterina G. Spinaris, Michael D. Denhof, and Julie A. Kellaway, "Post-traumatic Stress Disorder in United States Corrections Professionals: Prevalence and Impact on Health and Functioning," U.S. Department of Justice O.J.P. National Criminal Justice Reference Service, 2002, www.ojp.gov/ncjrs/virtual-library/abstracts/posttraumatic-stress-disorder-united-states-corrections.

30. Jaime Brower, "Correctional Officer Wellness and Safety Literature Review," U.S. Department of Justice OJP Diagnostic Center, July 2013, info.nicic.gov/virt/sites/info.nicic.gov.virt/files/09Correctional_Officer_Literature_Review.pdf.

31. F.E. Cheek and M.D. Miller, "The Experience of Stress for Correction Officers: A Double-Bind Theory of Correctional Stress," *Journal of Criminal Justice* 11, no. 2 (1983): 105–20. doi.org/10.1016/0047-2352(83)90046-6.

32. Amy E. Lerman, Jessie Harney, Meredith Sanin, "Prisons and Mental Health: Violence, Organizational Support and the Effects of Correctional Work," *Criminal Justice and Behavior* 49, no. 2 (February 2022), 181–99.

33. Lisitsina, "Prison Guards."

34. Spinaris, Denhof, and Kellaway, "Posttraumatic Stress Disorder in United States Corrections Professionals."

35. Bruce Finley, "Prison Horrors Haunt Guards' Private Lives," *Denver Post*, March 23, 2007. www.denverpost.com/2007/03/23/prison-horrors-haunt-guards-private-lives.

36. See Amy E. Lerman, *The Modern Prison Paradox: Politics, Punishment, and Social Community* (Cambridge: Cambridge University Press, 2013), inside.ccsi.org/CCSIPortal/media/content/PDFs/modern-prison-paradox.pdf.

37. National Research Council, "Growth of Incarceration in the United States," 163; see Sam Howe Verhovek, "No Frills' for Prisoners? Wardens Balk," *New York Times*, February 11, 1996.

38. Peter Finn, "No-Frills Prisons and Jails: A Movement in Flux," *Federal Probation* 60, no. 3 (September 1996): 35–44, www.strengthtech.com/correct/issues/mediais/2000/flux.htm.

39. Andy Lee and Martin C. Brhel, "Why No-Frills Jails Work!" *Sheriff* 52, no. 6 (November-December 2000): 20–21.

40. Associated Press, "McInnis of Lucedale Among Mississippi 2013 Deaths," *Mississippi Link*, December 31, 2013, themississippilink.com/2013/12/31/ap-analysis-former-state-rep-mack-mcinnis-of-lucedale-among-mississippi-2013-deaths.

41. Ibid.

42. Finn, "No-Frills Prisons and Jails."

43. Clemmer, "Observations on Imprisonment."

44. Lerman, *The Modern Prison Paradox*.

45. Ibid.

46. Ibid.

47. Dan Reisel, "The Neuroscience of Restorative Justice," TED Talk, February 2013, www.ted.com/talks/dan_reisel_the_neuroscience_of_restorative_justice /transcript?language=en.

48. Ibid.

49. Ibid.

50. Ibid.

51. Ibid.

52. Robert Rooks, interviewed by the author.

53. Tinisch Hollins, interviewed by the author.

54. Ibid.

55. "Repairing the Road to Redemption in California," Californians for Safety and Justice, May 2018, afeandjust.org/wp-content/uploads /CSJ_SecondChances-ONLINE-May14.pdf.

56. Ibid.

57. Ibid.

58. Ibid.

59. Comments of Jay Jordan, "Searching for Justice—Making Reentry Work After Incarceration," PBS NewsHour, December 2, 2021, www.pbs.org /newshour/nation/watch-live-searching-for-justice-making-reentry-work-after -incarceration.

60. Jay Jordan, interviewed by the author, December 15, 2021.

61. Ibid.

62. Ibid.

63. Ibid.

64. Ibid.

65. Ibid.

66. Ibid.

67. James Rainey, "California Plans to Close Troubled Youth Prisons After 80 Years. But What Comes Next?" *Los Angeles Times*, February 15, 2021.

68. Maureen Washburn, "Decades of Abuse at California's DJJ Will End in 2023," Center on Juvenile and Criminal Justice, February 16, 2021, www.cjcj .org/news/13081.

69. Gary Mohr, interviewed by the author, December 22, 2021.

70. Ibid.

71. Ibid.

72. Ibid.

73. Sam Lewis, "Living Two Lives: A Conversation with Sam Lewis,"

December 2021, *A New Legacy*, podcast, www.anewlegacy.com/podcast/episode3.

74. Ibid.

75. Ibid.

76. Ibid.

77. Jessie Balmert, "Ohio Issue 1: War on Drugs Isn't Working. Is a Constitutional Amendment the Fix?" *Cincinnati Enquirer*, November 4, 2018, www.cincinnati.com/story/news/politics/elections/2018/11/04/ohio-issue-1-war-drugs-didnt-work-constitutional-amendment-fix/1808046002.

78. See Ballotpedia, Ohio Issue 1, 2018, ballotpedia.org/Ohio_Issue_1,_Drug_and_Criminal_Justice_Policies_Initiative_(2018).

79. Ibid.

Chapter 10: A New Victims' Right: Trauma Recovery for All

1. Alicia Boccellari, interviewed by the author, August 11, 2020.

2. Ibid.

3. Ibid.

4. Ibid.

5. Ibid.

6. Ibid.

7. Ibid.

8. Alliance for Safety and Justice, congressional briefing on trauma recovery centers, Tuesday, October 5, 2021, presented to members of Congress via video conference.

9. Ibid.

10. Alicia Boccellari, interviewed by the author, August 11, 2020.

11. Ibid.

12. Ibid.

13. Ibid.

14. Adela Barajas, interviewed by the author, December 8, 2021.

15. Ibid.

16 Ibid.

17. Ibid.

18. Ibid.

19. Ibid.

20. Ibid.

21. See Jane Meredith Adams, "Lawsuit Says Schools Are Legally Required to Address Student Trauma," EdSource, May 19, 2015, edsource.org/2015

/lawsuit-says-schools-are-legally-required-to-address-student-trauma/79952
/79952.

22. *Peter P. et. al. v. Compton Unified School District et. al*, CV-15-3726 (C.D. Cal., filed May 18, 2015).

23. Public Counsel and Compton Unified School District Joint Press Release, "Landmark Federal Class Action Lawsuit Results in Innovative Trauma Programming," February 20, 2021, www.compton.k12.ca.us/news-release /news/2021/class-action-lawsuit.

24. Ibid.

25. Ibid.

26 Mark Leno, interviewed by the author, October 10, 2020.

27. Ibid.

28. Ibid.

29. Alliance for Safety and Justice, Congressional Briefing on Trauma Recovery Centers, Tuesday, October 5, 2021 (presented to Members of Congress via Zoom).

30. Alliance for Safety and Justice, congressional briefing on trauma recovery centers.

31. Ibid.

32. Ibid.

33. Shakyra Diaz, interviewed by the author, August 13, 2020.

Chapter 11: A New Lens: Crime Survivors Speak

1. "Crime Survivors Speak: The First-Ever National Survey of Victims' Views on Safety and Justice," Alliance for Safety and Justice, 2017, allianceforsafetyandjustice.org/crimesurvivorsspeak; "Crime Survivors Speak: Florida Victims' Views on Safety and Justice," Alliance for Safety and Justice, 2018, allianceforsafetyandjustice.org/wp-content/uploads/2018/02 /ASJ_FloridaCrimeSurvivorBrief-online.pdf; "California Crime Survivors Speak: A Statewide Survey of California Victims' Views on Safety and Justice," 2018, allianceforsafetyandjustice.org/wp-content/uploads/2019/04 /201904-CALIFORNIA-REPORT-FINAL-FINAL.pdf; "Toward Shared Safety: The First-Ever National Survey of America's Safety Gap," Alliance for Safety and Justice, 2020, wesharesafety.us/wp-content/themes/shared-safety/assets/downloads/NatlSafetyGaps-09142020.pdf; "Crime Survivors Speak: Texas Victims Experiences with Recovery and Views on Criminal Justice," Alliance for Safety and Justice, 2019, allianceforsafetyandjustice.org/wp -content/uploads/2019/04/201904-ASJ-Texas-Report-Full-FINAL.pdf; "Illinois Crime Victims' Voices: The First-Ever Survey of Illinois Victims' Views on Safety and Justice," Alliance for Safety and Justice, 2017, allianceforsafetyandjustice.org/wp-content/uploads/2016/12/ASJ-Illinois-Crime_survivors

-FINAL-online.pdf; "Crime Survivors Speak: Michigan Victims' Views on Safety and Justice," Alliance for Safety and Justice, 2018, allianceforsafetyand justice.org/wp-content/uploads/2018/07/ASJ_MichiganCrimeSurvivorBrief -F2-ONLINE.pdf.

2. Ibid.

3. Ibid.

4. Ibid.

5. Ibid.

6. Ibid.

7. A. Verma, "The Law-Before: Legacies and Gaps in Penal Reform," *Law & Society Review* 49, no. 4 (2015): 847–82; A. Verma, "A Turning Point in Mass Incarceration? Local Imprisonment Trajectories and Decarceration Under California's Realignment," *Annals of the American Academy of Political and Social Science* 664 (2016): 108–35.

8. California All, "California Governor Tackles Adverse Childhood Experiences with $10m Proposal for Cross-Sector Training and Public Awareness," press release, January 10, 2020, www.acesaware.org/wp-content/uploads/2020 /01/ACEs-Aware-2020-2021-Budget-Release-1.pdf.

9. Ibid.

10. Jean Peters Baker, interviewed by the author, August 22, 2020.

11. Ibid.

12. Ibid.

13. Ibid.

14. Ibid.

15. Ibid.

16. Tinisch Hollins, interviewed by the author, August 8, 2020.

17. Heather Littleton, Amie Grills, Marlee Layh, and Kelly Rudolph, "Unacknowledged Rape and Re-Victimization Risk: Examination of Potential Mediators," *Psychology of Women Quarterly* 41, no. 4 (December 2017): 437–50, https://doi.org/10.1177/0361684317720187.

18. Heather Littleton, Danny Axsom, and Amie Grills-Taquechel, "Sexual Assault Victims' Acknowledgment Status and Revictimization Risk," *Psychology of Women Quarterly* 33, no. 1 (March 2009): 34–42, doi.org/10.1111/j.1471 -6402.2008.01472.x.

19. Robert Davis, Pamela Guthrie, Timothy Ross, and Chris O'Sullivan, "Reducing Sexual Revictimization: A Field Test with an Urban Sample," Report to the National Institute of Justice, 2006, 59–66, www.ojp.gov /pdffiles1/nij/grants/216002.pdf,

20. Trudy Govier, "What Is Acknowledgement and Why Is It Important?" OSSA Conference Archive 1, 1999, scholar.uwindsor.ca/ossaarchive/OSSA3 /keynotes/1.

Chapter 12: A New Investment: Scaling Safety

1. Niraj Chohski, "California Voters Seem Ready to End the Tough on Crime Era," *Washington Post*, October 31, 2014.

2. Ballotpedia ballot argument in opposition to Proposition 47, October 2014.

3. Ballotpedia ballot argument in opposition to Proposition 47, October 2014.

4. Thomas G. Hoffman, "Commentary: Contrary to Critics, Proposition 47 Is Not Creating More Crime in California," *Fresno Bee*, February 16, 2022, www.fresnobee.com/opinion/op-ed/article258462583.html.

5. "Proposition 47 Grant Program: Demographics and Recidivism Update," presentation to the Board of State and Community Corrections, February 10, 2022, www.bscc.ca.gov/wp-content/uploads/Attachment-G-1-Prop-47-PowerPoint-Presentation-1.pdf.

6. Proposition 47 Issue Brief, Californians for Safety and Justice, June 2020, 14, safeandjust.org/wp-content/uploads/Prop47-2020-12.3.2020..pdf.

7. See "San Diego Misdemeanants At-Risk Track (SMART): The SMART Approach to Addressing the Chronic Misdemeanor Offender" (fact sheet), 2017, www.sandiego.gov/sites/default/files/smart_fact_sheet_171010.pdf.

8. *Scaling Safety: A Roadmap to Close America's Safety Gaps*, Alliance for Safety and Justice, April 2022.

9. *Scaling Safety*, Alliance for Safety and Justice, April 2022.

10. Gary Mohr, interviewed by author, December 22, 2021.

11. Jorja Leap, Karrah Lompa, Madison Thantu, and Whitney Gouche, *Newark Community Street Team Narrative Evaluation*, UCLA and Newark Community Street Team Narrative Evaluation, December 2020, www.newarkcommunitystreetteam.org/wp-content/uploads/2021/02/NCST-Evaluation_FINAL.pdf.

12. Ibid.

13. Ibid.

14. Ibid.

15. Ibid.

16. Ibid.

17. Mark Remillard and Aaron Ferrer, "Gun Violence in America: Newark; Overall Crime Has Dipped Every Year Since 2016 in the City," ABC News, July 30, 2021, abcnews.go.com/US/gun-violence-america-newark/story?id=79148257.

18. Richard Cowan, "Violent Crime Up Slightly in Newark This Year, While Arrests Are Down, Officials Say," NJ.com, December 29, 2021, www.nj.com/essex/2021/12/violent-crime-up-slightly-in-newark-this-year-while-arrests-are-down-officials-say.html.

19. K. Higuera, G. Jensen, and E. Morton, "Effects of the Male Community Reentry Program (MCRP) on Recidivism in the State of California," Stanford Digital Repository, 2021, purl.stanford.edu/bs374hx3899.

20. Rob Waters, "Enlisting Mental Health Workers, Not Cops, in Mobile Crisis Response," *Health Affairs* 40, no. 6 (June 2021), doi.org/10.1377/hlthaff .2021.00678.

21. "Toward Shared Safety: The First-Ever National Survey of America's Safety Gaps," Alliance for Safety and Justice, September 2020, alliancefor-safetyandjustice.org/wp-content/uploads/2020/09/NatlSafetyGaps-Report -PREVIEW-20200908-1751.pdf.

22. Ibid., 9.

23. Ibid., 8–10.

24. Dionne Wilson, "After My Husband Was Murdered," TEDxSanQuentin, YouTube, April 20, 2017, www.youtube.com/watch?v=USSLb-nOsRA; Tracey Kaplan and Mark Emmons, "Cop Widow Becomes Unlikely Public Face for Proposition 47," *Mercury News*, August 15, 2014, updated August 12, 2016, www.mercurynews.com/2014/08/15/cop-widow-becomes-unlikely -public-face-for-proposition-47; Dionne Wilson, Californians for Safety and Justice profile, May 21, 2013, www.youtube.com/watch?v=wAvTsxz3hvs.

25. Ibid.

26. Ibid.

27. Ibid.

28. Ibid.

29. Day of Healing, Sacramento, April 2013.

30. Ellen McDonnell, interviewed by the author, December 10, 2021.

31. Ibid.

32. Ibid.

33. Ingrid Archie, interviewed by the author, December 8, 2021.

Chapter 13: A New Justice: Stopping the Cycle of Trauma and Poverty

1. Jehan Gordon-Booth, interviewed by the author, October 20, 2021.

2. Ibid.

3. Ibid.

4. Ibid.

5. Tinisch Hollins, interviewed by the author, February 15, 2021.

6. Ibid.

7. Shakyra Diaz, interviewed by the author, January 10, 2022.

8. Simone Levine, "Community Demand for Change and Accountability: A History of Court Watch NOLA, New Orleans' Community Courtwatching Program," *New England Journal of Public Policy* 32, issue 1, article 14 (2020), scholarworks.umb.edu/nejpp/vol32/iss1/14; see also Andy Grimm, "A Decade After Danziger Bridge Shooting, Killings Still Cast a Shadow," *Times-Picayune*, September 5, 2015, updated July 18, 2019, www.nola.com /news/crime_police/article_00bb8d39-aa35-5959-b613-873905a4e734.html.

9. Simone Levine, interviewed by the author, March 8, 2021.

10. Ibid.

11. "New Orleans DA Seeks End to Lawsuit over Fake Subpoenas," 4WWLTV newsclip, December 16, 2020, www.youtube.com /watch?v=wJNXpi45HEw; see also Jeff Adelson, "DA's Jailing of Crime Victims Is 'Barbaric' and 'Misogynistic,' New Orleans City Council Says," Nola .com, February 7, 2019, www.nola.com/news/article_adfc2051-02c8-51b6 -a243-8b831e1e8216.html; Jeff Adelson, "New Orleans Prosecutors Dropping Charges in 90% of Misdemeanor Domestic Violence Cases, Council Is Told," Nola.com, December 3, 2019, www.nola.com/news/courts/article_f494905e -1630-11ea-a656-d3eff0872fe8.html.

12. Simone Levine, interviewed by the author, March 8, 2021; see also Levine, "Community Demand for Change and Accountability."

13. Associated Press, "Settlement Ends Lawsuit Over Fake Subpoenas, Jailed Victims," *U.S. News and World Report*, October 5, 2021, www.usnews .com/news/politics/articles/2021-10-05/settlement-ends-lawsuit-over-fake -subpoenas-jailed-victims.

14. Tara Mikkilineni, interviewed by author, March 3, 2022.

15. Renata Singleton, interviewed by author, March 3, 2022.

16. Victoria Law, "When Abuse Victims Commit Crimes," *The Atlantic*, May 21, 2019, www.theatlantic.com/politics/archive/2019/05/new-york -domestic-violence-sentencing/589507.

17. April Grayson, "New Bill Would Let Judges Weigh Survivors' History in Human Trafficking Cases," *Cal Matters*, August 16, 2021, calmatters.org /commentary/2021/08/new-bill-would-let-judges-weigh-survivors-history-in -human-trafficking-cases.

18. For excellent overviews of their proven abilities and promises, see sujatha baliga, "Whose Harm? The Role of the State in Restorative Justice," *New Political Science* 43, no. 1 (2021): 35–45; Daniel Van Ness and Karen Heetderks Strong, *Restoring Justice: An Introduction to Restorative Justice* (Routledge, 2014); H. Zehr, *The Little Book of Restorative Justice: Revised and Updated* (Simon and Schuster, 2015); Gerry Johnstone, *Restorative Justice: Ideas, Values, Debates* (Routledge, 2013); Lawrence Sherman and Heather Strang, *Restorative Justice: The Evidence* (Smith Institute, 2007); S. Han, M. Valdovinos Olson, and R.C. Davis, "Reducing Recidivism Through Restorative Justice: An Evaluation of Bridges to Life in Dallas," *Journal of Offender Rehabilitation* 60, no. 7

(2021): 444–63; and Bailey Maryfield, Roger Przybylski, and Mark Myrent, "Research on Restorative Justice Practices, Justice Research and Statistics Association," December 2020, www.jrsa.org/pubs/factsheets/jrsa-research -brief-restorative-justice.pdf.

19. "Proposition 47, Record Change and Resource Fair," October 28, 2015, Health Happens Here YouTube channel, www.youtube.com /watch?v=pfOrmCQ0G50; "How Proposition 47 Is Changing Records and Changing Lives," May 22, 2014, Californians for Safety and Justice YouTube channel, www.youtube.com/watch?v=JKKT6nGx4yQ.

20. Adela Barajas, interviewed by author, December 8, 2021.

21. For more information, see www.timedone.org.

Index

37–40; and California tough-on-crime movement, 33–42; California's Proposition 8 campaign and Victims' Bill of Rights, 35–36, 37; changed outlook, 273–74; courtroom procedural rights for victims, 7, 32, 36–37, 60, 74–76, 205; Crime Victims United (CVU), 38–39, 41, 233; "determinate sentencing" in the name of victims' rights, 34–35; disregard for victims while hiding behind language of victims' rights, 18–20, 41–45, 54–56, 103, 148; and expansion of criminal justice bureaucracies, 6–7, 10–15; and feminist movement, 32; law-and-order origins and tough-on-crime movement, 6–7, 11–15, 29–47; and mass incarceration, 7–8, 11–12, 16–20, 46–47, 271; and Oklahoma City bombing, 74–76; opposition to incarceration reforms in California, 41–42, 214–15; political partnership with law enforcement, 30–47, 129, 137; Reagan and, 36–37, 115, 214; and restorative justice, 273–74; "superpredator" bandwagon, 120–21; three main types of policy reform, 7; victim assistance and compensation programs, 31, 32, 34–35, 76–77, 205; "victim impact statements" in sentencing, 74–76

Violence Against Women Act (1994), 147

Violent Crime Control and Law

Enforcement Act (1994), 26, 27, 128

voting rights, 185

Waco raid (1993), 74
War on Crime (Johnson administration), 114
War on Drugs (Reagan administration), 115–16, 136–37. *See also* drug crimes
Warnken, Heather, 88
Warren, Earl, 30, 34
Warren Court decisions, 30, 34
Washington, Alma Lee, 138
Washington County, Oregon, 53
Washington Post, 231
Washington state's three-strikes law, 25
We Are Survivors campaign, 227, 255
Weekly Standard, 120
Weld, William, 181
Wetterling, Patty, 145–46
White, Walter, 71
Williams, LaTaevia, 256–57
Williams, Robin, 25
Wilson, Dionne, 247–48
Wilson, Orlando, 114
Wilson, Pete, 25, 27–28, 121
Winans, Ray, 92–95, 99

Young Women's Freedom Center, 260
You're Dead, So What? (Neely), 87
youth prisons, 16–17, 120–21, 174–76, 187; California Youth Authority, 174–76, 180, 187–88; solitary confinement and isolation, 16, 175. *See also* juveniles and the justice system

About the Author

Lenore Anderson is the founder and president of the Alliance for Safety and Justice, which has won reforms to reduce incarceration and expand community safety programs across the country. She is a former chief of policy at the San Francisco District Attorney's Office, former director of public safety for the Oakland mayor, and the recipient of the James Irvine Foundation Leadership Award and the American Bar Association's Frank Carrington Crime Victim Attorney Award. She was a 2020 Social Entrepreneurs in Residence (SEERS) fellow at Stanford University. This is her first book. She lives with her family in Oakland, California.

Publishing in the Public Interest

Thank you for reading this book published by The New Press. The New Press is a nonprofit, public interest publisher. New Press books and authors play a crucial role in sparking conversations about the key political and social issues of our day.

We hope you enjoyed this book and that you will stay in touch with The New Press. Here are a few ways to stay up to date with our books, events, and the issues we cover:

- Sign up at www.thenewpress.com/subscribe to receive updates on New Press authors and issues and to be notified about local events
- www.facebook.com/newpressbooks
- www.twitter.com/thenewpress
- www.instagram.com/thenewpress

Please consider buying New Press books for yourself; for friends and family; or to donate to schools, libraries, community centers, prison libraries, and other organizations involved with the issues our authors write about.

The New Press is a 501(c)(3) nonprofit organization. You can also support our work with a tax-deductible gift by visiting www.thenewpress.com/donate.

CPSIA information can be obtained
at www.ICGtesting.com
Printed in the USA
LVHW031014141022
730661LV00003B/3/J